PG
3462
.F6

Gorky, Maksim,
1868-1936.

Foma Gordeyev

219704

DATE DUE			

28.00

FOMA GORDEYEV

Library of Contemporary Soviet Novels

General Editor: YVONNE KAPP

FOMA GORDEYEV was first published in Russia in
1900, and an English translation appeared in 1901. Later,
Gorky revised the entire novel, and it was republished in
his revised and final version in 1923. The present English
edition, the first to follow Gorky's 1923 text, is based on
that published by the Foreign Languages Publishing
House of the U.S.S.R. in 1955, translated by Margaret
Wetlin.

FOMA
GORDEYEV

by
Maxim Gorky

GREENWOOD PRESS, PUBLISHERS
WESTPORT, CONNECTICUT
219704

Library of Congress Cataloging in Publication Data

Gor'kii, Maksim, 1868-1936.
  Foma Gordeyev.

    The present English edition, the first to follow
  Gorky's 1923 text, is based on that published by the
  Foreign Languages Publishing House of the U. S. S. R.
  in 1955, translated by Margaret Wettlin.
    Reprint of the 1956 ed. published by Lawrence &
  Wishart, London, in series: Library of contemporary
  soviet novels.
    I. Title. II. Series: Library of contemporary
  soviet novels.
  PZ3.G678Fo15 [PG3462.F6]   891.7'3'3   74-10361
  ISBN 0-8371-7670-0

To
ANTON PAVLOVICH CHEKHOV

I

SOME SIXTY YEARS ago when fortunes of millions were made
overnight on the Volga, a bailer named Ignat Gordeyev
worked on a barge belonging to the rich merchant Zayev.

Gordeyev was strong and handsome, far from stupid, and one
of those people who are always successful—not because they are
talented and hard-working, but because, endowed with enormous
stocks of energy, they do not spurn—are, in fact, incapable of
spurning—any means that leads to the achieving of their end,
and recognize no law save their own desires. Sometimes these
people speak with awe of their consciences, they may even endure
real torture struggling with them. But only a weak man is unable
to conquer his conscience; a strong one easily subdues it and
makes it serve his purpose. He may sacrifice several nights of
sleep to the struggle; his conscience may even win in the end,
but if it does, his spirit is not broken by defeat and he goes on
living just as vigorously under its rule as he did before.

. . . By the time he was forty, Ignat Gordeyev himself was the
owner of three steamboats and ten barges. He was respected all
along the Volga as a man of wealth and brains, but was given
the nickname "Fury", for his life did not flow smoothly down a
main channel as did the lives of others of his kind, but kept
seething with rebellion, leaping out of its bed, tearing away from
the pursuit of wealth, which he looked on as the main purpose
of existence. It was as if there were three Gordeyevs, three spirits
inhabiting Ignat's body. One of them, and the most important
one, was acquisitive and nothing else, and when it held sway Ignat
was a man possessed by a passion for work. This passion burned
in him day and night, consuming him body and soul, and he
went about snatching up hundreds and thousands of roubles as
if he could never get enough of the sweet rustle and clink of
money. He rushed up and down the Volga, casting and tightening
the nets he caught his gold in; he bought corn in the villages and

took it to Rybinsk in his barges; he cheated—sometimes without being aware of it, sometimes deliberately—always laughing triumphantly in the face of his victims. His craze for money reached poetic intensity. Yet for all the energy he put into the acquisition of wealth, he was not greedy in the narrow sense of the word. Indeed, he would sometimes display complete indifference to his own wealth.

One day when the ice was breaking on the Volga, he stood on the bank watching the floes crush his new two-hundred-and-fifty-foot barge against a steep embankment.

"That's right . . . stave her in . . . go on," he muttered through clenched teeth. "Now, once again!"

"Looks as if the ice were squeezing a cool ten thousand out of your pocket, eh, Ignat?" said Mayakin, his best friend.

"Let it. I'll make another hundred thousand. But look what the Volga's doing! Lord, what power! She could turn up the earth like a knife through curds if she had the mind to. Look! There goes my *Boyarina*. And she was only afloat one season. Well, let's have a drink to mark her end, shall we?"

The barge was shattered. Ignat and his friend sat at a window of a tavern on the river-bank drinking vodka and watching the fragments of the *Boyarina* drifting away down the river together with the ice.

"Sorry to lose your barge, Ignat?' asked Mayakin.

"No sense being sorry. The Volga gave, the Volga has taken away. It's not my hands she chopped off."

"All the same . . ."

"All the same—what? At least I've seen with my own eyes how it happened. A good lesson for the future. I'm sorry I wasn't there to see when my *Volgar* was burned. What a sight it must have been—a bonfire that size out on the water in the middle of the night! She was a big boat!"

"I suppose you weren't sorry to lose her either?"

"That steamer? No, I can't say that. I really was sorry. But that's just foolishness. What's the use? Cry if you like, but tears won't put out a fire. Let the boats burn. I don't give a damn if they all burn, so long as the fires inside me keep burning too."

"H'm," said Mayakin with a little laugh. "A man who talks like that is rich even if he hasn't a shirt to his back."

Despite his philosophical acceptance of the loss of thousands of roubles, Ignat knew the value of every kopek. He rarely gave

8

money to beggars, and then only to those who were unable to do any work at all. If he saw that a beggar was not hopelessly incapacitated he would say sternly:

"Get along with you! Can't you work? Here, go and help my yard porter clear away that pile of manure and I'll give you two kopeks."

When the obsession for work seized him he became hard and merciless to those about him—but he was just as merciless to himself as he chased the rouble. And then all of a sudden (this would usually occur in the spring, when the world is full of charm and loveliness and the soul is aware of some gentle reproach in the clear gaze of the sky), Ignat Gordeyev seemed to sense that he was not the master of his affairs, but their despicable slave. Then he would grow thoughtful, glance inquiringly out from under shaggy knit brows, and go about morbid and irritable, as though asking himself something he dared not give voice to. And another spirit awoke within him—the fierce, lustful spirit of a hungry beast. He was rude to people and profane in his speech; he drank, indulged his coarse instincts, and got others to drink with him, enjoying a very frenzy of excess, as though a volcano were erupting filth inside him. He seemed to be tearing at the chains he had forged and clamped on to himself—tearing wildly at them without being able to break them. Dirty, unkempt, his face swollen with drink and lack of sleep, his eyes wild, his voice hoarse and bellowing, he went from one tavern to another, taking no account of the money he squandered; he grew maudlin when soulful songs were sung, he danced, he fought with anybody at hand, but none of these things brought him relief.

The townsfolk made up legends about his orgies and severely condemned him for them, but nobody ever refused an invitation to take part in them. He would go on in this way for weeks at a time. And then he would come home unexpectedly, reeking of the tavern, but subdued and depressed. Silently and with downcast eyes, which now expressed nothing but shame, he would accept the reproaches of his wife, meek as a lamb, then go to his room and lock himself in. For hours on end he would kneel before the holy images, his head drooping, his arms hanging limply at his sides, his shoulders sagging. But he did not utter a word, as if he dared not pray. His wife would tiptoe to his door and listen. Great sighs, like those of a stricken and weary horse, came from inside the room.

9

"Dear Lord, Thou seest," Ignat would murmur at last, pressing his hands hard against his massive chest.

As long as his penance lasted he lived on rye bread and water. Every morning his wife would put a large bottle of water, a pound and a half of bread, and some salt outside his room. He would open the door to take it in then lock himself in again. No one disturbed him at such times; indeed, everyone avoided him.

After a few days of this he would turn up on the exchange, laughing and joking and signing contracts for grain deliveries, sharp-eyed as a bird of prey, keen judge of his affairs.

But in all three aspects Ignat was possessed of one great desire—the desire to have a son. The older he grew, the stronger the desire became. He often spoke to his wife about it. At breakfast or the midday meal he would scowl at his stout, shapeless wife with her rosy cheeks and sleepy eyes, and say:

"Well, don't you feel anything?"

She knew very well what he meant, but she invariably replied:

"How can I help feeling something? You've got fists like ten-pound weights."

"I'm asking about your belly, you fool."

"As if a woman who took such beatings could carry a child!"

"It's not the beatings that matter, it's your guzzling. You cram yourself so full of food there's no room for a baby."

"As if I hadn't borne you children!"

"Girls!" said Ignat contemptuously. "It's a son I want, can't you understand that? A son and heir. Who'll I leave my money to when I die? Who'll pray for me after I'm dead? Give it all to a monastery? I've given them enough as it is. Leave it to you? A fine intercessor you'd be! Your mind's full of fish pies even when you're in church. And when I die you'll get married again and all my money will fall into the hands of some fool. Do you think that's what I work for? Bah!"

And he would grow peevish and morose, convinced that his life was meaningless without a son who would carry on after him.

In the nine years of their married life his wife had borne him four daughters, but all of them had died. Although he had eagerly awaited each of the births, he grieved little over the deaths; he did not want girls. He began to beat his wife in the second year of their marriage. At first he beat her only when he was drunk, and did it without malice, merely in accordance with the saying:

"Love your wife like your life, but shake her like the pear-tree." But as each child she bore him frustrated his hopes, he began to hate her and take pleasure in beating her for not giving him a son.

Once when he was in the province of Samara on business, he got a message saying that his wife had died. He crossed himself, and after some deliberation wrote to his friend Mayakin:

"Bury her without me. Keep an eye on the property."

He went to church and had the funeral service read, and when he had prayed for the repose of her soul, he resolved to marry again as soon as possible.

At that time he was forty-three years old. He was tall and broad-shouldered and had a deep bass voice. The glance of his large eyes, overshadowed by dark brows, was bold and intelligent. There was much rude and healthy Russian beauty in his sunburnt face with its thick black beard, and in his whole powerful frame. A consciousness of his own strength informed the ease of all his movements and his leisurely gait. Women were attracted to him, and he did not avoid them.

Before his wife had been dead six months he asked for the hand of the daughter of a Cossack Old Believer who lived in the Urals, and with whom he had business connections. The Cossack consented to the marriage even though Ignat's reputation of being "a fury" had reached the Urals. The girl's name was Natalia. Tall, graceful, with enormous blue eyes and a long chestnut plait, she was a worthy mate for the handsome Ignat. He was proud of his new wife, and loved her with the love of a healthy male. But soon he began to study her thoughtfully.

Seldom did a smile cross his wife's lovely oval face. She was always pensive, and at times her blue eyes, coldly tranquil, would be troubled by a look that was dark and forbidding. When free of household duties, she would go into the largest room of the house, sit down at the window, and remain sitting there motionless for two or three hours. Although she gazed out into the street, her expression was at once so indifferent to all that was going on beyond the window and so full of concentration that she seemed to be searching her own soul. She had a strange walk: she did not move freely about the spacious rooms of the house, but slowly and cautiously. The house was furnished in a heavy style that was vulgarly ostentatious. All its glittering appointments proclaimed the owner's wealth, but the Cossack woman sidled past the expensive furniture and the sideboards loaded with silver as if she were afraid they might seize her and crush her. The pulsating life of this large trading town held no interest for her, and when she went out for a ride with her husband she kept her eyes fixed on the coachman's back. If her husband asked her to go visiting with him, she did not refuse, but she was just as quiet in company as she was at home. If guests came to see her, she pressed her food and drink upon them without taking any interest in what they talked about or caring more for one than for another. The only person who could coax the faintest shadow of a smile to her face was Mayakin, a clever, witty man.

"She's not a woman; she's a stick," was what he said of her. "But just wait—life is a bonfire, and this young nun will be kindled by it yet. All she needs is time. Then we'll see how she will bloom!"

"Well," said Ignat banteringly to his wife, "a penny for your thoughts! Are you homesick? Come, cheer up!"

She looked at him calmly without answering.

"You spend too much time in church. It's too soon for that. You'll have plenty of time to pray away your sins—commit them first. If you don't sin, you won't have anything to repent, and if you don't repent, you won't find salvation. So come, do a little sinning while you're young. Let's go for a ride, shall we?"

"I don't think I will."

He sat down beside her and put his arms round her, but she was cold and unresponsive.

"Natalia," he said, peering into her eyes, "what makes you so moody? Do you find me tedious?"

"No," she said briefly.

"Then what is it? Do you miss your own people?"

"Not particularly."

"What are you thinking about?"

"Nothing."

"Then what's the matter?"

"Nothing."

One day he got her to express herself more fully:

"There's something hazy in my heart. And in my eyes too. It seems to me that all this is not real."

With a wave of her hand she indicated the walls, the furniture, all her surroundings. Ignat did not bother to reflect upon her words, he merely gave a little laugh and said:

12

"Well, you're wrong. They're all real—all good and solid and expensive. But if you like, I'll burn them, I'll sell them, I'll give them away, and buy everything new. Do you want me to?"

"What for?" she asked impassively.

He marvelled that one so young and healthy could live as in a daze, without wanting anything, without going anywhere except to church, without seeing anyone.

"Just wait, you'll bear me a son and then life will be different," he consoled her. "It's not having any cares that makes you so unhappy; he'll give you plenty to do. You *will* bear me a son, won't you?"

"God willing," she said, dropping her eyes.

As time went on her moodiness began to irritate him.

"Well, you nun, you, why are you so down in the mouth? You walk as if you were treading on glass and look as if you had killed somebody. You're a luscious wench, but you've got no spirit. A little fool, that's what you are."

One day he came home slightly tipsy and began to make love to her. She resisted him. This made him angry.

"Natalia!" he cried. "Take care!"

She looked him straight in the face and said, unperturbed: "What will happen if I don't?"

Ignat was infuriated by her words and her fearless glance.

"What?" he roared, making for her.

"Perhaps you would like to strike me?" she said, without retreating a step or blinking an eye.

Ignat was used to seeing people tremble before his wrath and he was maddened and insulted by her composure.

"There, then!" he shouted, swinging his arm. Unhurriedly, but in good time, she evaded the blow, seized his arm, and pushed it away from her.

"If you touch me, never come near me again," she said without raising her voice.

Her enormous eyes were narrowed, and their piercing glint brought Ignat to his senses. Her face told him that she, too, was a strong animal, and that she would not give in even though he beat her to death.

"Bah!" he growled, and went out.

He had surrendered to her this time, but he would never do it again. It would be humiliating to have a woman, and that

13

woman his wife, refuse to bow down before him. Yet he sensed she would never yield to him in anything, and this meant that a fierce battle would be fought between them.

"Very well, we'll see who will win," he said to himself the next day as he followed her every movement with glum curiosity. Deep down in his heart a storm of impatience was gathering: the sooner he began the fight, the sooner would he enjoy his victory.

But four days later Natalia informed him that she was with child. He trembled with joy. He threw his arms about her and said in a voice hoarse with feeling:

"Natasha, if it's a son . . . if you give me a son . . . I'll smother you in gold! But that's nothing. I'll be your slave for life! I swear to God I will! I'll lie down at your feet and you can trample on me!"

"It is not for us, but for God to say what the child will be," she reminded him mildly.

"Ah, yes . . . for God," said Ignat with bitterness, hanging his head. From that moment he was as solicitous for his wife as if she were a small child.

"Why are you sitting at the window? You'll catch a chill if you're not careful," he said with gruff affection. "Why do you run up and down the stairs? You may hurt yourself. Here, eat some more; eat for two, so that he shall have his share."

Natalia grew even more quiet and thoughtful with her pregnancy. She withdrew further into herself, absorbed in thoughts of the new life she was cherishing within her. But the smile on her lips became clearer, and at times there was a new light in her eyes as faint and fleeting as the first flush of dawn.

Her birth pangs began early in the morning of an autumn day. Ignat turned pale at his wife's first cry of pain. He wanted to say something to her, but no words would come. With a despondent wave of his hand he left her and went downstairs to the little room that had been his mother's prayer room. He ordered some vodka and sat there miserably, drinking and listening to the turmoil in the house. The faces of the holy images, dark and aloof, were dimly outlined in the corner lighted by the icon lamps. He heard the shuffle of feet upstairs, the sound of something heavy being dragged across the floor, the clatter of basins and vessels. Everything was being done in a hurry, but time dragged on.

14

"She doesn't seem able to give birth," someone said in a hushed voice. "Perhaps we ought to send to the church and ask them to open the gates of the tabernacle."

A pious old woman who lived as a hanger-on in the house entered the room next to where Ignat was sitting and began to pray in a loud whisper:

"Dear Lord and Saviour . . . descended from heaven to be born of the Holy Virgin . . . knowing the weakness of Thy creatures . . . forgive this, Thy faithful servant. . . ."

But suddenly a heart-rending cry rang out, drowning all other sounds, and a long-drawn moan floated through the rooms of the house, dying away in corners darkened by the shadows of evening. Ignat threw anguished glances at the icons, sighed deeply, and thought: can it be another girl?

From time to time he stood up, and crossed himself bowing low before the icons; then he would sit down at the table again, go on drinking vodka (which did not make him drunk now) and doze off. In this way he spent the evening, the night, and the next morning.

At last the midwife came running down the stairs and cried in a thin, happy voice:

"Congratulations on the birth of a son, Ignat Matveyevich!"

"Do you—you aren't lying, are you?"

"Oh, dear no, why should I?"

He drew in a breath that filled his whole massive chest, then dropped to his knees.

"Praise be to Thee, oh God," he muttered in a shaking voice, his hands pressed to his breast. "It is clear Thou didst not wish to see my line cut off. My offspring shall make amends for the sins I have committed against Thee. I thank Thee, dear Lord!" The next moment he was on his feet and giving orders in a loud voice: "Hullo! Let someone go to St. Nicholas for the priest! Say Ignat Matveyevich sent for him! Say he is to read a prayer for a woman delivered of child!"

The maid came in and said in an anxious voice:

"Ignat Matveyevich! Natalia Fominishna is asking for you. She's feeling bad."

"Bad? She'll get over it," he roared, his eyes flashing with joy. "Tell her I'm coming! Tell her I'm proud of her. Tell her I'll come with a fine present. Wait! Get some food ready for the priest and send for Mayakin."

15

The intoxication of joy seemed to make his big form even bigger. He flung about the room, rubbing his hands together, casting grateful glances at the icons, crossing himself and waving his arms. At last he went up to his wife.

The first thing that caught his eye was a little red body that the midwife was bathing in a tub. The minute he saw it he clasped his hands behind his back and tiptoed towards it, pursing up his lips comically. It was squealing and twisting in the water—naked, helpless, pitiful.

"Be careful how you handle him. He hasn't got any bones yet," whispered Ignat to the midwife in pleading tones.

She gave a toothless laugh and tossed the baby lightly from one hand to the other.

"Go to your wife."

He turned obediently.

"Well, Natalia?" he said as he walked over.

On reaching the bed he pulled back the curtain.

"I'll never get over it," came a faint voice.

Ignat stared at the face of his wife, sunk deep in a white pillow over which, like dead snakes, were spread her dark locks. He had difficulty in recognizing this yellow, lifeless face with dark rings round the enormous wide-open eyes. Nor did he recognize those dreadful eyes, fixed motionless on some point beyond the wall. A premonition of disaster slowed down the joyful beating of his heart.

"That's all right . . . it's always like this. . ." he said, bending down to kiss her. But she repeated, looking him straight in the face:

"I'll never get over it."

Her lips were white and cold, and as soon as his own lips touched them he knew that death already dwelt within her.

"Dear God!" he murmured, fear clutching his heart and cutting off his breath. "Natalia, you can't! He . . . he needs you. What are you thinking of?"

He all but shouted at his wife. The midwife was dancing about him, waving the crying baby in the air and trying to make him understand what she was saying, but he heard nothing and was unable to tear his eyes off the fearful face of his wife. Her lips were moving and he could catch occasional words, but he did not understand them. He sat down on the edge of the bed and said in a dull, fumbling voice:

"But . . . he can't get on without you . . . he's just been born. Come, take yourself in hand . . . don't let yourself think such a thing . . . drive the thought out of your head . . . drive it away. . . !"

He spoke—and knew that his words were useless. Tears welled up within him and he felt something as heavy as lead, as cold as ice, in his chest.

"Forgive me. Farewell. Look after him. Don't drink," murmured Natalia tonelessly.

The priest came and covered her face. With many sighs he began to chant words of supplication:

"Great God and Father of the Universe, who curest all ills, cure Thy humble servant Natalia, just delivered of child . . . raise her up from the bed on which she lieth . . . mindful of the words of the prophet David: 'Behold I was shapen in iniquity; and in sin did my mother conceive me'."

The old man's voice broke, his thin face was stern, a smell of incense came from his clothes.

". . . and save the child she has borne from all evil . . . from all violence . . . from all storms . . . and from the evil spirits that fly by day and by night. . . ."

Ignat wept quietly. His tears, large and warm, fell upon his wife's hand. But she could not have felt them, for the hand did not move nor the skin tremble as the tears fell. When the prayer was over, she became unconscious and died two days later without uttering another word to anyone—died as silently as she had lived. Ignat gave her an elaborate burial, had his son christened Foma, and then, reluctantly, placed him in the family of his godfather, Mayakin, whose wife had just had a baby herself. The death of his wife left many a grey hair in Ignat's dark beard, but it also added something new—something gentle and kind— to the expression of his eyes.

II

MAYAKIN lived in a huge two-storeyed house surrounded by a large garden in which handsome old lime-trees grew. Their leafy branches covered the windows with dark shadow-lace, and it was all the sun could do to penetrate this leafy curtain and enter the small dark rooms crowded with numerous trunks and all kinds of furniture, so that an austere twilight always reigned there. The family was devout. Sighs of repentance and snatches of prayers hovered in the air, and the smell of wax, incense, and icon lamp-oil filled the house. All observances were strictly kept, and with delight, for the people who lived in this house poured all their excess energy into piety. Through the sombre, stuffy, oppressive rooms floated female figures clad in dark robes, with soft slippers on their feet and sanctimonious expressions on their faces.

Mayakin's family consisted of himself, his wife, his daughter, and five relatives, the youngest of whom was thirty-four years old. All these relatives were equally pious and colourless, and all were under the heel of Antonina Ivanovna, Mayakin's wife, a tall thin woman with a dark complexion and stern grey eyes with an intelligent and domineering gleam in them. Mayakin also had a son called Taras, but his name was never mentioned in the family. The townspeople knew that nineteen-year-old Taras had gone to Moscow to study and had married there three years later against his father's wishes, for which Yakov Mayakin had disowned him. Nobody knew what had become of the boy after that, but it was rumoured that he had been exiled to Siberia for some offence.

Yakov Mayakin was small and thin and wiry. He had a fiery red goatee, and the look in his greenish eyes seemed to say to one and all:

"That's all right, friend, I can see straight through you, but if you keep your hands off me, I won't give you away."

He had an egg-shaped head that was too big for his body. His high forehead, deeply furrowed, merged into his bald crown, so that he seemed to have two faces: one that everyone could see—very astute and penetrating, with a long gristly nose; another that was eyeless and mouthless and covered with wrinkles, behind which Mayakin seemed to hide his eyes and lips until the right time should come, when he would look out upon the world with different eyes, and smile a different smile.

He was the owner of a rope factory and had a shop on one of the wharfs. In this shop, stocked to the ceiling with rope, hemp and tow, he had a tiny office entered through a glass door with squeaky hinges. The office contained a big desk, old and ugly, with a deep armchair in front of it in which Mayakin spent his days drinking tea and reading the *Moskovskiye Vedomosti*. He enjoyed the respect of his fellow merchants, and had the reputation of being a "brainy" fellow. He was fond of boasting of his ancestry.

"We Mayakins have been merchants since the days of Catherine," he would say in his wheezy voice. "In other words, I've got pure blood in my veins."

In this family the son of Ignat Gordeyev spent the first six years of his life. At the age of six Foma, who had a handsome head and broad shoulders, seemed to be older, because of his size and the serious expression of his dark almond-shaped eyes. He was a quiet boy, but one who stubbornly insisted on having his own way. All day long he and Lyuba, Mayakin's daughter, played with their toys under the silent surveillance of one of the relatives, a fat, pockmarked old maid who, for some reason, had been nicknamed "Buzya". She was a shrinking creature; even to the children she spoke in monosyllables and under her breath. She knew an endless number of prayers but apparently no stories, for Foma had never heard one from her.

Foma got on well with Lyuba, but if she teased him or made him angry he turned pale and rolled his eyes comically, his nostrils would dilate, and he would beat her for all he was worth. She would cry and run to tell her mother, but Antonina Ivanovna loved Foma and paid little attention to her daughter's complaints. This served to strengthen the children's friendship. Foma's days were long and all alike. When he got up in the morning he washed himself and knelt down before the icons to say endless prayers, prompted by Buzya. Then the family sat down to breakfast, at which they drank tea and ate a great many buns, cakes and meat patties. After breakfast in the summer the children went out into the leafy garden that ended in a deep dark gully. Vapours and something frightening rose out of it. The children were not allowed to go near the gully, and this made them fear it all the more. In the winter they played indoors until dinner if the weather was very cold; if it was not, they went tobogganing down a steep hill.

At noon they had dinner "in good old Russian style", as Mayakin said. The first thing to be put on the table was a big tureen of cabbage soup without any meat in it but with cubes of rye toast and a great deal of fat floating on top. Then the same soup was served with slices of meat in it. This was followed by a roast of some sort: pork, goose, veal or tripe stuffed with buckwheat porridge. Giblet soup or broth with noodles followed. All this was finished off by something sweet and rich. The standing beverage was kvass made of juniper, bilberries or bread— Antonina Ivanovna always had several varieties. They ate in silence, sighing wearily with the effort. The two children's food was served in a separate bowl; all the other members of the family ate out of the same one. After a meal like this, the only thing to do was sleep and so, for two or three hours, nothing was to be heard in Mayakin's house but snores and somnolent sighs.

When they woke up they drank tea and exchanged gossip about the deacon, the members of the choir, the latest wedding or the shocking behaviour of some merchant of their acquaintance.

When tea was over Mayakin would say to his wife:

"Well, Mother, fetch the Bible."

His favourite reading was from the Book of Job. When he had put his heavy silver-rimmed spectacles on his hawk-like nose he would cast a glance over the company to see that everyone was present. He would find them all in their accustomed places wearing their usual dull, pious expressions.

"There was a man in the land of Uz," began Mayakin in his wheezy voice, and Foma, who was sitting next to Lyuba on the divan in the corner, knew that at this point his godfather would pause and run his hand over his bald crown. As he listened, Foma drew a mental picture of this man from the land of Uz. He was tall and naked, with eyes as enormous as those of the Saviour on the *Nerukotvorny Spas* icon, and with a voice like the brass trumpet the soldiers played in camp. With every minute the man grew bigger and, when he was as tall as the sky, he plunged his dark hands into the clouds and tore them apart, crying out in a dreadful voice:

"Why is light given to a man whose way is hid, and whom God hath hedged in?"

Foma trembled with fear. Every trace of sleepiness fled as he watched his godfather pluck at his beard and say with a slight smile:

"There's a bold fellow for you!"

Foma knew he was referring to the man from the land of Uz and was reassured by his godfather's smile. The man would not pull down the sky and tear it apart with his dreadful hands. Once more Foma saw the man in his mind's eye. This time he was sitting on the ground and "his flesh was clothed with worms and clods of dust," and his skin was "broken and become loathsome." Now he was little and weak and looked for all the world like one of the beggars who stood on the porch of the church.

"Who can bring a clean thing out of an unclean?" he was saying.

"He asks this question of God," explained Mayakin. "How, he asks, can I be righteous if I am born of the flesh of woman? That's the question he puts to God."

And Mayakin looked at the women inquiringly, a glitter of triumph in his eye.

"He proved himself worthy, the righteous man," they sighed.

Mayakin gave a mocking laugh.

"Fools!" he said. "Go and put the children to bed."

Ignat Gordeyev came to the Mayakins every day. He brought his son toys, picked him up in his arms and hugged him fondly, but sometimes he seemed displeased.

"What makes you so solemn?" he would ask with ill-disguised anxiety. "Why don't you laugh more?"

And once he said to his friend Mayakin:

"I'm afraid Foma's going to be like his mother. He's got such mournful eyes."

"It's too soon to worry about that," laughed Mayakin.

Mayakin was fond of his godson, and was sincerely grieved when Ignat announced one day that he intended to take him home.

"Let him stay here," he said. "He's got used to us. Look, he's crying."

21

"He'll stop. Do you think I had a son just to give him to you? And besides, it's dreary in your house—as dull as a monastery. That's bad for a child. And I'm lonely without him. I come home to an empty house—nothing to cheer me up. I can't move in with you for his sake. It's not I who was meant for him, but he for me. That's how it is. My sister Anfisa has come to live with me and she'll take care of him."

So the child moved into his father's house.

He was met at the door by a funny old woman with a long hooked nose and a big toothless mouth. She was tall and round-shouldered, wore a grey dress and had a little black silk cap on her grey hair. At first the boy did not like her—he was even afraid of her. But when he saw her black eyes smiling so kindly at him out of her wrinkled face, he quickly pressed his face to her skirts.

"My poor little motherless boy!" she said in a velvety vibrating voice as she stroked his head. "Just see how he's cuddled up to me, the little darling!"

There was something peculiarly sweet in her caresses, something Foma had never known before, and he gazed into the old woman's eyes with an expression of curiosity and expectation. This old woman was to initiate him into a world whose very existence he had not suspected. When she had put him to bed that first day, she sat down beside him, leaned over him, and said:

"Shall I tell you a story?"

After that Foma always fell asleep to the sound of her velvety voice conjuring up pictures of a magic world. He eagerly drank in the beauty of folk tales. Inexhaustible was the treasure the old woman drew forth from her memory and imagination. Sometimes as Foma dozed off she seemed to him to be the Baba-Yaga of her fairy-tales—a good and kind Baba-Yaga. At other times he saw her as the beautiful Vasilisa the Wise. As he lay with wide-open eyes and bated breath gazing into the quivering shadows dimly lighted by the icon-lamp, his fancy filled them with wonderful scenes from fairy-tales. Across walls and floor glided shadows that were none the less alive because they were speechless. The boy found it both terrible and delightful to watch them, to give them form and colour and life, and then to destroy them in an instant with a single flick of his eyelashes. His dark eyes took on a new expression, less solemn, more simple and childlike. Darkness and loneliness roused in him a tense feeling of expectation, stirred his curiosity, made him brave the eeriness of some dark corner to find out what was hidden there. He found nothing, but he did not lose hope that one day he would.

He was afraid of his father, but he loved him. Ignat's great size, his resounding voice, his bearded face, his thick grey hair, his long and powerful arms and his flashing eyes—all these things made him look like a robber out of a fairy-tale.

One day when Foma was seven years old he asked his father, who had just come home after a long journey, where he had been.

"Down the Volga," his father replied.

"On a raid?" asked Foma in a hushed voice.

"Wha-a-at?" exclaimed Ignat with a lift of his eyebrows.

"But you *are* a robber, aren't you, Father? I know you are," said Foma, screwing up his eyes cunningly, delighted that he had so easily forced his way into his father's secret life.

"I'm a merchant," said Ignat sternly, but after a moment's consideration he smiled good-naturedly and added: "And you're a little simpleton. I'm a grain dealer and I own steamers. Have you ever seen the *Yermak*? That's my boat. And yours, too."

"It's pretty big," said Foma with a sigh.

"I'll buy you a little one to play with as long as you yourself are little, shall I?"

"Oh, yes," said Foma, but when he had thought things over a minute he added with regret: "I was sure you were a robber."

"I'm a merchant, I tell you," said Ignat sharply, looking at the disappointed face of his son with perturbation, almost with fear.

"Like Grandad Fyodor who sells buns?" asked Foma after a pause.

"Yes, like him, but I'm richer; I have more money than Fyodor."

"Lots of money?"

"Well, I suppose some people have more."

"How many chests?"

"What's that?"

"Of money?"

"You silly, people don't measure money by the chest."

"Oh, yes they do," said Foma with animation, looking up at his father and hastening to explain: "Once Maxim, the robber, stole twelve chestfuls of money and lots of silver besides from a rich man, and then he robbed the church and ran his sword through another man and threw him out of the belfry for trying to sound the alarm—"

23

"Has your aunt been telling you all that?" asked Ignat, pleased to see his son's animation.

"Yes, why?"

"Nothing," laughed Ignat. "Now I see why you turned your father into a robber."

"Perhaps you were once upon a time?" asked Foma hopefully.

"No, I never was. Put the thought out of your head."

"Never?"

"No, never, I tell you! What a little rascal you are! Do you think it's nice for a man to be a robber? They're all sinners, those robbers of yours. They don't believe in God and they rob churches, and for that the churches call the wrath of God down on their heads . . . H'm . . . But this is what I wanted to say to you, son: you've got to begin to study. It's high time, poor little devil. Study all winter, and when spring comes and the fishing season begins I'll take you with me down the Volga."

"Am I to go to school?" asked Foma timidly.

"First you'll study at home with your aunt."

And so the boy sat down at the table every morning and repeated after his aunt, as he pointed to the Slavonic letters:

"Az . . . buki . . . vedi. . . ."

When he got to "bra . . . vra . . . gra . . . dra. . .", the syllables sounded so funny he could not help laughing. He mastered his letters quickly and in a short time he was reading the first psalm.

"Bless-ed is the man . . .that. . . ."

"That's right, my darling; that's right, Fomushka," encouraged his aunt, delighted with his success.

"That's fine, Foma," said Ignat gravely when he was told of the progress his son was making. "You and I will go down to Astrakhan in the spring, and in the autumn I'll send you to school."

The boy's days rolled along as smoothly as a ball going downhill. His aunt was his playmate as well as his teacher. Sometimes Lyuba Mayakina would come to see them and then the old woman became a child with them. They played hide-and-seek and blind-man's-buff. The children laughed with glee to see the old woman blunder about the room with a handkerchief over her eyes and her arms outstretched, bumping into chairs and tables in spite of her caution, feeling in out-of-the-way places for them as she muttered under her breath:

"The little rogues, the little monkeys, where could they have hidden themselves?"

The sun beamed tenderly down upon this ancient body harbouring a youthful soul—this old life pouring out its last stores of strength to brighten the lives of the children.

Ignat went to the exchange early in the morning, often remaining there until evening, and then he would go to visit friends, or to the city council, or elsewhere. Sometimes he would come home drunk. At first Foma ran away and hid from him on such occasions, but later he became accustomed to him and liked him better drunk than sober: he was more simple and affectionate when he was drunk, besides being rather comical. If it was night when he came home, his booming voice would waken the boy.

"Anfisa-a! Let me in to see my son and heir! Come, let me in, that's a good sister!"

"Go away and sleep it off, you drunken wretch," Foma's aunt would cry reproachfully, "standing there blubbering, and you with your hair turned grey already."

"Anfisa, aren't you going to let me have a look at my son— just one little peep?"

"May your eyes fall out from your swilling!"

Foma knew his aunt would not let his father in, and so he went back to sleep and let them go on with their bickering.

If it was daytime when Ignat came home drunk, he would snatch his son up in his great paws and laugh with drunken delight as he carried him through the rooms, shouting:

"What do you want me to buy you, Foma? Speak up. Sweets? Toys? Come, ask me for something. There's nothing in the world I wouldn't buy you, remember that. I've got a million roubles. And I'll have still more. And it's all yours!"

But suddenly his boisterousness would be extinguished as a candle is snuffed out by the wind. His bloated cheeks would twitch, his inflamed eyes would fill with tears and his lips stretch in a frightened grin.

"Anfisa," he would say, "what if he should die? What would I do then?"

The thought would bring on a fit of madness.

"I'd burn everything!" he would roar, staring wild-eyed into some dark corner. "I'd wipe everything out! I'd blow it to smithereens!"

25

"Enough of that, you monster! Do you want to frighten the child? Or bring an illness upon him?" wailed Anfisa. This was enough to make Ignat beat a hasty retreat, muttering as he went:

"All right, all right, I'm going. Don't shout, don't frighten him."

Whenever Foma fell ill his father would drop all his business. He would stay at home, wandering gloomily from room to room with fear-ridden eyes, moaning and groaning, pestering his sister and his son with foolish questions and advice.

"You'll bring the wrath of God down upon your head," Anfisa would say. "Look out or your mutterings will reach His ear, and He'll punish you for the poor return you make Him for all He's done for you."

"Ah, sister! Can't you understand that if anything should happen to him my life would be ruined? What would I have to live for? Nothing."

At first the boy was frightened by these scenes and by the abrupt changes in his father's mood, but soon he got used to them, and whenever he looked out of the window and saw his father climbing with difficulty out of his sleigh, he would remark indifferently:

"Papa's come home drunk again, Auntie."

Spring came, and Ignat kept his promise to his son. He took him with him on the boat, and here a new and entirely different life unrolled itself before the boy's eyes.

Swiftly down the current glided the handsome *Yermak*, a tugboat belonging to the merchant Ignat Gordeyev, while the Volga banks on either side came up to meet it, the left bank stretching away to the very horizon in a thick green carpet bathed in sunlight, the right thrusting its wooded bluffs up to the sky, where they were caught and held in its stern tranquillity. The broad-bosomed Volga flowed majestically between them. Noiselessly, solemnly, slowly ran her waters, ornamented by the dark shadows cast by the high banks on the right, by the green and golden velvet of water-meadows and sandy shores on the left. Villages came into sight, now on the cliffs, now in the meadows; the sun sparkled on the glass windows of huts, glistened on the brocade of thatched roofs, glittered on the gold crosses of churches half hidden in the tree tops; the grey arms of windmills revolved lazily in the breeze; factory chimneys spun threads of smoke into the sky. The silence of the river was broken by the shouts of children in red, blue and white shirts, who stood on the shore watching the steamer go by and waiting for the merry little waves sent out by its paddle-wheel to roll over their feet. A crowd of little boys jumped into a boat and rowed furiously out into midstream to rock on the swell. Crowns of tall trees protruded from the water—in places whole groves had been submerged and stood like islands amid the flood. From the shore came the strains of a doleful song sung in laboured gasps:

"Ah-ah-! One, two, and—pull!"

The *Yermak* passed some rafts of timber and engulfed them in its waves. They rocked wildly and the blue-bloused raftsmen, thrown off their balance, laughed and shouted. A trim little freighter sidled upstream; the yellow scantlings she was loaded with shone like gold in the sunshine and found blurred reflection in the murky waters of spring. A passenger steamer blew her whistle as she came to meet the tugboat; dull echoes of the sound fled away to hide in the woods and the crevices of the bluffs. The waves made by the two boats collided in midstream and came back, rocking the tug and the freighter. On one of the slopes of the right bank gleamed green strips of sprouting winter wheat, brown strips of fallow land, black strips of earth ploughed for spring sowing. Above them swarmed birds that were no more than tiny dots seen from the river, and yet were clearly visible against the blue expanse of the sky. Herds that looked like toys were grazing not far away, and their toy-like shepherd stood leaning on his staff and gazing out over the river.

As far as the eye could see there was space, freedom, sparkle, the cheerful green of the meadows, the tender blue of the sky. Restrained power was felt in the calm flow of the water. Above it blazed the generous May sun. The air was heavy with the sweet smell of evergreens and young leaves. The banks kept coming to meet the boat, gladdening the eye and the spirit with their beauty, unfolding one new scene after another.

Everything moved slowly; everything, nature and people alike, led a lazy, languid existence. Yet it seemed that behind this laziness lurked an enormous force, an irrepressible force that was not yet aware of itself and so as yet without clear aims and purposes. And this unawareness cast a shadow of sadness over the lovely expanses. Even in the cry of the cuckoo wafted on the wind could be heard a note of patient endurance, of submissive

27

waiting for some surge of new life. The mournful songs were like a plea for help. At times one could detect in them the recklessness of despair. The river sighed in response. The trees bowed their heads in meditation. Silence reigned.

Foma spent all his time on the captain's bridge beside his father. Silently, wide-eyed, he watched the endless panorama of the river-banks, and it seemed to him that he was moving down a wide silver pathway to the wondrous kingdoms inhabited by the knights and wizards of old. Sometimes he would ask his father questions about what he saw. Ignat willingly answered him, but Foma was not satisfied with the answers: they were flat, he did not understand them, they did not tell him what he longed to hear.

"Aunt Anfisa knows better than you," he once sighed.

"What does she know?" laughed Ignat.

"Everything," declared the child with conviction.

They never came to the wondrous kingdoms. But often they came to towns just like the one where Foma lived. Some were larger, some smaller, but the people and houses and churches were all exactly like those he knew so well. He went ashore with his father to see them, but he did not like them and would come back to the boat tired and depressed.

"Tomorrow we'll reach Astrakhan," Ignat said one day.

"Will it be just like all the others?"

"Of course. What did you expect?"

"And what's beyond Astrakhan?"

"The sea. The Caspian Sea, it's called."

"What's in it?"

"Fish, you silly. What else could live in water?"

"The town of Kitezh stood in the water."

"Ah, Kitezh! But that was a very special town. Only the righteous lived in Kitezh."

"Aren't there any righteous towns in the sea?"

"No," said Ignat, and then, after a moment's consideration: "Sea water is salty, you can't drink it."

"And after the sea, is there land again?"

"Of course. The sea has to come to an end some time, doesn't it? It's like a bowl."

"And then are there more towns?"

"Yes. But not our towns. Persian ones. Remember that Persian you saw at the fair: 'Peaches, apricots, pe-e-e-e-stachios'?"

"Oh yes," said Foma, going off into a dream.

One day he said to his father:

"Are there lots more lands?"

"Lots, son; ever so many."

"And are they all the same?"

"What do you mean?"

"I mean the towns and things."

"They are. All the same."

After a number of such talks the boy's black eyes no longer stared so expectantly into the distance.

The crew came to love him, and he in his turn loved all these strapping, weatherbeaten fellows who spoke so jocularly to him. They made him fishing rods and boats out of birch-bark, and they played with him and took him rowing when his father was in some town on business. The child often heard them grumble about his father, but he paid no attention to it and never told his father what they said. But once in Astrakhan, when the boat was taking on a load of fuel, Foma heard Petrovich, the mechanic, say:

"Fool! Telling us to take on so much timber! He'll sink the boat to the gunwales, and then shout: 'What do you mean by spoiling the engines! What do you mean by using up all that oil!'"

"And it's just because he's so damned greedy," came the voice of the grave, grey-haired pilot. "A greedy devil, if ever there was one."

"He's greedy all right."

This word, repeated so often, impressed itself on Foma's memory, and that evening when he was having supper with his father, he suddenly said to him:

"Father!"

"Yes?"

"Are you greedy?"

When his father questioned him, he told him what the pilot and the mechanic had said. Ignat's face grew dark and his eyes flashed with anger.

"So that's how it is!" he said, with a shake of his head. "Well, don't you . . . don't listen to them. They're not your sort; keep out of their way. Don't forget that you're their master and they're your servants. We can throw them all off the boat if we want to. They're cheap and there's as many of them as stray dogs. Understand? They'll always say nasty things about me, and the reason

29

is that I'm their lord and master. I'm rich and successful, and a rich man is always envied. Everybody's the enemy of a lucky man."

Two days later the boat had a new pilot and a new mechanic.

"Where's the pilot Yakov?" asked the child.

"I got rid of him—gave him the sack."

"What for?"

"For what he said."

"And Petrovich?"

"Petrovich too."

Foma liked the ease with which his father could dispose of people. He smiled at him, then went down on deck, where he found a boat-hand sitting on the floor unwinding rope to make a swab.

"We've got a new pilot," said Foma.

"I know. Good morning, Foma Ignatiyevich. Did you sleep well?"

"And a new mechanic too."

"And a new mechanic too. Don't you feel sorry for Petrovich?"

"No."

"No? And he was always so nice to you."

"Why did he have to say bad things about my father?"

"Oh, did he?"

"He did. I heard him myself."

"H'm. And your father heard him too?"

"No, I told him."

"So you told him, did you?" drawled the boat-hand, going back to work without further comment.

"Father told me I was the master here; he told me I could get rid of anybody I wanted to."

"Did he?" said the boat-hand, glowering at the boy who was bragging of his power with such enthusiasm.

Foma noticed that the men treated him differently after that: some of them became even more obliging and solicitous, others changed their bantering tone to a sharp one, or stopped talking to him altogether. The boy loved to watch them scrub the decks: they would run nimbly about with swabs in their hands, their trousers rolled up to the knee, sluicing the deck with pails of water, throwing it over each other, laughing, shouting, tumbling about. Water flowed everywhere, its splash forming a cheery background to the voices of the men. Not only had the child never been looked upon as being in the way when this easy and pleasurable job was being done, he had even joined in it, splashing water over the men and running away with a merry shriek when they threatened to splash him in turn. But after the dismissal of Yakov and Petrovich the men no longer gave him friendly looks. He sensed that he was in the way and that nobody wanted to play with him. Sad and perplexed, he would leave the deck and go up on the bridge, where he would sit gazing sulkily out at the blue river-banks and the fringed outline of the woods. Down below the crew were swilling the water about and laughing gaily. He longed to join them, but something held him back.

"Keep away from them," were the words his father had said to him. "You're their master."

He had an impulse to shout at them in a tone of command, as his father did. He tried hard to think of something suitable to say, but he could not. Two or three days passed in this way and in the end he was convinced that the men did not like him. He grew sick of the boat, and more and more often he caught a glimpse of the loving face of Aunt Anfisa smiling through the rosy mist of new impressions that had obscured it—Aunt Anfisa, whose smiles and tales and gentle laughter had always warmed his heart and filled it with happiness. He still lived in the world of fairy-tales, but the cruel hand of reality had torn away the pretty cobweb of fancy through which he had viewed everything about him. The incident with the pilot and the mechanic forced him to notice his surroundings; his eyes became sharper; a look of inquiry came into them and the questions he put to his father were prompted by a desire to understand what wheels and springs made people behave as they did.

One day he witnessed the following scene:

The boat-hands were carrying logs on barrows, and one of them—a cheerful, curly-haired lad named Yefim—said angrily as he walked down the deck:

"Oh, no, that's going too far! I never agreed to haul logs for him. A boat-hand—everybody knows what a boat-hand's supposed to do. And I'm not hauling logs for him, thank you. That would be skinning me twice over, and I didn't agree to that. He's got no conscience, that man. Sucking a man dry this way!"

The child heard him and knew he was talking about his father. And he saw that, although Yefim complained, he piled more logs on to his barrow than anyone else did and worked faster. The other men paid no attention to his grumbling; even the chap at the other end of his barrow complained only when Yefim put too many logs on it.

"Enough," he would say grumpily. "It's not a horse you're loading."

"Hold your tongue. Once they've put you in harness, haul the load without balking. Hold your tongue even if they suck the blood out of you. There's nothing you can do about it."

Suddenly Ignat appeared from nowhere and walked over to Yefim.

"What's that you're saying?" he asked sternly.

"I'm . . . I'm saying. . ." stuttered the lad, ". . . saying that our agreement didn't have anything in it about . . . about me keeping my mouth shut."

"And who is it that sucks people's blood?" asked Ignat, stroking his beard.

Finding himself caught and unable to wriggle out, the boat-hand threw down the log he was holding, wiped his hands on his trousers, and looked Ignat straight in the face.

"Well, aren't I right?" he asked boldly. "Don't you suck our blood?"

"Me?"

"Yes, you."

Foma saw his father's arm swing up and heard a thud as the lad fell heavily on the pile of logs. Quickly the boat-hand got up and went back to work without a word. His face was cut and blood dripped on to the white bark of a birch log. He wiped his face on his sleeve, looked at the stain, heaved a sigh, but still said nothing. When he passed Foma with his barrow the child saw two big tears trembling in the corners of his eyes.

Foma was very absent-minded during dinner and stole frightened glances at his father.

"What are you looking so glum about?" Ignat asked him gently.

"Nothing."

"Don't you feel well?"

"I'm all right."

"If anything's wrong, tell me."

Suddenly the boy said in a pensive tone:

"You're awfully strong!"

32

"Me? Yes, I am rather. God didn't withhold strength when He made me."

"What a blow you gave him!" cried the child softly, bending his head.

The exclamation made Ignat stop as he was about to put his caviar sandwich to his mouth and look wonderingly at the drooping head.

"You mean that Yefim?" he asked.

"Yes. He was bleeding. And when he walked away he was crying," said the boy in a low voice.

"H'm," murmured Ignat, biting into the sandwich. "Do you feel sorry for him?"

"Yes," said Foma, his voice trembling with tears.

"So . . . that's the kind of youngster you are," said Ignat.

He poured himself out a glass of vodka without a word, gulped it down, and then said impressively:

"There's no reason to feel sorry for him. He got what he deserved for airing his views. I know him; he's a good chap: strong, hard-working and with a sound head on his shoulders. But he's got no business to say what he thinks. I'm the only one that can do that, because I'm the boss. And it's not so simple to be the boss. That little knock won't hurt him—it'll do him good. Ah, Foma! You're just a baby; you don't understand anything yet. I've got to teach you how to get on in life. Perhaps there's not much time left to me in this world."

Ignat mused awhile and drank another glass of vodka before he went on instructing his son:

"It's right to feel sorry for people—I'm glad you do. But you've got to know when to feel sorry. First look at a person and find out what he's like and what he's worth. If you see he's strong and capable, feel sorry for him and help him. But if he's weak and a bad workman, spit on him and pass him by. Remember this: if a chap's always complaining, he's not worth his salt. There's no sense in feeling sorry for such a person, and no good will come of any help you give him. You'll just spoil him and make him softer than ever by feeling pity for him. Your godfather has all kinds of jelly-fish living in his house: pious old hags, beggars, hangers-on and other riff-raff. Put them out of your mind. They're not people; they're just empty shells, of no use to anybody. Like fleas and bugs and other vermin. It's not God they serve; they have no God, they just use His name to make fools

33

feel sorry for them and give them something to fill their bellies. It's their bellies they serve. They don't know how to do anything but eat and drink, sleep and groan. They make pulp of a man. They're always getting under your feet, and they're as sure to spoil a good man as rotten apples spoil a good one lying among them. The trouble is you're too little to understand what I'm saying. It's right to help a person who takes his troubles like a man. He may not even ask for your help, but if you see he needs it, give it to him without his asking. And if he's a proud one who takes offence if you help him, try to do it so that he doesn't notice it. That's the only way. Or here, take a case like this: two boards, say, have fallen in the mud. One of them's rotten, the other's a good strong board. What ought you to do? The rotten board isn't worth a pin. Leave it alone, let it lie in the mud; you can walk over it to keep your feet dry. But pull out the good board and put it in the sun. It will come in handy some day. That's how it is, son. Listen to what I say and try to remember it. There's no sense in feeling sorry for Yefim—he's a clever chap and knows his own worth. You can't knock the spirit out of him by giving him a blow. I'll keep an eye on him for a week or so, and then I'll put him on the bridge, and before you know it he'll be a pilot. And if I make a captain of him, he'll be a good one. That's how a person grows to be something. That's the sort of schooling I had too—I took many a blow when I was his age. Life's not a loving mother to any of us, son; it's a stern taskmaster."

For two hours Ignat talked to his son about his youth and his labours, about human nature and the dreadful strength inherent in weakness, and about how people like to pretend to be unfortunate so that they can live at other people's expense. And then he talked about himself again, telling him how he had risen from a simple workman to be the owner of a big enterprise.

As the child sat with his eyes riveted upon his father's face, drinking in his every word, he felt a growing kinship with him. What his father told him lacked the fascination of Aunt Anfisa's tales, but it was new, and it was clearer and more comprehensible than the fairy-tales, without being less interesting. His little heart beat fast and hard, and he felt drawn to his father. Ignat must have read this in his son's eyes, for he suddenly got up, took the boy in his arms and hugged him to his breast. And Foma put his arms round his neck, pressed his cheek to his, and sat there without a word.

"Son!" whispered Ignat hoarsely. "My life, my joy! Learn while I'm still with you. Life is not easy!"

The whispered words sent a pang through the child's heart. He clenched his teeth and hot tears sprang to his eyes.

The steamer was going up the Volga now. On a hot July night, with the sky hidden by thick black clouds and the river wrapped in sinister silence, they came to Kazan and dropped anchor near Uslon, at the end of a long caravan of boats. Foma was awakened by the clank of the anchor chain and the shouts of the crew. He looked out of the window: nothing was to be seen but some tiny lights gleaming in the distance, and the water, which was as dark and thick as oil. The boy's heart contracted with fear and he strained his ears in the silence. From somewhere far away came a plaintive song, mournful as a chant; watchmen on the boats in the caravan were calling to each other; there was a sound of hissing as the boat let off steam. The black water lapped softly and sadly at the sides of the vessels. By staring so intently into the darkness that his eyes ached, Foma was able to make out black forms with faint lights on them. He knew they were barges, but the knowledge did not reassure him; his heart beat fitfully and his imagination conjured up dark and terrifying images.

"O-o-o-o!" came a long-drawn cry from the distance, ending in what sounded like a sob. Someone crossed the deck.

"O-o-o!" came the cry again, but this time it was closer.

"Yefim!" called someone on deck in a low voice. "Damn it all, get up! Bring the boat-hook!"

"O-o-o-o!" The cry was close at hand this time and Foma sprang away from the window with a shudder.

The strange sound came closer and closer, now rising to a wail, now fading away in the darkness. Up on deck a frightened voice whispered:

"Yefim! Get up! A guest is floating past."

"Where?" was the hurried response.

There was a pattering of bare feet on deck, a shuffling about, two boat-hooks were slipped down past Foma's window and dropped into the thick water almost without a sound.

"A gue-e-e-st!" wailed someone nearby, and this was followed by an eerie little splash.

The mournful cry made the child tremble with fear, but he could not tear his hands away from the windowsill nor his eyes from the water.

"Light a lantern—I can't see a thing."

Presently a circle of dim light fell on the water. Foma saw that the water was heaving slightly and little ripples swept over its surface, as if it were shivering with pain.

"Look . . . look!" came a frightened whisper.

Into the circle of light floated a horrible human face with big white teeth exposed in a grin. It rocked on the water as it floated past, and the teeth looked straight at Foma and seemed to say:

"Ah, little boy, little boy, it is cold in here."

The boat-hooks quivered, were drawn up, dropped into the water again.

"Push it away—guide it. Look out—see it doesn't get caught in the paddle-wheel."

The hooks scraped along the side of the boat, making a noise like the grinding of teeth. Little by little the pattering feet withdrew to the stern of the boat, from where the mournful wail came again:

"O-o-o-o! A gu-e-e-est!"

"Father!" screamed Foma. "Father!"

His father jumped up and ran over to him.

"What is it? What are they doing?" cried the boy.

Ignat gave a savage roar and was out of the cabin in three large bounds. He came back quickly, even before Foma had time to stagger wide-eyed from the window to his father's bed.

"Did they frighten you? It's nothing, son," said Ignat, taking the boy in his arms. "Here, get into bed with me."

"What was it?" whispered Foma.

"Nothing, son. Somebody was drowned, and his body was floating down the river. That's all right, don't be afraid, he's gone now."

"Why did they push him away?" asked the boy, clinging tightly to his father and shutting his eyes in horror.

"Oh, they have to do that. If he got caught in the paddle-wheel we'd have to answer for it. The police would see it in the morning and make a lot of trouble—ask all sorts of questions—hold us up. And so they push him along. What difference does it make to him? He's dead already—it doesn't hurt his body or his feelings. But it could make a lot of trouble for us. Go to sleep, son."

36

"And so he'll go on floating?"

"For a while. Until somebody pulls him out and buries him."

"Won't the fish eat him?"

"Fish don't eat human flesh. Crabs do."

Foma's fear subsided a little, but he still had visions of that horrible face with the bared teeth rocking on the black water.

"Who was he?"

"The Lord only knows. Pray God to bring peace to his soul."

"Dear God, bring peace to his soul," whispered Foma.

"Good. Now go to sleep and don't be afraid. He's far, far away by this time. Floating on. Let that be a lesson to you—be careful when you go near the railing. You may fall into the water, God forbid! . . . And—"

"Did he fall in?"

"Yes. Perhaps he was drunk. Perhaps he threw himself in on purpose. People do sometimes. Just go and throw themselves in. Drown themselves. Life's like that: sometimes death is a blessing to a man, and sometimes a man's death is a blessing to everybody else."

"Father—"

"Go to sleep, son."

III

O N his first day at school Foma, who was dazed by the wild
uproar the boys made as they played their pranks and
games, instantly spotted two who seemed to be more interesting
than the others. One of them sat directly in front of him. He
could not help stealing glances at his broad back, his fat neck
generously sprinkled with freckles, his big ears and close-cropped
head covered with a stubble of bright red hair.

When the teacher, a man with a bald head and protruding
lower lip, called out: "Afrikan Smolin!" the red-haired boy got
up unhurriedly, walked to the front of the room and gazed
calmly into the teacher's eyes as the arithmetic problem was read
to him. Then he picked up the chalk and began to trace big
round numbers on the blackboard very precisely.

"Good. That will do," said the teacher. "Go on with the
problem, Nikolai Yezhov."

A fidgety little boy with the sharp black eyes of a mouse
jumped up from the bench he shared with Foma and made his
way down the aisle, twisting his head from side to side and bumping into everything as he went. When he reached the blackboard
he snatched up the piece of chalk, strained up on his toes, and
scribbled illegible little figures with an intensity that made the
chalk screech and crumble.

"Not so fast," said the teacher, screwing up his yellow face
as if he were in pain.

"The answer is: the first pedlar made a profit of seventeen
kopeks," rattled off Yezhov in a loud voice.

"That will do. Gordeyev! How are we to find out how much
profit the second pedlar made?"

Foma had been so absorbed in watching these two boys, so
different from each other, that he was taken unawares and could
not answer.

"Don't know? Tell him, Smolin."

Smolin, who was painstakingly wiping the chalk off his fingers, put down the rag without glancing at Foma, finished the problem, and began to wipe his fingers again, while the smiling Yezhov hopped back to his seat.

"What's the matter?" he whispered as he sat down next to Foma and gave him a little punch in the ribs. "Why couldn't you answer? How much profit was there all together? Thirty kopeks. How many pedlars? Two. One got seventeen kopeks, so how much did the other get?"

"I know," murmured Foma uncomfortably as he watched Smolin walk staidly back to his bench. He did not like Smolin's face. It was round and freckled and its blue eyes were buried in fat. Yezhov gave Foma's leg a painful tweak.

"Who's your father? The Fury?" he asked.

"Yes."

"Really? Listen, do you want me to tell you all the answers?"

"Yes."

"What will you give me for it?"

Foma considered a moment.

"Do you know all the answers?" he asked.

"Me? I'm the top pupil."

"Stop talking, there," called the teacher. "Are you at it again, Yezhov?"

Yezhov leaped to his feet.

"It wasn't me, Ivan Andreyevich, it was Gordeyev," he said glibly.

"They were both talking," announced Smolin.

The teacher, screwing up his face again and flapping his protruding lower lip comically, scolded all three of them, but his scolding did not keep Yezhov from whispering:

"All right, Smolin, I'll give it to you for sneaking!"

"Why did you put the blame on the new boy?" asked Smolin without turning round.

"You'll see, you'll see," whispered Yezhov.

Foma said nothing, merely glancing out of the corner of his eye at his lively neighbour, thinking it would be well to keep a safe distance from him for all his attractions. During the break Yezhov told him that Smolin, too, was rich—the son of the owner of a leather factory—but that he himself was poor, his father being a watchman at the Treasury building. It was clear that he was poor: his clothes were made of grey fustian patched at knees and elbows, his face was pale and drawn, his body meagre. He spoke in a low metallic voice, emphasizing his speech with gestures and grimaces, and he often used words whose meaning was known to him alone.

"You and I will be chums," he said to Foma.

"Why did you have to sneak to the teacher about me?" said Foma, glancing at him distrustfully.

"Pooh! What of it? You're new and rich; the teacher's always easy on rich fellows. I'm a poor chap. He doesn't like me because I'm noisy and never give him presents. If I wasn't so good at my lessons he'd have thrown me out long ago. Know what? I'm going to the *gymnasium* after I leave here. I'm going as soon as I finish the second form. One of the students there is tutoring me. Won't I study hard when I get there! How many horses have you got?"

"Three. Why are you going to study so hard?" asked Foma.

"Because I'm poor. Poor boys have got to study hard. Then they'll get rich too—they'll be doctors and officers and officials. I want to be a clanker—with a sword at my side and spurs on my boots—clank, clank! What are you going to be?"

"I don't know," mused Foma, studying his comrade.

"You don't have to be anything. Do you like pigeons?"

"Ye-es."

"What a milksop you are! Ye-es, no-o-o," said Yezhov, imitating Foma's hesitant speech. "How many pigeons have you got?"

"None."

"Think of that! Rich, and hasn't got a single pigeon! Even I've got three: a pouter, a speckled hen and a tumbler. If my father was rich I'd have a hundred pigeons and send them flying all day long. Smolin's got some nice ones. Fourteen. He gave me my tumbler. But even so, he's tight-fisted. All rich people are tight-fisted. Are you, too?"

"I—I don't know," said Foma.

"Come over to Smolin's place and the three of us'll race pigeons."

"All right. If I'm allowed to."

"Why, doesn't your father like you?"

"He does."

"Then he'll let you. But don't tell him I'll be there too. He may not let you come if he knows. Ask him to let you go to Smolin's, see? To Smolin's."

40

The fat boy came up and Yezhov greeted him with a shake of his head.

"You red-haired sneak, you. How can a fellow be chums with you, you old cobble-stone."

"What are you grumbling about?" asked the unperturbed Smolin, gazing fixedly at Foma.

"I'm not grumbling, I'm just telling the truth," said Yezhov twitching all over with excitement. "Listen, him and me are coming to your place on Sunday after mass even if you *are* cold mush."

"All right, come," nodded Smolin.

"We will. The bell will go in a minute and I want to sell this bird first," said Yezhov, taking a paper bag out of his pocket with something fluttering inside. The next moment he had slipped away like quicksilver.

"Whe-e-ew!" whistled Foma, astounded by Yezhov's liveliness.

"A quick one," said the red-haired boy in response to Foma's questioning look.

"And jolly," added Foma.

"Mm," agreed Smolin. They looked each other over without speaking for a moment.

"Will you come with him to see me?" asked the red-haired boy.

"Yes."

"Good. It's nice at our place."

Foma made no reply.

"Have you got many chums?" asked Smolin.

"None at all."

"I didn't have either until I went to school. Nobody but my cousins. Now you've got two chums."

"Yes," said Foma.

"It's fun having a lot of chums. And it's easier to study. They tell you the answers."

"Are you good at your lessons?"

"Me? I'm good at everything," said Smolin complacently.

The bell tinkled as if it were scuttling away in fright.

Foma felt more at ease when he was back in the classroom, and he began to compare his chums with the other boys. He soon decided that they were the best in the whole school, that they stood out from the others as distinctly as that 5 and that 7 stood out on the blackboard. And it pleased him to think that he had the best boys in the school as his chums.

The three went home together when school was over. Yezhov soon turned off into a narrow side-street, but Smolin went all the way with Foma.

"You see, we can walk to school together too," he said in parting.

There were celebrations when Foma got home: his father presented him with a heavy silver spoon bearing an elaborate monogram, his aunt with a scarf she had knitted herself. As soon as he had taken off his things they sat down to dinner, which consisted of his favourite dishes, and his father and aunt began asking him questions.

"Well, how did you like school?" asked Ignat, gazing lovingly at his son's flushed cheeks and sparkling eyes.

"All right. I liked it," said Foma.

"Bless your heart," murmured his aunt dotingly. "Don't let the other boys take advantage of you. If they do anything to hurt you, go straight to the teacher and tell him."

"Nothing of the sort!" snorted Ignat. "Don't listen to her. Always fight your own battles; give the boys a taste of your fists. Are they nice chaps?"

"Yes," said Foma, smiling as he recalled Yezhov. "One of them's the liveliest fellow you ever saw."

"Whose son is he?"

"A watchman's son."

"Lively, you say?"

"Fearfully."

"Well, well. And the other?"

"The other's red-haired. Smolin—"

"Ah, must be Dmitri Ivanovich's son. Make friends with him, he's your sort. Dmitri's got a good head on his shoulders. If his son takes after him, he's all right. But that other boy . . . I'll tell you what, Foma: ask them to come and see you on Sunday. I'll buy something nice to treat them to. We'll see what they're like."

"Smolin asked me to come and see *him* on Sunday," said Foma, glancing uncertainly at his father.

"Oh, he has, has he? Well, go then. Yes, go. You'll get to see what sort of people there are in the world. A fellow can't go on living all by himself, without any friends. Take me, for instance; I've been friends with your godfather for more than twenty years, and I've benefited by many good ideas of his. So you do the same: try to make friends with those who are better and cleverer

42

than you are. Rub up against a good man for some time and, like a copper coin that has rubbed against silver, you'll pass for silver yourself."

Ignat laughed, pleased with his simile, then added:

"But I'm only joking. Try to be the real thing, not imitation. Live by your own brains, even if you haven't many. Well, have you got much homework to do?"

"Lots," sighed the child, and his sigh was echoed by his aunt.

"See that you do it. Don't lag behind the others. But this is what I want to tell you: you'll never learn anything but reading, writing and sums in that school—not if you study there twenty years. Oh, to be sure, you may learn to do mischief, but God help you if you do. I'll give you a thrashing. And I'll cut your lips if you smoke tobacco."

"Keep the fear of the Lord in your heart, Fomushka," said his aunt. "Never forget the Lord God."

"That's right. Fear God and your father. But I was saying that text-books aren't everything. You need them as a carpenter needs a hammer and saw; they're your tools, but tools can't teach you what use they're to be put to. Understand? Here, let's put it this way: a carpenter's given an axe and told to bark a log. It's not enough to have hands and an axe; he's got to know how to swing the axe so that it hits the log and not his foot. In just the same way it's not enough to have a book; you've got to know how to use it. And this knowledge is worth more than any book, and it's not to be found in any book. Life's the only thing that can teach you this, Foma. A book's a dead thing: it won't cry out no matter how you squeeze it, or bend it, or tear it. But life's different: if you take a false step or get into the wrong place, you'll be shouted at from all sides, and may even get clubbed and knocked down."

Foma sat with his elbows on the table listening intently to what his father said, and as the man's voice boomed he imagined first the carpenter barking the log, then himself creeping with outstretched arms over treacherous ground toward some huge live thing that he wanted to catch even though it terrified him.

"A man must take care of himself for the sake of the work he has to do, and he must know exactly how to go about doing it. A man is like the pilot of a boat. In youth, as when the river is in spate, he can steer straight ahead—there's a channel everywhere. But all things in their time. Later on he'll have to be careful. The

43

water subsides, and then he'll have to look out for rocks, reefs, and shallows, to steer round them and bring his boat to a safe landing."

"I'll land safely!" said the child, looking with proud confidence at his father.

"Will you? Bravely said!" laughed Ignat. And the boy's aunt gave a fond little laugh too.

Ever since his trip on the Volga, Foma had been more vivacious and talkative in the presence of his father, his aunt, and Mayakin. But when he was in the street or among people he did not know, he withdrew into himself and cast furtive glances about him, as if he felt something hostile in the atmosphere, something hidden and lying in wait.

Sometimes he would wake up in the middle of the night and lie for a long time listening in the silence and staring wide-eyed into the darkness. Then the things his father had told him would rise before him in fleeting images. Without realizing it, he confused them with scenes from his aunt's fairy-tales, and the result was a medley in which the bright colours of fantasy were oddly interwoven with the sober tones of reality. They formed something enormous and baffling, and he would shut his eyes to drive the visions away and stop the flow of fancy that frightened him. But he could not fall asleep, and the room only became more crowded with images. Then he would call softly to his aunt.

"Auntie . . . Auntie."

"What? What's the matter?"

"May I get in with you?" he would whisper.

"Why? Go to sleep, darling; go to sleep."

"I'm afraid."

"Say 'The Lord is Risen' over and over to yourself and you won't be afraid any more."

Foma shut his eyes and repeated the prayer to himself. He saw the silence of the night as an endless expanse of black water standing perfectly still. It covered everything and there was not a ripple on its surface, not the faintest sign of motion, nor was there anything in the water, although it was deep as the sea. It was very terrible to be all alone, gazing down through the darkness at that dead water. Suddenly the night watchman sounded his rattle, and the boy saw the water stir, saw bright little balls skip over its surface, covering it with ripples. The clock on the tower struck,

44

and the water gave a mighty surge, and then went on heaving for a long time from the striking of the clock, and a circle of light fell on the surface and radiated out until it died away in the shadows at the rim. Then again there was the aching desolation of those black expanses. . . .

"Auntie," implored Foma under his breath.

"What is it?"

"I'm coming to you."

"Come along, come along then, darling."

When he had climbed into his aunt's bed, he snuggled up to her and said:

"Tell me a story."

"In the middle of the night?" objected his aunt sleepily.

"Oh, please!"

He did not have to press her. The old woman yawned, closed her eyes, and began to drone in a sleepy voice:

"Once upon a time in a far-off kingdom there lived a man and his wife who were as poor as poor. They were so poor they had nothing to eat. Every morning they set out to beg alms, and the crusts they were given were their daily bread. Later on a child was born to them. Once a child is born, it must be christened; but they were too poor to hold a feast for the godparents and the guests at a christening, and so no one would be godparent to their child. They asked this one, they asked that one, but everyone refused. At last they prayed to the Lord: 'Lord, oh Lord', they prayed."

Foma knew the dreadful tale of the Lord's godchild; he had heard it many times, and as soon as his Aunt began it, he pictured the godchild riding forth on a white horse in search of a godfather and godmother, riding through the darkness, through the wilderness, where he saw the damned suffering torment and heard their groans and their prayers:

"Ah, mortal man, ask the Lord when you see Him how much longer we are to suffer so!"

And it seemed to Foma that it was he who was riding the white horse, and it was to him those groans and prayers were addressed. His heart contracted and tears came to his eyes. He squirmed under the blanket and shut his eyes tightly, afraid to open them again.

The old woman interrupted her gruesome tale to say to him:

"Go to sleep, little one, and may the Lord bless you."

45

The next morning Foma got up as usual, washed himself hurriedly, swallowed down a cup of tea, and ran off to school with his pockets full of sweet buns and cakes to give to the hungry Yezhov, who was now fed regularly by his rich and generous new friend.

"Did you bring me some grub?" he asked, wrinkling his little pointed nose. "Let's have it; I left home without a bite this morning. Overslept, damn it. Sat up till two o'clock doing my lessons. Have you done your arithmetic?"

"No."

"You muggle-wuggle, you! Well, come along, I'll work it out for you."

He sank his sharp little teeth into a bun, purred like a cat, and tapped the floor with his left foot as he undertook to solve the problems.

"See that? Eight pailfuls leaked out in one hour. How many hours were there? Six. What good food you have at home! So we've got to multiply it by eight. Do you like buns stuffed with green onions? I'm mad on them. So we have forty-eight pailfuls leaking out of the first tap in six hours. Altogether there were ninety pailfuls in the tank. So what have you got to do next?"

Foma liked Yezhov better than Smolin, and yet he was more friendly with Smolin. He was in awe of Yezhov's wit and liveliness, he could see that the little chap was cleverer than he was, he resented this and envied him for it, and at the same time he pitied him with the condescending pity of the well-fed for the hungry. Perhaps this was why he could not feel as friendly towards him as to the dull, red-haired Smolin. Yezhov enjoyed poking fun at his well-fed companions.

"Hey, you baskets-of-buns!" he would call out.

His joking piqued Foma.

"You beggar, you pauper!" he once retorted angrily.

Yezhov's sallow face broke out in red blotches.

"Very well," he said slowly, "I won't help you with your lessons any more, and you can show yourself up for the lump you are."

For three days they did not speak to each other, causing the teacher the distressing necessity of giving unsatisfactory marks to the son of the respected Ignat Gordeyev.

Yezhov knew everything. He told his schoolmates that the prosecuting attorney's housemaid had had a baby by him, for which his wife had soused him in hot coffee. He knew the best time to go fishing, the best place to catch perch, how to make bird traps and cages. He explained how and why the soldier had hanged himself in the attic of the barracks. He knew which of the boys' parents had given the teacher a present, and what the present was.

Smolin's knowledge and interests were confined to the lives of the local merchants. He took an interest in their relative wealth, knew the exact value of their houses and ships, and discussed these things with enthusiasm.

His attitude to Yezhov was as condescending as Foma's, but more friendly and constant. Whenever Foma quarrelled with Yezhov, he tried to smooth things over.

"Why are you always quarrelling with him?" he once asked Foma as they were coming home from school.

"He's too stuck-up," said Foma testily.

"That's because you don't know your lessons and he helps you. He's clever, and it's not his fault if he's poor, is it? He can learn anything he wants to, and some day he'll be rich too."

"A mosquito, that's what he is," said Foma scornfully. "Always buzzing about. One of these days he'll bite."

But there was one thing that formed a bond between the boys and enabled them to spend hours together oblivious of differences in caste and character. All three were pigeon fanciers; every Sunday they would gather at Smolin's and climb up to the dovecote on the roof of one of the outhouses to let the birds out.

The sleek, beautiful creatures would shake their wings and fly out, one after another, and sit in a row on the top of the roof, cooing and preening themselves in the sunshine to the delight of the boys.

"Shoo them off!" Yezhov would say, twitching all over with impatience.

Smolin would wave a long stick with some rags tied to the end and give a piercing whistle.

The frightened birds rose into the air, filling it with a whir of wings. Then in wide graceful circles they soared into the blue, higher and higher, their plumage shimmering in the sunlight like snow and silver. Some of them sought to reach the very dome of heaven, soaring with a falcon's even flight, wings outstretched and almost motionless; others tumbled playfully

47

in the air, falling like snowballs, rising with the swiftness of arrows. Now the whole flock seemed frozen against the vast background of the sky—seemed to be sinking in it, drowning in it. The boys watched them in ecstasy, saying not a word, their heads thrown back, their eyes fixed on the sky—their tired eyes whose happy glow was tinged with envy for these winged creatures who could leave the earth with such ease and soar into pure, quiet, sun-drenched spaces. The children's imagination was fired by the sight of these scarcely visible dots clustered against the blue sky, and Yezhov expressed the thoughts of all when he said, softly and pensively:

"If only *we* could fly like that."

At one in their delight, silently, eagerly awaiting the return of the birds from out of the depths of the sky, the little boys pressed close together, as far removed from the world as the birds from the earth. In that moment they were wholly children, knowing neither anger nor envy. Estranged from all else, they were near to each other; without words, by the mere light in their eyes, they understood what each was feeling, and they were as happy as the birds in the sky.

At last the pigeons would come back to the roof, tired out by their flight, and be locked up in the dovecote again.

At this point one Sunday, Yezhov, instigator of all their adventures, said:

"Come on, fellows, let's go for apples!"

His challenge dispelled the tranquil mood induced by the contemplation of the birds, and, like animals on a scent, alert to the slightest noise, they crept toward the far end of the neighbour's orchard. Their fear of being caught was outweighed by a longing to make a successful raid. Stealing, too, is labour, and very dangerous labour. And how sweet its fruits! The harder the effort, the sweeter the reward. Cautiously the boys climbed the fence and ran towards the apple-trees, bent double and looking furtively about them. The slightest noise made their hearts pound. They were just as afraid of being seen and recognized as of being caught, and they preferred to be chased without being recognized —merely shouted at. Shouts would send them flying in all directions and later, when they came together again, they would laugh and chatter excitedly about how they had felt when they heard the cries and footsteps that had sent them tearing through the orchard.

Foma put more spirit into these robber raids than into any of their other games or adventures, and he displayed a recklessness that amazed and distressed his companions. He would purposely throw caution to the winds when he found himself in a neighbour's orchard, would talk in a loud voice, break branches noisily, and if he happened to pick an apple that was worm-eaten, would throw it at the owner's house. More stimulated than intimidated by the danger of being caught in the act, he would clench his teeth, his eyes would darken, and his face take on a proud, forbidding look.

"You do put on airs," Smolin once said, making a wry face.

"I'm no coward," replied Foma.

"I know you're not. But only fools put on airs. You can do things well without that."

Yezhov's view was slightly different.

"What the devil is the use of a chum who *asks* to get caught?" he said. "You're no friend of mine. If they catch you, they'll turn you over to your father and he won't touch you, but they'll give me such a beating there won't be a whole bone left in my body."

"Coward!" said Foma.

One day Foma was caught by a skinny old man named Chumakov, a retired army captain. He had crept up on the boy as he was stuffing apples inside his shirt.

"Now I've got you, you thief!" he cried, seizing Foma by the shoulder.

Foma was nearly fifteen years old at the time, and he easily freed himself from the old man's grasp. But he did not run away.

"You dare lay hands on me!" he warned, scowling and showing his fists.

"Lay hands on you? I'll turn you over to the police, that's what I'll do! Who's your father?"

Foma was so taken aback that all his anger and bravado deserted him. He was sure his father would never forgive him if he were taken to the police.

"Gordeyev," he faltered, with a little shudder.

"Ignat Matveyevich's son?"

"Yes."

Now it was the captain who was taken aback. He straightened up, threw out his chest and cleared his throat impressively. But the next moment he wilted.

"Aren't you ashamed of yourself?" he chided paternally. "The son of such a well-known and highly respected personage! I would never have expected such a thing of you! You can go home, but if I ever catch you again I shall have to report you to your father—to whom, by the way, I have the honour of sending my best regards."

The swift change of expression on the old man's face told Foma that he was afraid of Ignat. Foma, instead of going home as he had been told he could, stood scowling like a wolf cub at the captain, who shifted from one foot to the other and twisted his grey whiskers with a ridiculous air of importance.

"You may go," repeated the old man, pointing down the path leading to his house.

"And what about the police?" asked Foma sullenly. The instant he had said it he was frightened by the thought of what the answer might be.

"Oh, I was only joking," smiled the captain. "I just wanted to frighten you."

"You're afraid of my father," said Foma and, turning his back on the old man, he went deeper into the orchard.

"Afraid? Ho! A fine thing to say!" called the captain after him, but from the tone of his voice Foma knew he had been stung. The boy felt so ashamed that for the rest of the day he roamed about alone. On coming home in the evening his father greeted him with a stern face.

"Foma, did you climb into Chumakov's orchard?" he asked.

"Yes," said the boy unwaveringly, looking his father straight in the face.

Evidently Ignat had not been expecting this answer and for a second or two he stroked his beard in silence.

"Why did you do that, you little scamp? Haven't you got apples enough of your own?"

Foma dropped his eyes and said nothing.

"You're ashamed, aren't you? I suppose it was that Yezhov of yours who put you up to it. I'll give it to him when I see him! I may even forbid you to play with him altogether."

"I did it myself," said Foma firmly.

"All the worse. But *why* did you do it?"

"Just because."

"Just because!" mocked his father. "If you do a thing, you ought to know why. Come here."

Foma went over to where his father was sitting. Ignat stood him between his knees, put his hands on his shoulders, and looked into his eyes.

"Ashamed?" he said with a little laugh.

"Mm," sighed Foma.

"You little fool! Disgracing yourself and me!"

He pressed his son's head to his breast and stroked his hair.

"Why on earth did you go stealing apples?" he asked again.

"I don't know," stammered Foma. "We always play the same old thing . . . and I got tired of it. But this . . ."

"This was exciting?" laughed his father.

"Yes."

"H'm. I suppose that's true. But don't do it again, Foma. If you do, I'll give you a thrashing."

."I'll never do it again," promised the boy.

"I'm glad you stand on your own legs. What you'll turn out to be in the end the Lord only knows, but you're all right now. It's good for a person to answer for what he does—to pay his own bills. Another chap might have put the blame on to his friend, but you spoke out and said you were to blame. That's the way, Foma. You play, you pay. That Chumakov—he didn't . . . er . . . hit you, did he?" asked Ignat.

"I'd have paid him back if he had," said Foma promptly.

"H'm," murmured his father.

"I told him he was afraid of you. That's why he came and sneaked on me. He wasn't going to."

"He wasn't?"

"No. He said I was to give you his regards."

"Oh, he did, did he?"

"Yes."

"The worm! Some people are queer: you steal from them and they bow and scrape and send you their regards! Oh, I know it was only a kopek's worth you stole, but a kopek is to him what a rouble is to me. And the kopek isn't the thing; the thing is that it belonged to him and nobody else had a right to it unless he chose to give it to them. But enough of this. Tell me where you were and what you saw."

The boy sat down beside his father and told him all the impressions of the day. Ignat's brows drew together thoughtfully as he studied his son's glowing face.

51

"We scared an owl in the gully," said Foma. "What fun it was! The owl flew up, and—bang!—straight into a tree! It even let out a squeal. It was hurt, I suppose. We scared it again, and it flew up again and the same thing happened. Every time it flew it bumped into something. How the feathers did fly! It went banging about the gully for a long time before it found a place to hide in. We didn't bother to look for it—we felt sorry for it, banging itself like that. Can't owls see anything at all in the daytime, Father?"

"Nothing at all, son," said Ignat. "There are people who go banging about life like your owl—fluttering here, fluttering there—looking for some place to fit into. All that comes of it is that the feathers fly. They lose their feathers, hurt themselves, get ill, and in the end throw themselves headlong into the first thing they come upon—anything to end their struggles. Alas for such people, son! Alas!"

"What makes them like that?"

"It's hard to say. Some of them are blinded by pride—they have big ambitions, but nothing much else. Others are just stupid. Oh, there are lots of reasons."

And so, slowly, day by day, Foma's life unfolded. It was, on the whole, a quiet, peaceful life, without much to disturb it. At times the boy's soul would be stirred by some impression that stood out strikingly against the background of his tranquil existence, but this would not last long. His soul was a quiet lake as yet—a lake sheltered from the storms of life, and all that touched its rim, or glided over its surface, or fell into its depths, disturbing the sleeping waters for a brief moment, dissolved in widening circles, leaving the lake as placid as before.

At the end of five years of study, Foma, who had finished only four forms (he was not a brilliant pupil), left school. He was a handsome lad with black hair, brown skin, heavy eyebrows and a dark line of down on his upper lip. There was a meditative, innocent look in his large dark eyes, and his lips were still soft and childlike. But if he was crossed in anything, the pupils of his eyes would dilate, his lips form a tight line, and his face grow hard.

"The girls will find you sweeter than honey, Foma, but you haven't given signs of much brain yet," chuckled his godfather.

This drew a sigh from Ignat.

"High time you set the lad on his way, Ignat."

52

"Wait a little."

"Why wait? Two or three years on the Volga, and then the altar. My Lyuba's a big girl now."

At this time Lyuba Mayakina was in the fifth form of a boarding school. Whenever Foma passed her in the street she would give him a condescending nod of her fair head, with its smart little hat. Foma liked her, but her pink cheeks, gay brown eyes, and scarlet lips could not make up for the offensiveness of those condescending nods. She was friendly with a group of students from the *gymnasium*, and although Foma's old friend Yezhov was one of them, he had no inclination to join the group for he did not feel at home with them. It seemed to him they always tried to show off their knowledge in front of him and laughed at his ignorance. They would gather at Lyuba's and read books out loud, but if he came while they were reading or arguing noisily, they would instantly break off. He felt the affront of this. One day when he was at the Mayakins, Lyuba invited him to walk in the garden, and as he was walking at her side she made a little face and said:

"What makes you so unsociable? You never open your mouth."

"How can I talk if I have nothing to talk about?" he answered simply.

"Read books and learn."

"I don't want to."

"Those boys know a lot and can talk about anything. Yezhov, for instance."

"He's a windbag."

"You're just jealous. He's awfully clever; oh, yes he is! When he finishes the *gymnasium* he's going to Moscow to enter the University."

"Let him."

"And you'll go on being an ignoramus."

"What of it?"

"How intelligent you are!" said Lyuba ironically.

"I'll get on in the world without any learning," sneered Foma. "And I'll get the better of all those learned friends of yours. It's for beggars to study, not for me."

"Ugh, what a nasty, stupid, horrid person you are!" cried Lyuba and walked away, leaving him alone.

His eyebrows shot up and he sent a hurt look after her. Then he sauntered away with drooping head.

53

He began to taste the joy of solitude, the sweet poison of meditation. Often on summer evenings, when the world was aglow with sunset hues that kindle the imagination, his heart would be heavy with some incomprehensible longing. Sitting in a secluded corner of the garden, or lying on his bed, he would conjure up visions of fairy princesses. They would come to him in the form of Lyuba or other girls of his acquaintance, and float silently in the shadows of twilight, bending soft, mysterious glances upon him. Sometimes these visions would make the blood race in his veins and fill him with strength, so that he would leap up, square his shoulders, and draw in great breaths of the fragrant air; at other times they made him sad—made him feel like crying and, though he felt ashamed to cry and did his best to hold back the tears, they would come in spite of himself.

Little by little his father taught him the business. He took him to the exchange, told him how to give orders and make contracts, talked to him about his colleagues, telling him how they had "got on in the world", pointing out which ones had made a fortune, and describing their personalities. Foma easily mastered the business and took it seriously.

"Our turnip is growing into a handsome poppy," laughed Mayakin, winking at Ignat.

But even when Foma was nineteen years old there was something childish and innocent about him that made him different from other young men of his age. They laughed at him and thought him stupid and he remained apart, offended by their attitude. His father and Mayakin, who both kept a watchful eye on him, were seriously disturbed by his irresolute character.

"I don't understand him," said Ignat unhappily. "He doesn't drink or run after the women, he's respectful to you and me and listens to us, but he's more like a girl than a man. And yet he isn't stupid, is he?"

"Not particularly, I should say," answered Mayakin.

"It's as if he was waiting for something, as if he had scales on his eyes. His mother was like that—went about groping her way. Afrikan Smolin is only two years older, but look at him. You can't tell who's the brains there—him or his father. He wants to go away to study—to some factory or other. He's always quarrelling with his father: says he didn't teach him anything worth knowing. That's the sort he is. But my son? I can't make him out." And Ignat heaved a deep sigh.

54

"Look, this is what you must do," said Mayakin. "Throw him into some big job—let him sink or swim. After all, gold is tested by fire. We'll see what he's like when he's given his head. Send him off on a commission down the Kama by himself."

"As a sort of test, eh?"

"What if he bungles things? You'll be out of pocket, but at least you'll know the stuff he's made of."

"You're right; that's what I'll do," resolved Ignat.

And that spring Ignat sent his son down the Kama with two barges of corn. The barges were towed by the *Prilezhny*, with Foma's old friend, the former boat-hand Yefim (now respectfully called Yefim Ilyich), in command. He had grown into a stocky, lynx-eyed man of thirty and had turned out to be a very strict, steady and sensible captain.

They sailed along swiftly and in high spirits, for everyone was pleased. Foma was proud to have been entrusted with his first big responsibility. Yefim was glad to be under this youthful master who did not swear at him for every slip he made. And the good humour of the two chiefs was as sunlight shining upon the rest of the crew. They set out with their freight in April and reached their destination at the beginning of May. When the barges were anchored near shore, the steamer came alongside them. Foma's orders had been to unload the corn as quickly as possible, collect the money and set out for Perm, where he was to take on a cargo of iron which Ignat had contracted to deliver to the market.

The barges were anchored near a hamlet at the edge of a pine wood. On the morning after their arrival a noisy group of men and women on foot and on horses came down to the river-bank. Shouting and singing, they clambered up on the decks of the barges, and instantly work was in full swing. The women went down into the holds and poured the corn into sacks which the men threw over their shoulders and carried up on deck and down the gang-planks to the shore. Soon a long line of carts piled high with the long-awaited corn was winding slowly up the road leading to the hamlet. The women sang as they worked, the men joked and swore good-naturedly, the crew, transformed into guardians of law and order, shouted at the workmen, the gang-planks slapped the water as the men walked up and down them, horses whinnied, carts creaked, the sand made a grating sound as the wheels passed over it.

55

The sun had just risen, and the air, redolent of pine, was fresh and invigorating. The placid water reflected the blue of the sky and murmured softly as it lapped against the sides of the boats and the anchor chains. The gay sounds of people at work, the youthful beauty of the spring landscape gleaming in the rays of the sun—all this was charged with an exhilarating force that excited Foma pleasantly and evoked vague new feelings and desires in him. He was sitting on deck in the shade of an awning having tea with Yefim and a red-haired, near-sighted, bespectacled clerk from the District Council who had been sent to receive the corn. The clerk's shoulders twitched nervously as he spoke, in a cracked voice, of how the peasants were starving, but Foma paid little attention to what he said; his eyes kept wandering from the people at work down below to the high bank edged with pines on the other side of the river—a quiet, deserted place.

"I'll have to row over there," thought Foma, while to his ears, as if from far away, came the rasping voice of the clerk:

"You wouldn't believe the state things are in! Listen to this: in Osa a peasant brought his daughter, a girl of about sixteen, to an educated gentleman and said to him: 'Here, I've brought you my daughter, your honour.' 'What for?' asks the gentleman. 'I thought you might take her, you being a bachelor,' says the peasant. 'But why? What for?' 'Well,' says the peasant, 'time and again I've walked round the town trying to place her as a servant, but nobody will have her. So you take her—as your mistress, if you can't find any other use for her'. Think of that! Offering his own daughter, his *daughter*, mind you, to this man as a mistress! The man, of course, was indignant and told the peasant what he thought of him. But the peasant said, very sensibly: 'What am I to do with her in times like these, your honour?' he says. 'She's just a burden. I've got three boys besides; they'll grow up to be workmen, so I've got to try to keep them alive. Give me ten roubles for my girl and I'll be able to save my boys'. What do you think of that, eh? Dreadful, I tell you."

"Not a pretty picture," sighed Yefim. "Hunger, as the saying goes, is not a fairy-godmother. The belly has its own idea of right and wrong, it seems."

For some reason he could not explain, Foma was deeply interested in the fate of the girl.

"Did the gentleman buy her?" he asked quickly.

"Of course not," said the clerk reproachfully.

"What happened to her?"

"Oh, they found some good people who took her in."

"Ah!" gasped Foma; then suddenly, in a harsh voice: "I'd have given it to that peasant! I'd have broken his head!" and he raised a clenched fist.

"But why?" cried the clerk, snatching the spectacles off his nose.

"How is it possible to sell a human being?"

"Savagery, I'll admit, but—"

"And a young girl at that! I'd have given him his ten roubles, all right!"

The clerk shrugged his shoulders without replying. This irritated Foma. He got up and walked over to the railing, from where he could see the workmen hurrying to and fro on the barge. The bustle made him giddy, and the vague feelings that had been hovering in his soul crystallized into a longing to work himself, to possess fabulous strength and gigantic shoulders on which he could carry hundreds of sacks of grain at a time, so that everyone should be struck with wonder.

"Quick, there! Stir your stumps!" he called down. Several heads were raised, he caught a glimpse of faces, and one of them—the face of a woman with black eyes—smiled at him gently, alluringly. At the sight of that smile something flared up inside him, his blood went hot and flowed through his veins like molten lava. He tore himself away from the railing and returned to the table, aware that his cheeks were burning.

"Look," said the clerk, turning to Foma, "wire your father to give us some extra corn to make up for the loss in spilling. Just see how much goes to waste, and every grain is worth its weight in gold. You ought to know that. But that father of yours . . . h'm . . ." ended the clerk with a grimace.

"How much do you want him to throw in for good measure?" asked Foma in an off-hand way. "A hundred poods? Two hundred?"

"Oh! Dear me, that would be splendid!" exclaimed the astonished clerk. "If you have the right—"

"I'm the master," said Foma brusquely. "And I'll ask you not to make slurring remarks about my father and turn up your nose."

57

"I beg your pardon. I don't doubt that you have the right. I thank you from the bottom of my heart . . . you and your father . . . on behalf of all these people."

Yefim looked askance at his young master. He pursed up his lips and smacked them, but the young master stood with a proud look on his face as the clerk poured out words of gratitude and squeezed his hand.

"Two hundred! That's real Russian generosity, young man! Here, I shall tell these peasants about your present. You'll see how grateful they will be!" and he shouted down: "The owner is making you a present of two hundred poods, men!"

"Three hundred," corrected Foma.

"Three hundred poods! Thank you! Three hundred poods of corn, men!"

But the effect was not what the clerk had expected. The peasants raised their heads for a moment, then went back to work without a word. A few voices were heard to say falteringly, even reluctantly:

"Thank you."

"God bless you for that."

"Many thanks."

And someone called out with gay mockery:

"Corn? Ah! If he was to give us each a glass of vodka, now, that *would* be kindness ! The corn isn't for us, it goes to the Council!"

"They don't understand," cried the distressed clerk. "Here, I'll go down and explain to them."

And he went. But Foma did not care what the muzhiks thought of his gift: he saw the black eyes of the woman gazing at him with an odd little smile. They were thanking him, caressing him, calling him, and he could see nothing else. She was dressed like the town women—in a cotton blouse, with shoes on her feet and a special sort of kerchief binding up her black hair. Tall and willowy, she was sitting on a pile of wood mending sacks, her arms, bare to the elbow, flashing as she worked, her lips smiling at Foma.

"Foma Ignatiyevich," he heard Yefim saying reproachfully, "aren't you showing off a bit too much? Fifty poods, say, would be all very well. But handing it out right and left like that! If you don't look out we'll come to grief, you and me."

"Mind your own business!" snapped Foma.

"Do as you like. I can keep my mouth shut. But you're young yet, and I was told to keep an eye on you. I may get a punch on the nose for letting a thing like this pass."

"I'll tell my father," said Foma.

"That's all right. You're the boss, but—"

"Then that's enough, Yefim!"

Yefim heaved a sigh and was silent. Foma looked down at the woman and thought to himself:

"If somebody would only sell a woman like that—to me!"

His pulse quickened. As yet a virgin, he had picked up a knowledge of the intimate relations between men and women from chance conversation. It had come to him in coarse, obscene words that repelled him, yet excited his curiosity. He tried hard to imagine what it was like, but none of the images he conjured up were comprehensible to him. Deep down in his heart he did not believe that the relations between men and women were as gross and matter-of-fact as he had been told. When he was scoffed at and assured that they were, and that nothing else was possible, he grinned foolishly, but went on believing that this shameful form was not the only one in which man's relation to woman could be expressed; that there must surely be another, more pure and delicate, less insulting to human nature.

But now, as he stood gazing in admiration at the black-eyed woman, it was just this coarse attraction that he felt for her. This frightened and humiliated him. Yefim, who was standing next to him, said gravely:

"And now here you are staring at that woman. Say what you will, I can't keep my mouth shut. You've never seen her before, but if she keeps on making eyes at you it's clear that, young as you are, and with the character you've got, you may do things that'll send the lot of us home on foot, and lucky if we've still got trousers left to go in."

"What do you want of me?" said Foma, reddening.

"I don't want anything. But you'd better listen to me. I can certainly teach young fellows something about dealing with women. It's all very simple: give her a bottle of vodka and something to eat, then a couple of bottles of beer, and when it's all over, give the lady twenty kopeks. For that price she'll show you all the love that's in her."

"That's a lie!" said Foma under his breath.

"A lie? Why should I lie when I've played this game myself at least a hundred times? Look here, let me manage this affair for you. I'll see that you make the lady's acquaintance."

"Very well," said Foma, who felt as if someone had him by the throat.

"I'll bring her along this evening."

For the rest of the day Foma went about in a daze, unconscious of the deferential, ingratiating looks the peasants cast at him. He was horrified; he felt he had wronged somebody, and this made him meek and gentle with everyone as if in apology.

That evening the workmen gathered on the river-bank to cook their supper over a huge camp-fire. The flames made red and yellow splashes on the river and their reflections danced on the smooth water and on the glass window of the cabin where Foma sat huddled in one corner of the sofa. He drew the curtain over the window and did not light the lamp. The glow of the camp-fire came through the curtain, throwing a faint, quivering light, which kept growing and waning, on table and walls. It was very quiet; the only sound that broke the silence was the murmur of voices on the bank and the lapping of the water against the sides of the boat. Foma imagined that someone was hiding in the shadows of the cabin and watching him closely. . . . Ah, here they were! Heavy footsteps running up the gang-plank . . . the plank slapping the water spitefully . . . laughter and lowered voices outside his door. . . .

"Go away!" was the cry that rushed to his lips. He even got up from the sofa, but before he had time to speak or act the door was thrown open and he saw a tall woman standing there. She closed the door behind her soundlessly.

"Goodness gracious, how dark it is!" she said in a low voice. "Is anyone here?"

"Yes," said Foma faintly.

"Well then, good evening." And the woman took an uncertain step forward.

"I'll—I'll light the lamp," stammered Foma, but he merely sank down upon the sofa and huddled into the corner again.

"Oh, it's all right as it is. When your eyes get used to it, you can see in the dark."

"Sit down," said Foma.

"Thank you."

She sat down on the sofa, within hand's reach. Foma was aware of the sparkle of her eyes and the smile on her lips. Her smile seemed to be different now—more sad and pathetic. It encouraged him. Her eyes dropped when they met his, and this made him breathe more easily. But he did not know what to say to her, and there was a strained silence. She was the first to break it.

"You must feel lonely all by yourself, don't you?"

"Ye-es," said Foma.

"How do you like our part of the river?"

"Very pretty. Lots of woods."

Again there was silence.

"Your river's even prettier than the Volga," Foma forced himself to remark.

"I've been on the Volga. At Simbirsk."

"Simbirsk," repeated Foma, unable to think of anything else to say. But she, having sized up her companion by this time, suddenly exclaimed in a lively whisper:

"Come, why don't you treat me to something, master?"

"Ah, yes," said Foma, pulling himself together. "Of course. What a stupid fellow I am! Here, help yourself."

And he began fumbling about in the darkness, picking up and putting down the bottles, bumping into the table, laughing guiltily and self-consciously. She went over and stood next to him, smiling as she looked at his blushing face and trembling hands.

"Are you ashamed?" she whispered suddenly.

He felt her breath on his cheek.

"Yes," he whispered back.

At that she put her hands on his shoulders and gently drew him to her breast, whispering soothingly:

"It's nothing . . . don't be ashamed . . . after all, you can't do without it . . . you're so young . . . and handsome . . . and I feel so sorry for you. . . ."

Her whispered words made him feel like crying. A sweet langour enveloped his soul; he pressed his head against her breast and clasped her in his arms, murmuring something unintelligible, something he himself did not know the meaning of. . . .

"Go away," said Foma, staring at the wall with wide-open eyes.

61

She kissed his cheek, got up obediently, and went to the door. "Good-bye," she said.

Foma was unbearably ashamed in her presence, but as soon as she was gone he jumped up and then again sat down on the sofa. He had not sat there long before he staggered to his feet, overwhelmed by a sense of loss—the loss of something precious which he had not even known he possessed until it was gone. At almost the same moment he was filled with a brave new feeling of pride in himself. This obliterated his shame, and instead of shame, he felt pity for the woman who had gone out alone into the darkness of the cold May night. Quickly he left the cabin and went on deck. The night was starry and moonless; he felt its chill, plunged into its darkness. The embers of the camp-fire were still glowing red and gold on the river-bank. Foma listened: an oppressive silence hung in the air with no sound to relieve it but the plash of the water as it struck the anchor chains. Nowhere was a step heard. He wanted to call to the woman, but he did not know her name. For several minutes he remained standing on deck, eagerly drinking in the fresh air and, suddenly, from the bow of the boat on the other side of his cabin, came a sound as of sobbing. He gave a start and moved forward quietly, certain he would find her there.

She was sitting on the deck and crying, her head resting on a coil of rope. Foma could see the rise and fall of her bare white shoulders and hear her forlorn weeping. He himself felt forlorn.

"What is it?" he asked timidly, bending over her.

She shook her head without answering.

"Have I hurt you?"

"Go away," she said.

"But—but why?" said Foma anxiously, touching her hair. "Don't be angry with me; after all, you yourself. . . ."

"I'm not angry," she whispered. "Why should I be angry with you? You're not a beast; your heart is pure. Oh, my bird of passage, sit down beside me."

She took Foma's hand and pulled him down beside her as if he were a child, holding his head to her breast and leaning over to press her hot lips to his.

"What are you crying for?" asked Foma, stroking her cheek with one hand and gripping her shoulder with the other.

"For myself. Why did you send me away?" she asked plaintively.

"I was ashamed," said Foma, dropping his head.

"Dear boy, be honest with me! You didn't like me, did you?" she said laughingly, and big hot tears fell on Foma's chest.

"What are you saying?" said the youth almost in fright. Then he broke into ardent expostulations, telling her how lovely and how tender she was, how he pitied her, and how ashamed he felt when he was with her. And as she listened she kept kissing his cheeks, his neck, his head, and his bare chest.

When he had finished she began to speak in a soft, sad voice, as if she were speaking about the dead:

"So I was mistaken," she said. "When you told me to go away, I got up and went, but your words made me very bitter. There was a time, I thought, when they used to love and caress me without stopping, without growing tired; they would do anything I asked for one of my smiles. That was what I thought of, and it made me cry. I cried for my lost youth, for now I am thirty years old, and there isn't much time left to a woman after thirty. Ah, Foma Ignatiyevich!" she cried, raising her voice and quickening the rhythm of her melodious speech, whose sounds were a lovely echo of the lapping water. "Listen to what I say! Make good use of your youth! Nothing on earth is so precious. Youth, like gold, will bring you whatever you want. Spend it so that there will be something to remember when you're old. It was my youth I thought of and, though it made me cry, my heart was glad as I remembered how I had lived. And I felt young again, as if I had drunk of living waters. Ah, dear lad, I shall take my pleasure with you, if I am to your liking, and throw my whole soul into the taking! Once I've caught fire, I'll burn till I'm nothing but ashes!"

And she snatched Foma to her breast and kissed him passionately on the lips.

"Night wa-a-a-tch!" sang out a boat-hand on the neighbouring barge, snapping off the ". . .tch" abruptly. Then he took up his mallet and struck a piece of sheet iron serving as a bell. Clanging vibrations tore through the solemn stillness of the night.

A few days later, when the barges were unloaded and the boat was ready to weigh anchor for Perm, Yefim saw, to his great consternation, a cart driving down to the water's edge, and in the cart was the dark-eyed Pelagea with her trunk and bundles.

"Send some men to go and fetch her things," ordered Foma, nodding toward the cart.

63

Yefim gave a disapproving shake of his head and did what he was told with an ill will. Later he said in lowered tones:

"So she's going with us, is she?"

"She's going with me."

"I didn't suppose with all of us. Heigh ho!"

"What are you sighing about?"

"Look, Foma Ignatiyevich, it's a big town we're going to; there'll be plenty of her kind there."

"Hold your tongue!" said Foma severely.

"I will, I will; but this isn't right, you know."

Foma scowled.

"If I hear you or anyone else say anything indecent about her, I'll break your head, and don't you forget it!" said Foma imperiously, stressing every word.

"Ghosts and goblins!" murmured Yefim, gazing incredulously at his master and retreating a step. Ignat's son had bared his teeth like a wolf and the pupils of his eyes were dilated.

"Just dare!" he roared. "I'll show you!"

"You may be my master," said Yefim with dignity in spite of his fright, "but I was told to keep an eye on you, and I'm the captain here."

"Captain?" shouted Foma going white and quivering all over. "And who am I?"

"You needn't shout. And all because of some good-for-nothing woman."

Red blotches broke out on Foma's white face, he jumped from one foot to the other, jammed his hands into his pockets, and said in a firm, even voice:

"Listen, you captain! If you say another word you can go to the devil! I'll put you ashore. The pilot and I will go on without you, understand? Don't think you can give orders to *me*!"

Yefim was dumbfounded. He stood there blinking at Foma, unable to utter a word.

"I asked you if you understood?"

"Y-e-s," gasped Yefim. "But why all the noise? Just because of a damned—"

"Shut up!"

Foma's wild eyes and distorted face told the captain it would be prudent to withdraw, which he did in haste.

He was angry with Foma and considered that he had been unjustly treated; at the same time he recognized the strong hand of a real master and, since he was used to being ordered about, he liked to feel that the power over him was a strong one. He went straight to the cabin of the pilot and told him, not without approval, what had happened.

"What do you think of that?" he said on concluding his story. "A good hound, they say, shows its points the first time you take it hunting. You wouldn't think it to look at him—he seems a wobbly sort of creature. Well, let him have his fun. No harm will come of it—not with the temper he's got! The way he blared at me! Like a trumpet! It certainly hasn't taken him long to show what *he* is made of. You'd think he'd swallowed power and authority by the bucketful!"

What Yefim said was the truth: Foma had completely changed in the last few days. The passion that had flared up within him made him complete possessor of the woman's soul and body, and he drank greedily of the burning sweetness of possession. It burnt out all the incongruities that had made him seem a dull, morose lad, and filled his heart with youthful pride and a consciousness of his own individuality. Love for a woman is always beneficial to a man, no matter what sort of love, even though it brings him nothing but suffering, for suffering itself is not without benefit. Poison to sickly souls, love is to wholesome ones as fire to steel.

Foma's infatuation with this thirty-year-old woman, whose love for him was the swan song of her youth, did not distract him from the job on hand. He did not lose himself in either love or work, but kept himself whole for both. Like good wine, the woman roused in him an urge to activity as well as to lovemaking, and she herself grew younger under the spell of his caresses.

At Perm he found a letter from his godfather waiting for him. Mayakin wrote that Ignat was drowning his loneliness in drink, and since it was bad for him to drink so much at his age, Foma had better finish his business as quickly as possible and hasten home. The youth sensed a note of alarm in the letter that spoiled his heart's holiday, but this shadow was soon dispelled by the cares of business and the caresses of Pelagea. Time sped past with the swiftness of the river current; every day brought new experiences and new ideas. Pelagea's love had the intensity of passion that only a woman of her age, draining the last drops from the cup of delight, could achieve. At times she would experience another feeling that was just as strong as this passion and bound Foma to her even more securely—a feeling akin to that of a mother's anxiety to guard her son from making fatal mistakes, to teach him the wisdom of life. Often as they sat in each other's embrace on the deck at night, she would speak to him sadly and tenderly.

"Listen to me as to an elder sister," she would say. "I've had a lot of experience. I know people. How much I've seen in my time! Choose your friends with care, for there are people as contagious as disease. You can't tell this at first. A man may seem to be just like any other, and before you know it you've caught his sores. And be careful with women—may the Holy Virgin protect you. You're still soft; your heart has no crust on it yet. Lads like you—strong, handsome, rich—make fine pickings for women. Be wary of the quiet ones; they suck men like leeches, suck on and on in their sweet quiet way. But though they suck the very life out of a man, they keep themselves intact. They break men's hearts without giving anything in return. Better to take up with the lively ones, like me. They have no thought of gain."

Pelagea certainly had no thought of gain. At Perm Foma bought her clothes and trinkets. She was pleased with them, but as she looked at them she said anxiously:

"Don't squander your money. Your father will be angry. I love you anyway—without all this."

From the very first she had told him she would go with him only to Kazan, where her married sister lived. Foma did not believe she would leave him there, and when, on the night before they got to Kazan, she said it again, he was disconsolate and begged her not to go.

"Don't grieve in advance," she said. "There's a whole night before us. It will be time enough to shed tears when I'm gone, if you really miss me."

But he only begged her the harder not to leave him, and said that he wanted to marry her.

"Oho! so that's what you want!" she laughed. "Bless your heart, what a strange fellow you are! So you want to get married, do you? As if men married women like me! You'll have lots and lots of sweethearts before that time comes. Wait to get married until you've seen something of the world, until you've had your fill of the sweets of life and are longing for good black bread. Then

66

it will be time to get married. A healthy man shouldn't marry young; one woman is not enough for him, so he'll go to others. If you want to be happy, don't take a wife until you're sure that she alone will satisfy you."

But the more she spoke, the more loath Foma was to part with her.

"Listen to me," she said calmly. "If you're carrying a torch and have light enough without it, plunge it straight into the water so that it won't smoke or burn your hand."

"I don't understand what you mean."

"Try to. You have done me no wrong and I don't want to do you any. That's why I'm leaving you."

It is hard to say how their contest would have ended had not circumstances intervened. At Kazan Foma got a wire from his godfather saying briefly: "Return immediately passenger boat". Foma's heart sank, but a few hours later he was standing, pale and downcast, on the deck of a passenger boat that was drawing away from the landing. Motionless, without so much as blinking, he clutched the rail with both hands and gazed at the woman's face that seemed to be floating away from him together with the landing and the river-bank. Pelagea waved her kerchief to him and smiled, but he knew she was crying. The front of his shirt was wet with her tears, and they had left his anguished heart feeling cold and sodden. The figure of the woman grew smaller and smaller and as Foma watched it he was conscious that some strong new feeling had been added to his grief at losing the woman and his fear for his father. It was resentment against someone, but he could not say whom.

The crowd of people on the landing became a single dark blur without face or form or movement. Foma turned away and began to pace the deck unhappily.

The passengers, talking loudly, sat down to tea; waiters rushed back and forth laying the tables; a child's laugh rose from somewhere down in the third class; a concertina was played; the cook rattled dishes and pounded a steak with the flat side of a knife. The huge steamer ploughed swiftly against the current, shuddering with the strain of cutting through the waves, which were churned into foam. As Foma gazed down into the swirling water in the wake, he had a wild wish to break and tear and destroy. He, too, wanted to plough against the current and smash its force with his breast and shoulders.

67

"Fate!" said someone nearby in a languid, husky voice.

He had heard the word before; his Aunt Anfisa had often used it in answer to his questions, and the four letters represented for him a force similar to that of God. He glanced up to see who was speaking. One of the men was old and grey-haired and had a kindly face; the other was a younger man with large tired eyes and a pointed black beard. His big fleshy nose and hollow cheeks made Foma think of his godfather.

"Yes, Fate," the old man repeated in confirmation of what his companion had said. "It hangs over life as an angler hangs over a stream, throwing in its hook, which someone snatches up hungrily; the next thing you know, the victim lies gasping on shore with a breaking heart. That's how it is, my friend."

Foma shut his eyes as if a beam of sunlight had struck them.

"True!" he said aloud, shaking his head. "Oh, how true!"

The two men turned and stared at him—the old man with a faint appreciative smile, the younger disapprovingly, from under lowered brows. This embarrassed Foma, and he blushed and walked away, pondering Fate, wondering why it had treated him so kindly by giving him this woman, only to snatch her away so quickly and cruelly. And he realized that the gnawing feeling he had been carrying about with him was resentment against Fate for playing with him. He had been too pampered by life to accept this first drop of poison in his cup as a matter of course. He lay awake at night thinking about what the old man had said and nursing his resentment. But his resentment left him wrathful and eager for vengeance, rather than downcast and despondent.

Foma was met by his godfather, whom he pressed with anxious questions.

"Your father's taken leave of his senses," replied the old man, his green eyes flashing as he seated himself in the carriage next to his godson.

"Drinking?"

"Worse. He's out of his mind."

"What is it? For God's sake tell me!"

"It's like this: there's a certain young lady fluttering about him—"

"Well?" said Foma, thinking of his Pelagea with a little twinge of joy.

"She's fastened herself on to him and is sucking him dry."

"Is she the quiet sort?"

"She? Quiet as a house on fire. Blew seventy-five thousand out of his pocket like a feather."

"Good Lord! Who is she?"

"Sonya Medynskaya, the architect's wife."

"Saints in heaven! Do you mean to say—could my father—is she his mistress?" asked the astonished Foma under his breath.

His godfather started back and rolled his eyes.

"You're as mad as he is, lad! Quite as mad, upon my word. Think what you're saying! A mistress at the age of sixty-three, and at such a price! What are you thinking of? Just wait till I tell Ignat that!"

And he broke into a cackling laugh that made his scraggy beard shake in an ugly way. It took some time for Foma to find out what he wanted to know. The old man was not his usual self at all: he was nervous and uneasy; his speech, ordinarily so flowing, was disconnected, and he kept interrupting himself to swear and to spit. Foma could hardly make out what he was trying to tell him. It seemed that Sophia Pavlovna Medynskaya, wife of a rich architect, a woman known throughout the town as an indefatigable champion of charitable projects, had talked Ignat into donating seventy-five thousand roubles for the building of a shelter for paupers and a free public library and reading-room. The newspapers had lauded Ignat to the skies for his generosity. Foma had often seen this woman out walking; she was very small and had the reputation of being one of the prettiest women in town. People said unpleasant things about her.

"Is that all?" said Foma when he had heard his godfather out. "And here I was thinking all sorts of things!"

"You! You were thinking!" snorted his godfather. "You can't think. You've just been weaned!"

"What are you so angry about?" asked Foma in amazement.

"Seventy-five thousand roubles! Is that a lot of money or isn't it? Answer me that."

"Of course it is," said Foma after a moment's consideration. "But Father has plenty of money. I don't see why you—"

Mayakin shuddered and glanced contemptuously into the young man's face.

"You speak like that?" he asked in a feeble voice.

"Why not?"

"It's not you! It's the foolishness of your youth that speaks. And it's the foolishness of my old age, which has stood a thousand

69

tests, that says you're still a puppy and it's too soon for you to be barking!"

Foma had often felt the sting of his godfather's figurative speech (Mayakin always spoke more roughly to him than his father did), but this time he was cut to the quick.

"I don't know why you should talk to me like that; after all, I'm not a child any more," he said firmly and with restraint.

"Indeed!" exclaimed Mayakin mockingly, lifting his brows. This was too much for Foma. He looked the old man straight in the face and said very clearly and distinctly:

"Yes, indeed. I say that I've had enough of your bawling and I don't want to hear any more of it?"

"H'm!" He clicked his tongue. "I beg your pardon."

Mayakin screwed up his eyes, chewed his lips, looked away, and said nothing for a minute or two. The carriage turned into a narrow street and, on catching sight of the roof of his house, Foma involuntarily strained forward.

"Foma," said his godfather with a twinkle in his eye, "whom have you been sharpening your teeth on?"

"Why, are they sharp?" asked Foma, pleased to hear his godfather say this.

"Sharpish. That's a good thing, lad. A very good thing indeed. We were afraid, your father and me, that you'd turn out to be a nincompoop. Well, and have you learned to drink vodka, too?"

"Yes, I have."

"A little early. Do you drink a lot?"

"Why a lot?"

"Like it?"

"Not particularly."

"H'm. Well, there's nothing wrong in all this. Only you're too outspoken. Ready to confess any old sin to any old priest. Think it over, lad; it's not always best to come straight out with things. Sometimes by keeping quiet, the sin's forgotten and friends are won. A man's tongue is rarely cool and calculating. Well, here we are. Your father isn't expecting you. I'm not even sure he's at home."

He was. Through the open window came the sound of his deep, hoarse laughter. When the carriage stopped in front of the house he glanced out of the window and, on catching sight of his boy, he cried out joyfully:

"What? Back already?"

70

A minute later he was crushing Foma to his breast with one hand and bending back his head with the other to gaze with shining eyes into his face.

"Sunburnt! Put on weight! A healthy fellow!" he exclaimed delightedly. "How do you like my son, madam?"

"A very nice son," came a silvery voice.

Over his father's shoulder Foma caught a glimpse of a tiny woman with fluffy hair sitting with her elbows on the table in a far corner of the room. Dark eyes, delicate brows and soft red lips were set in a pale face. Behind her chair stood a big philodendron plant whose decorative leaves hung above her golden head.

"How do you do, Sophia Pavlovna," said Mayakin in mellifluous tones, going over to her with outstretched hand. "Still wheedling contributions out of us poor beggars, eh?"

Foma bowed to her without speaking and without hearing her reply or what his father was saying. The young woman gazed at him with a welcoming smile on her lips. Her girlish figure, clad in some dark material, blended with the wine-coloured upholstery of the chair, and this dark background lent a radiance to her golden hair and pale face. As she sat there in the corner under the green leaves of the plant, she resembled a flower, or an icon.

"Just see, he can't tear his eyes off you, Sophia Pavlovna!" said Ignat. "A fine young stallion, isn't he?"

She lowered her lashes, faint colour dyed her cheeks, and she gave a little laugh that was like the tinkle of silver bells. Then she got up.

"Good-bye," she said, "I won't intrude."

Foma caught a whiff of scent as she glided past him, and he saw her eyes were dark blue, her brows almost black.

"So she's gone, the little minx," said Mayakin softly, looking daggers after her.

"Well, tell us about the trip. Did you spend a lot of money?" said Ignat, pushing his son towards the armchair Medynskaya had just been sitting in. Foma gave it a sidelong glance and sat in another.

"A pretty little thing, eh?" chuckled Mayakin, probing Foma with his gimlet eyes. "If you stand in front of her with your mouth hanging open, she'll gobble up all your insides."

Foma gave a little start and, ignoring his godfather's remark, began to tell his father about his trip. But Ignat interrupted him.

71

"Just a minute. I'll get them to bring some cognac," he said.

"They say you've been drinking a lot," said Foma disapprovingly.

Ignat looked at him in astonishment.

"Is that the way to talk to your father?" he said.

Foma dropped his eyes.

"That's right," said Ignat good-naturedly, and called for the cognac.

Mayakin, after standing and peering at the two Gordeyevs for a minute or two, gave a sigh and took his leave, inviting them to have tea in the garden with him that evening.

"Where's Aunt Anfisa?" asked Foma, feeling uncomfortable for some reason when he was left alone with his father.

"Visiting a convent. Well, tell me all about it while I have a drink."

In a few minutes Foma had given his account, which he concluded by saying:

"I spent a lot of money on myself."

"How much?"

"Something like . . . six hundred roubles."

"In six weeks! That's a tidy sum. You're an expensive agent. What did you do with it all?"

"I gave away three hundred poods of corn."

"What's that? To whom?"

Foma told him.

"Quite all right," said his father. "Such gifts are all to the good. For the honour of your father and the firm. They can't be counted a loss because they're invested in a good name, and there's no better advertisement for a merchant, son. Well, and where else did the money go?"

"Oh, here and there."

"Speak out. It's not the money I'm interested in, but how you spent your time," insisted Ignat, studying his son's face carefully.

"Oh, I ate and drank," evaded Foma.

"Drank? Vodka?"

"Vodka, too."

"Isn't it a little early?"

"I didn't get drunk—ask Yefim if I did."

"Why should I ask Yefim? I want to hear it all from you. So you drink, do you?"

"I can do without it."

"I daresay! Well, have some cognac?"

Foma looked at his father and gave a broad grin. His father grinned back.

"Damn it all, drink if you want to, but keep within bounds. What's to be done about it? Drunkenness can be slept off, but stupidity can't. Keep that in mind, though it's little comfort. And did you try the women, too? Come, out with it! Are you afraid I'll give you a beating?"

"Yes. I had a woman on the boat. I took her from Perm to Kazan with me."

Ignat heaved a great sigh and said with a scowl: "You've defiled yourself pretty early."

"I'm twenty. And you're always saying they married boys off at fifteen in your day," remonstrated Foma.

"*Married* them. Oh, well, enough of this. You've had a woman, and what of it? A woman's like the smallpox: no escaping it. And I can't pretend to be an angel myself. I began before I was your age. But be on your guard with women."

Ignat sat for a long time without moving, without speaking, his head on his chest.

"Listen to me, Foma," he began at last in a firm and solemn voice: "I won't live much longer. I'm old. Something keeps pressing on my chest, cutting off my breath. I'll die soon. Then all my business will pass into your hands. At first your godfather will lend a helping hand, and mind you listen to him. You made a good beginning: did everything you were told and held the reins in a tight hand. I hope to God you keep it up. Remember one thing: business is like a mettlesome horse—you've got to know how to manage it, got to pull hard on the bit or it'll get out of hand. Try to hold yourself above your business so that you can always get a bird's-eye view of the whole and see the tiniest screw that holds it together."

As Foma looked at his father's broad chest and listened to his hearty voice, he thought to himself: you won't die so soon! This was a pleasant thought, and it gave rise to a sudden upsurge of love for him.

"Stick to your godfather," went on Ignat. "He's got enough brains in that head of his to supply the whole town. If he was as brave as he is clever, he'd have made a great name for himself. Well, as I was saying, there's not much time left me. If I did what I

73

ought to do, I'd begin getting ready to die: drop all my affairs, fast and pray, and do something to make people remember me kindly."

"Oh, they will do that!" Foma assured him.

"I don't know why they should."

"What about that shelter for the poor?"

Ignat glanced at his son and laughed.

"So Mayakin's had time to tell you about that, has he? I suppose he abused me for it?"

"A little," smiled Foma.

"He wouldn't be Yakov Mayakin if he didn't."

"He spoke as if it was *his* money you'd spent."

Ignat threw himself back in his chair and laughed harder than ever.

"The old crow! You're right about that—his money and mine is all the same to him, and that's what he's so upset about. He's got a bee in his bonnet, the old bald-head. What do you suppose it is?"

"I don't know," said Foma after a moment's consideration.

"He wants his money and mine to be joined together."

"How?"

"Guess."

Foma looked hard at his father and—guessed.

His face darkened, he leaned forward in his chair and said in a determined voice:

"I don't want that. I'll never marry her."

"You won't? Why not? She's a good strong girl, and not stupid. And she's her father's only child."

"What about Taras, the son that disappeared?"

"Once he's gone, he's gone, and that's all there is to it. There's a will that reads: 'All my property, movable and immovable, is to be passed on to my daughter Lyuba'. As for her being your godsister, we can get round that."

"It makes no difference," insisted Foma, "I won't marry her."

"Well, it's too early to speak about that. But why are you so set against her?"

"I don't like her sort."

"Just think of that, now! And what sort *do* you like, my fine gentleman?"

"I like them simpler. She's always with those students of hers . . . and with her books. She's too clever for me. She'd make fun of me," said Foma with feeling.

74

"You're right about that. She's a lively lass—too lively, in fact. But that's nothing: tarnish will always come off if you rub it hard enough. And your godfather's a clever old fellow. He's done nothing but sit about all his life, and that's given him a lot of time to think things over. He's worth listening to, son—he sees things inside out. And he's of good blood—goes back to Catherine the Great. Knows a lot about himself. When his line broke off with Taras, he decided to put you in Taras's place. Do you realize what that means?"

"I'll make a place for myself without his help," said Foma doggedly.

"You haven't got any sense yet," scoffed Ignat.

Their conversation was interrupted by the arrival of Aunt Anfisa.

"Fomushka! So you've come back!" she cried before she had reached the door. Foma got up and went to meet her with a loving smile on his lips.

Once more Foma's life flowed on slowly and monotonously. His father's tone when he spoke to him was still mockingly genial, but his manner was stricter. He held him to account for every little thing and kept reminding him that he had brought him up leniently, without any restrictions and without beating him.

"Other fathers take clubs to their offspring, but I never laid a finger on you."

"I don't suppose you had any reason to," Foma said one day.

Ignat was infuriated by the words and the complacent tone in which they were spoken.

"What's that?" he shouted. "It's made you bold, this soft upbringing, hasn't it? You know how to answer back, don't you? Be careful, or this soft hand of mine will get so hard it'll send the tears spouting out of your heels! Didn't take you long to grow up, did it? Sprang up like a toadstool that stinks before it's an inch high!"

"Why are you so harsh with me?" Foma once asked when his father was in a good humour.

"Because you can't bear your father finding fault with you. You always argue back."

"But you're unfair. I'm no worse than I used to be. And do you think I don't see how other boys of my age behave?"

75

"It doesn't hurt you to get a wigging now and then. And I give it to you because there's something in you I don't like. What it is I don't know, but I see it plain enough. And it'll harm you."

These words set Foma thinking. He himself was aware of some peculiar quality that distinguished him from other boys of his age, but he could not say what it was. He began to watch himself suspiciously.

He liked to be among the noise and bustle of the exchange, to mingle with prominent businessmen who were making deals involving thousands of roubles. He was flattered by the respectful tone in which the lesser tradesmen spoke to him, Foma Gordeyev. He was proud and happy whenever he was given a chance to handle some business for his father independently and earn a bantering word of praise from him. He longed to be looked upon as a grown-up man with good business sense, but he still kept aloof from people and felt no desire to make friends, although he was constantly thrown among merchants' sons of his own age. They often invited him to join in their orgies, but he refused their invitations off-handedly.

"I'm afraid to," he would say in a jocular tone. "If your fathers find out about your doings they'll beat you, and I'll get my ears tweaked, too."

He did not like the way they caroused without the knowledge of their fathers, on money stolen from their fathers' tills or borrowed on long-term notes at a high rate of interest. They disliked Foma in their turn because of his reserve, behind which they sensed a pride that offended them.

Foma often thought of Pelagea, and at first this made him long to be with her. But as time went on her image faded and without his realizing it her place in his dreams was taken by tiny, angel-faced Sophia Pavlovna Medynskaya. Almost every Sunday she came to Ignat with some request or other, all of them concerned with the building of the shelter. In her presence Foma felt clumsy, enormous, ungainly. He would blush crimson whenever he met the gentle glance of Sophia Pavlovna's large eyes. He noticed that they grew darker when she looked at him, and her upper lip trembled and lifted slightly, revealing small white teeth. This frightened him. His father noticed the way he looked at her, and one day he said to him:

"Don't stare too long at that face. It's like birch coals: smooth and harmless-looking on the outside, but full of fire within."

Medynskaya did not excite physical desire in Foma; she did not resemble Pelagea in the least, and Foma could not understand her. He knew that people said disparaging things about her, but he did not believe what they said. His attitude changed when, one day, he saw her riding in a carriage beside a fat gentleman in a grey hat with stringy hair falling down to his shoulders. His face was as red and puffy as a toy balloon; there was not a sign of beard on it, and he looked for all the world like a woman in disguise. Foma was told that this man was her husband. The information filled him with dark and contradictory emotions: he wanted to insult the architect, and at the same time he could not help envying and respecting him. Sophia Pavlovna seemed less beautiful and more accessible. He felt sorry for her, yet he thought to himself with some satisfaction: she must hate his kissing her.

Above and beyond all this, he was filled at times with an aching sense of emptiness that neither the impressions of the day nor memories of the past could fill—an emptiness that swallowed up the exchange, the business, his thoughts of Medynskaya. It was disturbing. He suspected that in the dark depths of this emptiness lurked some hostile force that was formless as yet, but was steadily, insistently seeking to assert itself.

Meanwhile Ignat, outwardly little changed, grew more restless and grumpy, and complained more often of his health.

"I don't sleep any more," he said. "Once upon a time you could have skinned me alive in my sleep and I'd not so much as blink. Nowadays I toss from side to side all night through and only manage to drop off in the morning. And my heart beats unevenly: now it races ahead—put-put-put!—now it almost stops, as if the next minute it would plunge down into some deep dark hole. Ah, God in heaven, take pity on me, a poor sinner!"

With a penitent sigh he would roll up eyes that had already lost their keen, lively sparkle.

"Death's hiding in the corner, waiting to take me," he said moodily, but with resignation. And true enough, it soon struck down his great frame.

It happened in August, early in the morning. Foma, who was still sound asleep, suddenly felt someone shaking him by the shoulder.

"Get up!" said a hoarse voice in his ear.

He opened his eyes and saw his father sitting on a chair beside the bed, repeating in a dull voice:

"Get up, get up."

The sun had just risen, and the rays that fell on Ignat's white linen undershirt were still of a rosy hue.

"It's too early," said Foma, stretching himself.

"You'll have time to sleep later."

"Do you need something?" asked Foma, snuggling down under the blanket.

"Get up, son, please do," exclaimed Ignat, adding in an aggrieved tone: "I wouldn't have waked you if I didn't need you."

Foma looked into his father's face and saw that it was grey and haggard.

"Are you ill? Shall I go for the doctor?"

"The doctor!" said Ignat derisively. "I'm not a child. I don't need him to tell me. . . ."

"What?"

"I know everything," said the old man mysteriously, casting odd little glances about the room. Foma began to dress himself.

"I'm afraid to breathe," said his father slowly, his head sinking upon his chest. "I have a feeling that if I take a deep breath my heart'll burst. . . . Today's Sunday. Go for the priest as soon as early mass is over."

"What are you thinking of, Father?" said Foma with a deprecating laugh.

"Nothing in particular. Wash yourself and go out into the garden. I told them to take the samovar out there. We'll have tea in the cool morning air . . . I want tea . . . hot, strong tea."

The old man got up heavily and staggered out of the room on his bare feet. As Foma watched him go his heart was gripped by cold fear. He washed quickly and hurried out into the garden.

He found his father sitting in a big oaken armchair under a great old apple-tree. The sunlight falling through the boughs lay in thin stripes on his white undershirt. It was so utterly still in the garden that Foma was startled by the rustle of the branches he touched in passing. The samovar was standing on the table purring like a well-fed cat and exhaling a wisp of steam into the air. In the quiet stillness of the green garden, which had been washed by rain in the night, this splash of glittering, murmuring metal seemed an intrusion; it was out of harmony with the time, the place, and the feeling that overwhelmed him as he looked at the sickly old man in white, sitting huddled up under a canopy of green leaves, among which ruddy apples were hiding modestly.

"Sit down," said Ignat.

"Hadn't I better send for the doctor?" said Foma timidly as he took a seat opposite his father.

"No. I feel better in the open air. Probably feel better still when I've had some tea," said Ignat as he poured it out. Foma noticed that the tea-pot shook in his hand.

Foma pulled his glass towards him without speaking and bent over it, listening with a heavy heart to his father's quick and strident breathing.

All of a sudden something struck the table with such force that the dishes rattled.

Foma started, looked up, and caught a frightened, wild look in his father's eyes.

"An apple fell . . . devil take it! Like a gun shot, eh?"

"You might put some cognac in your tea," suggested Foma.

"It's all right as it is."

They were silent. A flock of siskins darting across the garden filled the air with their merry twitter. When they were gone, solemn stillness settled once more over all this ripe beauty. Ignat's eyes were still haunted by fear.

"Dear Lord, Jesus Christ," he said under his breath, as he crossed himself furiously, "here it is . . . it's come . . . the last hour of life."

"Nonsense, Father," whispered Foma.

"When we've had our tea, go for the priest, then for your godfather."

"I'll go now."

"They'll be ringing for mass in a minute . . . you won't find the priest . . . and there's no hurry . . . it may pass. . . ."

And he began to sip his tea out of the saucer.

"I ought to live another year or two . . . you're still so young . . . I'm afraid for you . . . be honest and firm . . . don't covet other people's property, but hold on to your own. . . ."

Finding it hard to talk, he broke off and rubbed his chest.

"Don't put faith in people . . . and don't expect much from them . . . we all live to get, not to give. . . .Oh Lord, have mercy on me, a sinner!"

The stillness of the morning was broken by the tolling of a big bell somewhere in the distance. Ignat and his son crossed themselves three times.

The call of the first brazen tongue was taken up by a second and a third and soon from all sides came the sound of the summons— a stately, measured chiming.

"Ringing for mass," said Ignat, listening to the hum of the bell metal. "Do you know the voices of the different bells?"

"No," said Foma.

"That one . . . hear it? . . . deep-toned . . . that's the bell Pyotr Dmitrievich Vyagin presented to the church of St. Nicholas. And that one . . . the hoarse one . . . is at St. Praskovia's. . . ."

The air was vibrant with singing waves of sound that died away in the clear blue sky. As Foma watched his father's face, he saw the fear fade from it and a new light come into the eyes.

But suddenly the old man flushed a deep red, his eyes sprang so wide open that they seemed about to leap out of their sockets, he gasped as if in amazement, and gave a strange, guttural cry.

The next minute his head had fallen on one shoulder and his heavy body was slipping out of the chair, as if the earth were asserting its power to take it to itself. For several seconds Foma watched him in fear and wonder, unable to speak or move, then he rushed to his father's side, raised his head off the ground and gazed into his face. It was dark and rigid, and the wide-open eyes held no expression at all—neither pain, nor fear, nor joy. Foma glanced about him. The garden was empty, as before, and the air was still filled with the clamour of the bells. Foma's hands trembled. He dropped his father's head and it struck the earth with a little thud. A thin, sticky stream of blood trickled out of one corner of the mouth and down the livid cheek.

Foma struck his breast and let out a wild cry as he knelt beside the body. Horror made him shake all over, and he searched the garden with frenzied eyes in the hope of finding someone.

IV

FOMA was stunned by the death of his father. He experienced a strange sensation, as if his soul were filled with silence—a weighty, anchored silence that swallowed up all the sounds of life. People he knew hovered about him, came and went, spoke to him; he answered them, but their words made not the slightest impression upon him; they sank without trace into the bottomless depths of the silence in his soul. He did not cry or grieve or think about anything. Pale, sullen, scowling, he concentrated all his powers on listening to this silence that crowded out all feeling, laid waste his heart, and held his brain as in a vice.

Mayakin took charge of the funeral. The heels of his boots could be heard clattering across the floor as he hurried energetically from one room to another, shouting at the servants as if he were their master, slapping his godson on the back and saying by way of consolation:

"You're as if turned to stone, my boy. Your father was old, his body flabby. Death's waiting for all of us; there's no escaping it. All the more reason why we should keep ourselves as alive as possible in this world. You can't bring him back by grieving over him, and he has no need of your sorrow, for it has been written: 'The day cometh when the dread Angel shall wrench the soul from the body, and then all kith and kin shall be forgot'. In other words, it's all the same to him now whether you laugh or cry. It's for the living to care for the living. Have a good cry— that's the human thing to do. You'll feel better afterwards."

But these words, too, left no trace on Foma's mind or heart.

He revived on the day of the funeral, thanks to the persistence of his godfather, who strove uninterruptedly and in his own odd way to rouse the boy's crushed spirits.

The day dawned dull and grey. In the cloud of dust that rose behind Ignat Gordeyev's coffin moved a huge crowd of people. The vestments of the clergy glittered with gold, and the shuffle of feet in the slow procession blended with the solemn music sung by the bishop's choir. Foma was jostled from behind and both sides, but as he plodded on, he was aware of nothing but his father's grey head and the strains of music that found a mournful echo in his heart. Mayakin, who was walking beside him, kept whispering into his ear:

"Look, what a crowd! Thousands of them! The governor himself has come to see your father to his final resting place. And the mayor. And almost all the members of the council. And behind you—turn round—is Sophia Pavlovna. The town is paying great respect to Ignat."

At first Foma paid no heed to his godfather's whisperings, but when Mayakin mentioned Sophia Pavlovna he involuntarily turned round and caught sight of the governor. A tiny drop of pleasure fell on his heart as he saw this august personage with the bright ribbon over one shoulder and all the orders on his breast walking behind his father's coffin, his stern face looking very solemn.

"Sacred is the path," chanted Mayakin with a sniff; then, turning to Foma again: "Seventy-five thousand roubles—you couldn't expect fewer mourners for a sum that size. Have you heard that Sonya's laying the cornerstone of her shelter as soon as your father's forty days are over?"

Once more Foma turned round, and this time his eyes met those of Sophia Pavlovna. The tender glance she gave him brought a sigh from the very bottom of his heart and he instantly felt better, as if a warm ray of light had entered his soul and melted something there. But he also felt that it was unbecoming of him to be glancing round like this.

In the church Foma was crushed by the sad solemnity of the funeral service, and when the priest said the heart-breaking words: "Come to implant the last kiss", an anguished sob broke from his lips, making the crowd sway with the impact of such grief.

Foma, too, swayed on his feet. His godfather caught him by the arm and pushed him toward the coffin, chanting with a vigour that had something reckless about it:

" 'Kiss once more the late depa-a-a-arted!' (Kiss him, Foma! kiss him!) 'Ere he is lowered into the gra-a-a-ave, sealed with a sto-o-o-one . . . to live in da-a-a-arkness, to live with the de-e-ad!'"

When Foma's lips touched his father's forehead, he jumped back in horror.

"Careful! You almost knocked me down," Mayakin said under his breath, and these simple words spoken unfeelingly offered Foma better support than his godfather's arm.

" 'Oh friends and brothers, weep for me, who lie before you, bereft of light, bereft of breath!' " pleaded Ignat in the words of the ritual. But his son no longer wept: he was horrified by the sight of his father's swollen, discoloured face, and this horror served to shock him out of the spell cast by the long lament sung by the church over the body of its son. He was surrounded by people who uttered kind words of condolence, and he felt that they pitied and loved him. But his godfather whispered into his ear:

"Just see how they're truckling to you! The mice have smelt the cheese!"

Foma resented these words, but they were a help in that they forced him to respond in some way.

At the cemetery, when the chant "Eternal Rest" was sung, Foma wept again. Again his godfather took him by the arm, and as he led him away from the grave he said with some spirit:

"You *are* a weakling, lad! Do you think it's any easier for me? After all, I'm the only one who really knew your father's worth. You were only his son. But I'm not crying. He and I were as close as brothers for over thirty years. How we talked together! How we thought together! How we wept together! You're just a youngster—what do you know about grief? Your whole life's ahead of you, to be enriched by all sorts of friendships. But as for me . . . I'm old . . . and left like a beggar . . . burying the only real friend I ever had. It's too late for me to think of finding another."

The old man's voice quavered and grew squeaky. His face twisted, his lips spread and quivered, his wrinkles deepened, and down them ran a stream of little tears squeezed out of his slits of eyes. He looked so piteous and so unlike himself that Foma stopped and pressed him to his breast with the tenderness of the strong for the weak.

"Don't cry, godfather," he almost shouted. "Don't cry, dear godfather!"

"That's better," said Mayakin faintly, heaving a deep sigh. The next minute he was again the firm, astute old man.

"It won't do for you to weep," he said confidingly when he was sitting beside his godson in the carriage. "You're the captain now, and in battle a captain's got to lead his troops bravely.

83

Your troops are roubles, and you've got a big army of them. Show the stuff you're made of!"

Foma was amazed by the swiftness of his godfather's transformation and, as the old man's words fell on his ears, he was reminded of the sound made by the clods of earth as people threw them on to his father's coffin.

"Did your father ever tell you I was a clever old fellow and that you should listen to me?"

"Yes."

"Then see that you do. If we add my brains to your young strength we'll enjoy a great victory, you and I. Your father was a big man, but of narrow vision, and he paid little heed to my advice. It's less to his brains than to his heart he owes his success. But you'll turn out to be somebody. . . . Come and stay with us; you'll feel lonely in that house of yours."

"My aunt's there."

"Your aunt! A sick woman. She's not long for this world either."

"Don't say that," pleaded Foma softly.

"I will say it. Why should you be afraid of death? You aren't an old woman. Live on without fear, doing the task you've been appointed to. And man has been appointed to bring order into life. A man is capital. And, like the rouble, he's made up of worthless little coppers and kopeks. Of the dust of the earth, as it is written. Then he's put into circulation, and as butter and grease, sweat and tears are rubbed into him, signs of a heart and brain appear. And he begins to grow upward and downward. Before you know it, he's worth five kopeks, then fifty, then a hundred roubles, and some are above any price. Once he's in circulation, he's in duty bound to bring in interest. Life knows just what each of us is worth, and won't call us before our time. A wise man will do nothing to his own detriment. Are you listening?"

"Yes."

"Do you understand anything?"

"Everything."

"I daresay!" grunted Mayakin sceptically.

"I do . . . only . . . why must people die?" murmured Foma.

Mayakin glanced at him compassionately.

"That's a question no sensible person ever asks himself," he said, wetting his lips. "A sensible person sees that if there's a river, it has to flow somewhere; if it didn't, it would make a bog."

84

"You're just mocking me," said Foma glumly. "The sea doesn't flow anywhere."

"It's the meeting place of all rivers. And there are big storms at sea. In just the same way the sea of life is made stormy by human passions. And death refreshes the waters and keeps them from getting stagnant. No matter how many people die, there are always more than there were."

"Small comfort. My father is dead."

"And you will be too, some day."

"So what difference does it make to me that there are always more people than there were?" said Foma with a bitter laugh.

Mayakin sighed. "It makes no difference to anybody," he said. "I suppose that's what your trousers say: what difference does it make to us that there's lots of other cloth in the world? But you don't pay any attention to them—you just wear them out and throw them away."

Foma glanced at his godfather reproachfully, but on seeing that the old man was laughing, he was filled with wonder and respect.

"Aren't you really afraid of death, godfather?" he asked.

"The thing I'm most afraid of is a fool, child," said Mayakin caustically. "This is how I see it: if a fool gives you honey, spit it out; if a wise man gives you poison, drink it. And it's a faint-hearted hedgehog whose quills don't stand up."

The old man's levity hurt and angered Foma, and he turned away.

"Always speaking in riddles!" he said.

"What of it?" burst out Mayakin, his eyes flashing. "Everyone speaks in his own way. Do you find me harsh? Is that it?"

Foma did not answer.

"You're a fine one! Remember this: he who loves, teaches. Never forget it. And stop thinking about death. It's the height of folly for a living man to think of death. Ecclesiastes pondered it long, pondered it hard, and his conclusion was: a living dog is better than a dead lion."

They reached home. The street in front of the house was lined with carriages and through the open windows came the sound of loud talking. As soon as Foma entered the room he was seized by the arm and led to a table piled high with food and drink. People urged him to eat something. The room was as noisy as the market-place, and it was crowded and stuffy. Without a word Foma gulped down a glass of vodka, following it by a second and a third. All about him people were chewing and smacking their lips, he heard the gurgle of vodka being poured, the clinking of glasses. People commented on the fish, criticized the soloist in the bishop's choir, spoke of the fish again; then they said that the mayor had intended to speak at the funeral, but after the bishop's fine speech he was afraid of making a poor showing.

"This is what the deceased used to do," said someone in drooling tones: "he would cut off a slice of salmon, sprinkle lots of pepper on it, put another slice on top, and send it chasing a glass of vodka."

"So let's follow his example," came a booming voice.

Foma's heart was bursting with indignation as he watched the greasy lips and jaws devouring the rich food; he had a sudden desire to cry out, and to drive away all these people whose social prominence had so recently filled him with awe.

"Come, be more cordial, more talkative," whispered Mayakin, who suddenly appeared at his side.

"What do they mean by guzzling like this? Do they think they're in a tavern?" said Foma in a loud and angry voice.

"Shhh!" said Mayakin in fright, glancing swiftly about, an ingratiating smile on his lips.

But it was too late; his smile was of no avail. Foma had been overheard. The noise and talk died down, some of the guests fidgeted uncomfortably, others put down their knives and forks with an offended air and left the table, many cast sidelong glances at Foma.

Silent and fuming, he met their glances without flinching.

"Sit down, sit down," cried Mayakin, darting here and there like a spark among ashes. "Pray take your places. Pancakes are to be served next."

Foma shrugged his shoulders and walked over to the door.

"I don't want any dinner," he said.

He heard an unfriendly muttering behind him, then the voice of his godfather trying to explain:

"It's his grief," he was saying. "After all, Ignat was mother and father to him."

Foma went into the garden and sat down in the place where his father had died. Grief and loneliness lay like a weight on his chest. He unfastened the collar of his shirt to make breathing easier, put his elbows on the table and sat without moving, his head in his hands. A fine rain was falling and the leaves of the apple-tree murmured together in a melancholy way as the drops struck them. For a long time he sat there, watching the rain drip off the leaves on to the table. There was a roar inside his head from the vodka he had drunk, and a loathing for people in his heart. Vague thoughts came and went; he saw his godfather's bald pate with its crown of silver hair, and his dusky face that resembled the faces on old icons. This face, with its toothless mouth and crafty smile, roused Foma's dislike and distrust and increased his sense of loneliness. He recalled the gentle eyes of Sophia Pavlovna and her small and graceful figure, and beside her, for some reason, rose up the tall, handsome, red-cheeked Lyuba Mayakina, with her laughing eyes and thick auburn plait. The air was full of mournful sounds. The sky seemed to be weeping and cold tears trembled on the boughs of the trees. It was dark and chill in Foma's heart. A fearful sense that he was all alone in the world had taken possession of him, and this feeling gave birth to the question: How am I to go on living?

The rain drenched his clothes. Aware that he was trembling with cold, he went into the house.

Life tugged at him from all sides, giving him no chance to collect his thoughts. On the fortieth day after the death of his father he drove off in his best clothes, in high spirits, to the laying of the cornerstone of the shelter. The night before Sophia Pavlovna had sent him a note saying he had been elected to the committee supervising the building operations, and also an honorary member of the society of which she was president. This pleased him, and he grew very much excited at the thought of the part he was to play at today's ceremony. He tried to imagine what it would be like as he drove along, and how he should behave not to disgrace himself.

"Here! Wait a minute!"

He turned round to see Mayakin running along the pavement. He had an enormous umbrella in his hand and was wearing a high-crowned cap and a frock coat that reached his heels.

"Take me with you," said the old man, jumping into the carriage with the agility of a monkey. "As a matter of fact I was waiting for you. I thought it was about time for you to be passing."

"Are you going too?" asked Foma.

87

"Certainly. I want to see how my best friend's money gets dug into the ground."

Foma shot him a glance out of the corner of his eye but said nothing.

"What are you looking at me like that for? So you, too, it seems, are going in for charity?"

"What do you mean?" asked Foma coldly.

"I saw in today's paper that you've been elected a member of that shelter business, and an honorary member of Sonya's society as well. It'll eat into your pocket, that membership will," sighed Mayakin.

"I don't suppose it will make a pauper of me."

"That I can't say," said the wily old man, "but I *can* say that charity is a foolish business—and not a business at all: just a harmful waste of time."

"So you think it's harmful to help people?" asked Foma defiantly.

"Oh, you cabbage-head!" said Mayakin with a wry smile. "Come and see me, and I'll open your eyes to all this. You need instruction. Will you come?"

"I will."

"Good. Meanwhile, hold your head up proudly at this ceremony, and let everyone see you. If I didn't tell you to do so, you'd probably hide behind somebody's back."

"Why should I hide?" asked Foma, piqued.

"Why should you, indeed? Just what I say. It was your father who gave the money for this, and you ought to get the honour as his heir. Honour is as good as money: a merchant who has won honour is given credit anywhere; all doors are open to him. So keep to the fore, where everybody can see you, so that if you make a present of five kopeks, you will get a rouble back. It would be foolish to hide yourself."

All the town's important citizens had arrived when Foma's carriage drew up, and a crowd of people had gathered about the piles of timber, bricks and earth. The bishop, the governor, prominent townsmen and members of the local government, together with their richly dressed wives, formed a colourful group as they stood watching two stonemasons preparing bricks and lime. Mayakin and his godson joined this group.

"Don't be shy," whispered Mayakin to Foma. "Fine feathers don't make fine birds."

In a gay little voice that was yet full of respect, he greeted the governor before the bishop.

"How do you do, Your Excellency! Good day, Your Holiness!"

"Ah, Yakov Tarasovich!" exclaimed the governor heartily, and while he squeezed and shook Mayakin's hand, Mayakin strained towards the bishop's hand. "How are you getting on, you deathless old man?"

"Very well, thank you, Your Excellency. Good afternoon, Sophia Pavlovna," said Mayakin quickly, spinning like a top in the crowd. In a minute he had managed to exchange greetings with the judge, and the prosecuting attorney, and the mayor— with everyone, in fact, whom he considered it important to speak to. There were not many who fell into this category. He smiled and joked and made his little figure the centre of attention. Foma stood behind him with hanging head, stealing glances at the gold braid and expensive clothes about him, envying his godfather's dash, quailing before the crowd and, conscious of this, quailing the more. Presently his godfather seized him by the hand and drew him over.

"Here, Your Excellency, let me present my godson, Foma, the only son of the late Ignat."

"Ah," said the governor, "it's a pleasure. You have my heart-felt sympathy, young man," he said, grasping Foma's hand and making a little pause; then, pompously: "It is a great misfortune to lose one's father."

He waited a second or two for Foma to make some reply, and when none was forthcoming he turned back to Mayakin.

"An excellent speech you made in the council yesterday," he said. "Excellent. Very clever, Yakov Tarasovich. Those people who are proposing to use this money for a club don't understand the real needs of the population."

"And besides, Your Excellency, they haven't got the capital. In other words, the town would have to add its own money."

"Quite right! Quite right!"

"Temperance, I say, is highly commendable. Drinking is a bad thing, I agree. I don't drink myself and am against other people doing it. But why build reading-rooms if they—the common people, that is—don't know how to read?"

The governor gave a grunt of approval.

"What I say is: take that money and use it for technical developments. If you do it on a small scale, the sum will be enough, and if it isn't, you can apply to St. Petersburg. They'll give something. Then the town won't have to add anything of its own, and the money will be put to better account."

"Precisely. But how those liberals shouted at you!"

"That's what they're for—to shout, Your Excellency."

The archdeacon from the cathedral gave a cough that announced the opening of the consecration service.

Sophia Pavlovna came up and greeted Foma.

"It nearly broke my heart to see your face on the day of the funeral," she said in a low sad voice. "I could see how dreadfully you were suffering."

Her words were balm to Foma's heart.

"Your cries shook my soul. Ah, my poor boy, I can speak to you like this because I am an old woman already."

"You?" exclaimed Foma softly.

"Don't you believe me?" she asked, glancing artlessly into his face.

Foma dropped his head and said nothing.

"So you don't believe that I am an old woman?"

"I believe you, but . . . but it isn't true!" he protested in a low voice.

"What isn't true? That you believe me?"

"No, not that. But that you . . . that you . . . You must excuse me, I don't know how to put things," said Foma, red to the roots of his hair. "I'm not one of your educated young men."

"That's nothing to be ashamed of," said Sophia Pavlovna patronizingly. "You're still young, and anyone can get an education. But there are people who don't need it, who would be spoiled by it—people who are pure in heart and as sincere and trusting as children. You are one of them. You are, aren't you?"

How could Foma answer such a question?

"Thank you," was all he said.

Seeing that his words brought a merry twinkle to Sophia Pavlovna's eyes, he felt foolish and was angry with himself.

"So now you see what I'm like," he said huskily. "I say what I think. I don't know how to pretend. If I find something funny, I laugh out loud. I'm not clever enough to hide it."

"Now, now, why should you say such a thing?" chided the woman. As she rearranged the folds of her skirt, she happened to touch the hand in which Foma was holding his hat. Foma glanced down at his hand and gave a shy, happy smile.

"I suppose you will be at the banquet, won't you?" she asked.
"Yes."
"And tomorrow at the meeting at my house?"
"Without fail!"
"And then perhaps you'll drop in to visit me, without any particular excuse?"
"Oh, thank you! Indeed I shall!"
"I'm the one who should thank *you* for making such a promise."
Both of them fell silent. Through the air floated the reverential voice of the priest intoning a prayer as he held his hand out in blessing over the site of the shelter.

". . . that neither wind nor flood nor other disaster shall harm this sanctuary, and that those dwelling herein shall suffer no injury or violence. . . ."

"How beautiful and full of meaning our prayers are, aren't they?" asked Sophia Pavlovna.

"Yes," said Foma briefly, blushing again, for he had not understood what she said.

"They'll always go against the interests of us merchants," Mayakin was whispering emphatically into the ear of the mayor, who was standing near Foma. "What do they care? All they want is to win the praise of the newspapers; they never go to the root of things. They just live for show, not to improve life. Newspapers and Sweden—they're the two rules they measure everything by! That doctor fellow kept harping on Sweden all day yesterday. In Sweden, he says, public education and all sorts of things are of the very best. But what's Sweden, I'd like to know? Perhaps there's no such thing as Sweden, it's just made up and there's no public education and all the rest of it at all. The only thing we know about it, that Sweden of theirs, is gloves and matches. And anyway, *we're* not Sweden, and it can't serve as a model for *us*. We've got to do things in our own way, haven't we?"

The archdeacon had thrown back his head and was chanting: "Eternal rest to the soul of the founder of this charity!"

Foma gave a start, but his godfather was at his side in a trice and tugging at his sleeve.

"Are you going to the banquet?" he said.

Once more the warm, velvety hand of Sophia Pavlovna touched his own.

The banquet was torture to Foma. For the first time in his life he found himself in high society. He was aware that these people ate and talked and did everything else better than he did, and that it was not a table that separated him from Sophia Pavlovna, who sat directly opposite, but a veritable mountain. Next to him was the secretary of the society of which Foma had been elected an honorary member. He was a young clerk of the court who bore the strange name of Uhtishchev. As if to make his name appear even more absurd, he talked incessantly in a high tinkling voice, and this, together with his general appearance—short, fat, round-faced—made him resemble a bright new bell.

"The finest thing our society can boast of is its patroness," he was saying; "its most important task is to pay her homage; its most difficult task is to pay her compliments she will find acceptable; and its wisest is to worship her hopelessly and in silence. And thus we see, gentlemen, that we are in fact not members of a Society Devoted to the Cause of . . . but a society of Tantaluses serving our adored Sophia Pavlovna."

Foma listened to this prattle, watched the patroness as she carried on a serious conversation with the chief of police, grunted replies to his neighbour's remarks, pretended to be busy with his food, and longed for the whole thing to end. He felt that all eyes were upon him and that everyone found him foolish, absurd, contemptible.

Mayakin was waving his fork in the air and working his wrinkles as he expounded something to the red-faced, grey-haired, short-necked mayor, who stared at him like a bull and rapped on the edge of the table with his thumb from time to time in approval. The lively talk and laughter drowned what Mayakin was saying. Foma could not make out a word of it, especially with the shrill voice of the secretary in his ears all the time.

"Look," the secretary said at last, "the archdeacon is blowing up his lungs. In a minute he'll offer up a prayer to the memory of Ignat Matveyevich."

"Couldn't I leave?" asked Foma quietly.

"Why not? People will understand."

The booming voice of the cleric drowned, or rather crushed, the noise in the room; all these merchants gazed in admiration at the enormous, wide-open mouth from which the resounding syllables poured. Taking advantage of the moment, Foma got up and left the room.

A minute later he sank back against the seat of his carriage with a sigh of relief, thinking to himself that the society of those people was not for him. He found them too polished, he disliked their brilliance, he disliked their faces, their smiles, their talk; but the freedom and assurance of their movements, their ability to speak on any subject and their fine clothes—these things roused in him mixed feelings of envy and respect. He was hurt and saddened by the realization that he could not talk so much and so fluently on any subject as these people, and he recalled that Lyuba Mayakina had often made fun of him on this account.

Foma did not like Mayakin's daughter, and when he had learnt from his father that Mayakin intended him to marry Lyuba, he had avoided her. But since the death of his father he had been at the Mayakins' almost every day.

"Do you know," Lyuba once said to him, "you don't look at all like a merchant's son."

"You don't look like a merchant's daughter either," Foma retorted, glancing at her suspiciously. He could not make out whether she had said this to hurt him or not.

"Thank goodness!" she exclaimed, and gave him a bright and friendly smile.

"Why are you glad?" he asked.

"I'm glad we aren't like our fathers."

Foma looked at her in surprise.

"Tell me the truth," she said, lowering her voice. "You don't like my father, do you?"

"Not much," Foma admitted.

"I don't like him at all!"

"Why not?"

"Oh, for all sorts of reasons. When you get more sense you'll understand. Your father was better."

"Yes, he was!" said Foma proudly.

This confession led them to take an interest in each other, and their interest grew from day to day until it developed into an unusual sort of friendship.

Lyuba was the same age as Foma but her attitude to him was that of an older girl to a little boy. She spoke to him patronizingly, often chaffed him and was constantly using words he had never heard before, pronouncing them with particular emphasis and evident satisfaction. She liked especially to speak about her brother Taras, whom, though she had never seen him, she painted

93

in colours that made him resemble the brave and noble robbers of Aunt Anfisa's fairy-tales. When complaining about her father she would say to Foma:

"Some day you'll be the same sort of monster he is."

It was not pleasant to hear her say such things, and Foma took them to heart. But at times she was simple, outspoken and even affectionate. He would respond by opening his heart to her, and for a long time the two of them would sit telling each other their most intimate thoughts and feelings.

They spoke at length and sincerely, but Foma felt that all Lyuba's ideas were unacceptable to him and harmful to her. At the same time he could see that his own halting words did not interest her in the least and that she did not understand him. For all their talking, they only grew more dissatisfied with each other. It was as if an invisible wall of misunderstanding kept them apart. Neither of them had the courage to touch the wall or even admit its existence and so they went on with their futile discussions, each vaguely aware of qualities in the other that might have served to bring them together.

On the day of the banquet Foma returned to his godfather's house and found Lyuba alone. As soon as he entered the room he saw that she was not well or was upset about something. Her eyes had a feverish glitter and there were dark circles under them.

"I'm glad you've come," she said with a smile, drawing her woollen shawl tighter about her shoulders. "It was lonely, but I didn't feel like going anywhere. Will you have tea?"

"Yes. What's the matter, aren't you feeling well?"

"Go into the dining-room and I'll tell them to heat the samovar," she said, ignoring his question.

He went into a tiny room which had two windows opening out on to a front garden. Between the windows stood an oval table surrounded by old-fashioned leather-covered chairs. On the wall hung an old clock in a long glass case and in one corner stood a china closet filled with silverware.

"Have you come from the banquiet?" asked Lyuba as she came into the room.

Foma nodded.

"Well, how was it? In the grand style?"

"Awful!" said Foma with a little laugh. "I was on pins and needles. They were all like peacocks and I was like a stuffed owl."

94

Lyuba went on arranging the tea things without comment.

"What makes you look so woebegone?" asked Foma again as he glanced at her dismal face.

She took an impulsive step towards him.

"Oh, Foma! If you only knew what a wonderful book I've just read!" she cried in pain and rapture. "If only you could understand it!"

"It certainly must be a wonderful book if it does that to you!" laughed Foma.

"I read all night—didn't sleep a wink. When you read a book like that, it's as if the gates into an entirely new world were opened to you. The people are different, and what they say is different, and everything, everything! Life itself is different!"

"I don't like that kind of thing," said Foma disapprovingly. "It's all made up, just to mislead you. Like the theatre. They make the merchants look a pack of fools. Are they really so stupid? Of course they're not. Take your father, for instance."

"The theatre's just the same as school, Foma," said Lyuba instructively. "There *have* been merchants like that. How can a book mislead you?"

"As fairy-tales do. None of it's real."

"You're wrong. You haven't read books, so how can you say? On the contrary, it's the books that are real. They teach you how to live."

"Bah!" said Foma with a wave of his hand. "Drop your books! They can't teach you anything. Look at your father, he never reads books, but what a clever fellow he is! It made me envious to see him today. The way he gets on with people! He always knows the right thing to say, the right thing to do, and he feels at home everywhere. Anybody can see he's a man who'll always get what he wants."

"But what does he want?" exclaimed Lyuba. "Nothing but money. There are people who want happiness—happiness for everyone on earth, and for this they're willing to work and suffer and even sacrifice their lives. Can you compare my father with such people?"

"Why compare them? They like one thing, your father likes another."

"They don't like anything!"

"What's that?"

"They want to change everything!"

95

"There must be some reason behind it," said Foma sensibly enough. "Surely there's *something* they want."

"Happiness for everybody," repeated Lyuba vehemently.

"That's beyond me," said Foma with a shake of his head. "Who cares whether I'm happy or not? And, besides, how can they know what'll make me happy if I myself don't know? But you ought to have seen those others—those people at the banquet today."

"They aren't people," said Lyuba derisively.

"I don't know what you'd call them, but it's clear they know their place in life. They're very clever, very sure of themselves."

"Oh, Foma!" exclaimed Lyuba in a disappointed tone. "You understand nothing. And don't care either. You're horribly lazy."

"There you go again! It's just that I haven't had a good look at things yet."

"It's just that you're empty-headed, !" said Lyuba with conviction.

"How do you know what's in my head?" objected Foma serenely. "You don't know my thoughts."

"You have nothing to think about," said Lyuba with a shrug of her shoulders.

"Yes I have. I'm alone in the world, for one thing; and I've got to live, for another. I can't go on as I am, I know that well enough. I don't want to be a laughing-stock. I don't know how to talk to people, and I don't even know how to think," Foma ended up with a foolish little laugh.

"You ought to read, you ought to study," said Lyuba as she walked up and down the room.

"There's something stirring deep down inside me," went on Foma without looking at her, as if he were speaking to himself; "but I don't understand what it is. I suppose what your father tells me is sensible, but somehow it doesn't interest me. I find those other people far more interesting."

"Those 'aristocrats'?" asked Lyuba.

"Yes."

"Then you belong with them," said Lyuba, her lip curling contemptuously. "For shame! Do you call them human beings? Do you think they have souls?"

"What do you know about them? You've never met them."

"I've read about them."

Their conversation was interrupted by the maid bringing in the samovar. Lyuba made the tea in silence, and as Foma watched her his thoughts were about Sophia Pavlovna. If only he could talk to *her*!

"With every day I see more clearly how hard life is," said Lyuba pensively. "Take me, for instance; what am I to do? Get married? To whom? To a merchant who'll spend all his time robbing people, drinking and playing cards? I don't want to! I want to be a personality—and I am a personality, if only because I see how hideous life is. Study? As if my father would let me! Run away? I haven't the courage. So what am I to do?"

She clasped her hands tightly and let her head fall.

"If you only knew how I despise all these people! There's not a person with a spark of life. Father drove everybody away after Mother died. Some of my friends have gone away to study—Lipa, for instance. She writes and tells me to read books. Oh, but I do!" Lyuba cried in a tone of despair; then, after a moment's pause: "Books don't tell you what your heart longs to know, and I don't understand all they do tell you. And it's lonely, horribly lonely to do nothing but read by yourself. I want someone to talk to, and there isn't anyone. I'm sick of it all! A man only lives once, and it's high time I began, but the right man doesn't come along. What have I to live for? I'm living in a prison!"

Foma studied his fingers intently as he listened to her; he saw her deep suffering, but he did not understand it. And when she finished speaking, crushed by misery, the only words he found to say sounded like a rebuke.

"See?" he said, "You yourself admit that books can't help you and yet you're always telling me to read them."

She looked into his face and anger flashed in her eyes.

"If only you felt something of the torments I suffer! If only you lay awake at night, as I do, tortured by your thoughts! If only you loathed everything—even yourself—as I do! Oh, how I hate you all! How I hate you!"

Her face was flaming and she looked at him with such hostility and spoke with such vehemence that he was too much taken aback even to be offended. Never before had she spoken to him in such a way.

"What's the matter with you?" he asked.

"And I hate you too. You! What are you? A spineless ignoramus! How are you going to get on in life? What have you to offer others?" she hissed spitefully.

"I shan't offer them anything; let them get things for themselves," said Foma, intentionally stoking her anger.

So forceful was her condemnation that he could not help listening. He felt there was sense in what she said and he drew his chair closer to hers, but she turned away in rage and indignation and refused to say another word.

It was still light outside; the sunset was reflected on the branches of the lime-tree growing beside the window, but the room was filled with shadow. Every second the dull brass pendulum of the clock peeped out of its glass case, then took cover, now on the right, now on the left with a weary little grumble. Lyuba got up and lit the lamp hanging over the table. Her face looked pale and drawn in the sudden flare.

"You've hauled me over the coals," said Foma with restraint, "but I'm sure I don't know why."

"I don't want to speak to you," said Lyuba testily.

"As you please. But still, what have I done?"

"Can't you see I'm choking? I'm suffocating? What sort of life is this? What am I? My father's dependant. He keeps me to look after the house. Then I'm expected to get married—and look after somebody else's house."

"What has all this got to do with me?" asked Foma.

"You're no better than the rest of them."

"But what are you blaming me for?"

"You ought to *want* to be better."

"But I do," exclaimed Foma.

She was about to reply when the door-bell rang and she threw herself back in her chair.

"Father," she said.

"It's a pity he's come so soon," said Foma. "I wanted to hear what else you had to say. You speak so strangely."

"Ah, my children, my turtle doves!" said Mayakin as he appeared in the doorway. "Having tea? Pour me out a glass, Lyuba."

He sat down next to Foma, smiling sweetly and rubbing his hands together.

"And what might you two be cooing about?" he asked, giving Foma a playful dig in the ribs.

98

"Nothing in particular," said Lyuba.

"I didn't ask you," said her father, making a face. "Hold your tongue and tend to your woman's duties—"

"I was telling her about the banquet," interrupted Foma.

"I see, I see. Well, and now it's my turn to talk about the banquet. I've been keeping an eye on you, Foma, and I must say you don't know how to behave."

"What do you mean?" said Foma with a frown.

"I mean just that: you don't know how to behave. For instance, the governor speaks to you and you keep your mouth shut."

"What was I to say? He said it was a misfortune to lose one's father. I know that well enough, so what could I say?"

" 'Since the Lord saw fit to send me this misfortune, Your Excellency, I bear my cross in silence'. That's what you should have said, or something else to that effect. Governors like people who bear things in silence, my lad."

"Ought I to have looked at him like a sheep?" laughed Foma.

"Your looks were sheepish enough, and that's just what they shouldn't be. You don't want to be either a sheep or a wolf, but play at being something in between—this way, that way—'You're our dear father, Your Excellency, and we're your dear children' —and before you know it he's completely melted."

"Why should he melt?"

"It might come in handy some time. You can always make good use of a governor, lad."

"What are you trying to turn him into, Father?" said Lyuba indignantly.

"What do you think?"

"A toady."

"Wrong, you learned fool. It's diplomacy I'm teaching him, not toadying. The diplomacy of how to get on in life. But look, you'd better leave us. Get thou behind me, Satan, and serve us something to eat. Run along, run along."

Lyuba got up quickly, threw the napkin she was holding over the back of a chair, and went out. Her father narrowed his eyes and drummed on the table as he watched her.

"And now, Foma, I'm going to give you a lesson. I'm going to teach you the true and trustworthy science of philosophy. And if you understand it, you'll get through life without making any mistakes."

Foma looked up to see the wrinkles working on his godfather's forehead; they reminded him of lines of Slavonic writing.

"First of all, Foma, if you live in this world, you're obliged to give some thought to what's going on about you. Why? So that you won't suffer from your ignorance, and others won't suffer either. Now then, you must know that everything a person does has two sides to it. One is the outside—everybody can see it, and it's a false side. The other is hidden away, and it's the real side. It's this side you've got to find if you're to get at the meaning of things. For instance, take these shelters, workhouses, and other charitable institutions—can you guess what they're for?"

"Why guess?" said Foma wearily. "Everybody knows what they're for: for the poor and the incapacitated."

"Ah, brother, sometimes everybody knows a certain man's a scoundrel, and yet they call him Ivan or Pyotr instead of what he deserves."

"What are you driving at?"

"The same point. You say these homes and things are for paupers and beggars—in other words, for carrying out Christ's teachings. Very well. What is a beggar? A beggar is a man whose purpose in life is to remind us of Christ, he's the brother of Christ, he's a bell that the Lord rings to rouse our conscience, to stir our sated flesh. He stands under our windows and cries: 'A crust, in the name of the Lord!' and his cry reminds us of the Lord and of how He taught us to help one another. But people have ordered life in a way that makes it impossible for them to follow Christ's teachings; there's just no room for Jesus Christ in this life of ours. We've nailed Him to the cross not once, but a hundred thousand times, and still we can't get rid of Him as long as those brothers of His, the beggars, keep going about the streets calling upon His name and reminding us of Him. But lately we've thought of a good way out of the difficulty: we've decided to lock up the beggars in special homes to prevent them walking about the streets and rousing our conscience."

"Very clever," said Foma, gazing in wonder at his godfather.

"See the point?" Mayakin's little eyes were sparkling with triumph.

"How is it Father didn't see it?" asked Foma uneasily.

"But wait! Let me go on—the worst is yet to come. We thought of a scheme of locking them up in all sorts of homes, and then we put them to work, those old folk and cripples, to cut down the cost of their keep. And so now we don't have to give them alms and, since we've rid the streets of their rags, we no longer have to look on their poverty and misery and it seems to us that all people on earth have shoes and clothes and enough to eat. So that's what those homes of yours are for—*to hide the truth.* To banish Christ from our lives. Do you see?"

"Ye-e-es," said Foma, confused by his godfather's artful argumentation.

"And that's not all; we haven't scooped all the water out of the puddle yet," cried Mayakin, waving one hand in the air.

The wrinkles of his face were quivering, his long, hawk-like nose was twitching, his voice trembled with malicious delight.

"Now let's look at the case from another side. Who contributes most to all those homes, shelters and other charities? The rich people, the merchants. Very well. And who gives the orders and lays down how things shall be? Not us; it's the gentry who do that—the gentry, the officials, and others of their kind. The laws, the newspapers, science—all these things are their affair. They used to be wealthy landowners; the land was snatched from under their feet, so they've gone into office. But who are the strongest people today? The merchants are the real force in the land, because they have millions on their side. Isn't that so?"

"Yes," Foma assented, anxious to hear the conclusion that was already gleaming in his godfather's eyes.

"So listen well and try to understand what I say," went on the old man emphatically. "We merchants don't make life what it is; to this very day we have no voice in the making of it. We can't raise a finger in the matter. It's those others who have arranged life, it's they who bred all these cripples and beggars and good-for-nothings, it's they who cluttered up life with this trash, and if justice were done, it's they who ought to purify it. But we're the ones who do the purifying, we're the ones who give money to the poor, we're the ones who care for them. And why should we? Why should we mend somebody else's coat if we didn't tear it? Why should we repair somebody else's house if we don't live in it? Wouldn't it be wiser for us to stand aside for the present and watch the vermin swarm over those others? They won't be able to cope with them; they don't have the means. So they'll come and ask our help: 'Be so kind as to come to the rescue, gentlemen,' they'll say. And we'll answer: 'Then give us freedom to do things as we see fit. Give us a chance to say how life should be ordered'.

And as soon as they give us this chance, we'll get rid of the filth and the vermin in no time. And his Majesty the Tsar will see with his own bright eyes who are his faithful servants and how much wisdom they stored up as they sat with their hands tied. Do you understand?"

"Of course I do!" exclaimed Foma.

When his godfather spoke of the officials, Foma saw before him the faces round the banquet table, especially the face of the vivacious secretary, and the thought flashed through his mind that this rotund little man probably had an income of not more than a thousand a year, while he, Foma, had a million. Yet the secretary felt at ease and at home in the world, while Foma always felt uncomfortable and out of place. This contrast, added to what his godfather had just told him, roused a storm of ideas in his mind, but he managed to seize upon and formulate only one of them.

"When you get down to it, is it just for money we work? What's the use of money if it doesn't give you power?" he said.

"Aha!" exclaimed Mayakin, narrowing his eyes.

"How is it Father didn't see this?" said Foma. "Did you tell him?"

"I kept telling him for twenty years."

"And what did he say?"

"My words never reached him. He had a thick skull, your father had. He wore his heart on his sleeve, but his mind was set very deep. H'm, he made a big mistake. It's a very great pity about that money."

"I don't mind losing the money."

"Try earning one tenth of it, and then see what you'll say!"

"May I come in?" asked Lyuba from the doorway.

"You may," said her father.

"Are you ready for supper?" she asked as she entered.

"Serve it."

She went over to the sideboard and began rattling the dishes. Mayakin chewed his lips as he watched her, then he suddenly slapped Foma on the knee and said:

"So that's how it is, godson! Think it over."

Foma smiled in reply.

He's clever . . . cleverer than Father ever was, Foma thought to himself, but at the same time another voice within him seemed to say: cleverer, but Father was better.

V

THIS dual attitude towards his godfather persisted as time went on. Foma listened attentively and with keen interest whenever the old man expounded his views, but he felt his dislike for him growing. Sometimes Mayakin excited in him a feeling akin to fear, even of physical repulsion. This was usually the case when something had pleased the old man and made him laugh. His wrinkles worked when he laughed, causing a constant change in the expression of his face; his thin dry lips stretched out into a grin that exposed black stumps of teeth; his red beard glowed like fire and the sound of his laughter was like the rasp of rusty hinges. Unable to hide his feelings, Foma was often rude to Mayakin, but the old man ignored his rudeness and kept a sharp eye on him, supervising every step he took. He neglected his own shop, devoting himself almost completely to young Gordeyev's shipping business and, because of this, Foma himself was left with a great deal of leisure time. Thanks to Mayakin's influence in the town and his wide connections up and down the Volga, the business flourished; but the jealousy with which Mayakin guarded it strengthened Foma in his conviction that his godfather meant to marry him to Lyuba and this made him dislike the old man the more.

He was fond of Lyuba, but he considered her dangerous. She was still single, yet her father never spoke of marrying her off, never gave parties for her, never invited young people to the house nor allowed her to go out. All her girl friends were married by this time. Foma was startled by the things Lyuba said, but he listened to her as eagerly as to her father. She spoke of Taras with love and longing and Foma imagined that under this name she had in mind another person, perhaps Yezhov, who, as she told him, had had to leave the University and Moscow for some reason or other. There was a great deal of kindness and simplicity in Lyuba that Foma appreciated and often what she said made him feel sorry for her. It seemed to him that she went about in a sort of trance.

The story of Foma's behaviour at his father's funeral feast circulated quickly among the merchants, and it did great damage to his reputation. He noticed that his colleagues on the exchange looked at him with hostility and assumed a special tone when speaking to him. Once he even heard someone behind him say in a loud, contemptuous voice:

"The stiff-necked milksop!"

He did not turn round to see who had said it. He no longer admired these rich people in whose presence he had once trembled. More than once they had snatched a profitable order out of his very hands; he saw that they would do the same thing again, that all of them were greedy for money and ready at any time to cheat one another.

"What do you expect?" his godfather said on hearing his views. "Trade, like war, is a hazardous business. They're fighting for treasure, and where your treasure is there will your heart be also."

"I don't like it," declared Foma.

"There are some things about it I don't like either—too much trickery. But you can't be open and above-board when it comes to trade; you've got to be a diplomat. When you talk business, you've got to have money in your left hand and a knife in your right."

"Rather unpleasant," said Foma thoughtfully.

"The pleasant part comes later, when you've got the better of the bargain. The rules of life are very simple, Foma, lad: either you bite or you lie down and let others walk over you."

The old man grinned and the sight of the sharp stumps of his teeth made Foma think: you've done a lot of biting in your day.

"Isn't there a better way? Is that the only one?"

"What other way could there be? Every man wants the best for himself, and what does 'the best' mean? It means to forge ahead of others, to rise above them. Every man tries to win first place for himself—some do it this way, some that, but each tries to tower above his fellows like a steeple, so that all can see him. That's what man was made for, to rise in the world. It's even written in the Book of Job: 'Man is born unto trouble, as the sparks, to fly upward'. Even children try to outdo each other in their games. And every game can be won; that's what makes it interesting. Understand?"

"Yes, I understand," said Foma.

"But you must also *feel* it. Understanding alone won't take you far; you've got to wish, wish with all your heart and then mountains will be turned into molehills and seas into puddles. Oh, when I was your age, I was deep in the game. And here you are, still trying to make up your mind to get into it."

By harping on the same theme day after day, the old man at last achieved his end: Foma decided what his purpose in life was to be. You've got to be better than others, he kept saying to himself. The seeds of ambition sown by his godfather fell deep in his heart. They fell deep, but they did not fill it, for his relations with Sophia Pavlovna took their inevitable course. He was irresistibly drawn to her, he always longed to see her, but when he was with her he became clumsy and bashful and stupid. He knew this, and suffered because of it. He often went to her house, but rarely found her alone. Scented fops hovered about her like flies about a lump of sugar. They sang and laughed and spoke French to her, while he watched them in silence, consumed by hate and jealousy. For hours on end he would sit in some corner of her elaborately furnished drawing-room, his feet tucked under him, watching sullenly.

And she would cast gentle smiles and glances in his direction as she moved soundlessly back and forth over the soft carpet, surrounded by admirers who glided as deftly as snakes among the many tables, chairs, screens and all the fragile bric-à-brac scattered about with an artistic carelessness as perilous for the objects themselves as for Foma. When he entered the room the carpets did not deaden the sound of his steps and the bric-à-brac caught in his coat and crashed to the floor. Near the piano stood a bronze sailor in the act of throwing a life-belt ornamented with ropes of fine wire that invariably became entangled in Foma's hair. This made Sophia Pavlovna and her admirers laugh, but it made Foma go hot and cold by turns.

He felt no more at ease when he was alone with her. She would greet him with a tender smile and then, before talking to him, would curl herself up like a cat in a corner of the sofa and gaze at him with shadowy eyes that had a hungry gleam in them.

"I do so love to talk to you," she once purred, drawling her words musically. "I'm sick of all those others—they're boring, ordinary, jaded. But you are fresh and sincere. You don't like them either, do you?"

"I can't bear them," said Foma.

"And me?" she asked.

Foma looked away.

"You're always asking me that," he said with a sigh.

"And it's hard for you to answer?"

"Not hard, but—what's the use?"

"I want to know."

"You're just playing with me," said Foma gloomily.

"Playing with you? What does that mean?" she asked in wondering tones, opening her eyes very wide. Her face at that moment looked so very angelic that he could not doubt her sincerity.

"I love you, I love you deeply! How is it possible not to love you?" he said ardently; then, softly and sadly: "But that means nothing to you."

"There, you've said it again," said Sophia Pavlovna contentedly as she edged away from him. "I adore the way you say it; it always sounds so youthful, so impulsive. Would you like to kiss my hand?"

Without a word he seized her slender white hand and bent over it to kiss it long and ardently. Smilingly, gracefully, she pulled it away at last, unmoved by his ardour. Then she sat gazing at him as if he were a rare object, her eyes shining in that particular way that Foma always found so disconcerting.

"How strong and healthy and unspoiled you are!" she exclaimed. "Why, you merchants are a race of your own, a new unspoiled race, with unique traditions and enormous moral and physical resources. Take you, for example: a perfect jewel! If one were to polish you—"

Whenever she said: "you", "yours", "you merchants", Foma felt that she was using the words to thrust him away from her. This offended and saddened him. He would say nothing—just sit and gaze at her tiny figure, girlish in its delicacy, as fragrant as a flower, and always dressed with outstanding taste. At times he was seized by a wild, coarse desire to snatch her up and kiss her. But her beauty and fragility made him afraid he might hurt her, while her gentle voice and clear but wary glance chilled his emotion. It seemed to him that she saw into the depths of his soul and read his every thought. These outbursts of passion were rare, for his feeling for Sophia Pavlovna was rather one of adoration; he marvelled at everything about her—her beauty, her talk, her clothes. And hand in hand with this adoration went the painful recognition of the great gulf that lay between them, of her superiority to him.

Their relations developed very quickly. In two or three meetings Sophia Pavlovna had captivated him completely; and then began his slow torture. Evidently she took pleasure in having at her mercy this strong, healthy youth, in exciting and subduing the animal in him with a word or a glance; the game delighted her, for she was sure of her power. On leaving her he would be half sick with excitement, resenting her and angry with himself. And in two days' time he would come back for further punishment.

One day he said to her shyly:

"Sophia Pavlovna, have you ever . . . er . . . had children?"

"No."

"I thought not!" he exulted.

She looked at him as might a very small and innocent child, as she said:

"What made you think so? And why should you want to know whether I have had children or not?"

Foma blushed and dropped his eyes; his voice was hollow and he spoke as if every word weighed a pood and he were digging it out of the earth.

"Because once a woman is . . . that is, has had children . . . er . . . her eyes . . . aren't like yours."

"They aren't? What are they like?"

"They're . . . shameless," blurted out Foma.

Sophia Pavlovna laughed her silvery laugh and Foma looked up and laughed too.

"Forgive me," he said. "Perhaps I said something . . . something improper."

"Oh, no! You *couldn't* say anything improper. You're a pure, sweet boy. And so my eyes aren't shameless?"

"Yours are like an angel's!" breathed Foma rapturously, his own eyes shining.

And this time she looked at him as she had never done before— looked at him as a mother might look, sadly, her love tinged with fear for him.

"Go now, my dear. I'm tired and want to rest," she said, averting her eyes and getting up.

He went away obediently.

For some time after that she was more reserved and honest with him, as if she pitied him, but it was not long before she was playing with him again as a cat plays with a mouse.

Foma could not hide his relations with Sophia Pavlovna from his godfather.

"Foma!" the old man said to him one day, glancing at him craftily. "Feel your head every now and again to make sure it's still on."

"What do you mean?" asked Foma.

"Sonya. You spend a lot of time with her."

"What business is it of yours?" asked Foma rudely. "And what right have you to call her Sonya?"

"It's not my business and it won't hurt me in the least if she gobbles you up. As for calling her Sonya—that's what she's called, as everybody knows, and they also know that she likes other people to do her dirty work for her."

"She's a clever woman," declared Foma, scowling and putting his hands in his pockets. "Well educated . . ."

"She's clever, no denying that. And well educated. She'll give you an education. And so will all those loafers that hang round her."

"They're not loafers; they're clever too," retorted Foma, denying his own convictions in his anger. "I'll learn things from them. What do I know? Neither the words nor the tune. Nobody's ever taught me anything. All sorts of things are discussed at her house and everybody has his opinion. I mean to make something of myself, and don't you try to stop me!"

"Well, well! Just listen to him! As fierce as hail on the roof! All right, make something of yourself; but it would be better to hang round the tavern if you want to do that; at least the men there are better than those at Sonya's. It wouldn't be a bad thing for you to learn to size people up, young man—to tell who's what. Take Sonya, for instance. What is she? An insect for the adornment of nature—nothing more nor less."

Thoroughly outraged, Foma set his teeth, thrust his hands deeper into his pockets and went out.

But before long the old man brought up the subject of Sophia Pavlovna again. They were driving along in a roomy sleigh and chatting amiably about business, having just made an inspection of steamers wintering in a creek. It was March. Water sprayed out from under the runners of the sleigh, the snow had almost melted, the sun shone with lively warmth in the clear sky.

Mayakin suddenly interrupted their business talk to say:

"I suppose you'll run to that lady-friend of yours the minute you get home, won't you?"

"I will," said Foma, unpleasantly surprised.

"H'm. Do you often give her presents?" asked Mayakin good-naturedly.

"Presents? Why should I?" asked Foma in surprise.

"No presents? Think of that! Do you mean to say she lets you have her for nothing? Just for love?"

Foma reddened with shame and anger.

"You're an old man, but you say things it's a disgrace to hear," he remonstrated, turning sharply to his companion. "As if she'd do such a thing! As if she could!"

Mayakin smacked his lips.

"Of all the fools! Of all the blockheads! Bah!" he said, spitting in an excess of feeling. "All the pigs have swilled out of that trough and now, when there's nothing but their leavings in it, this fool comes along and starts worshipping it. Of all the damned idiots! Listen, go to her and say straight out: 'I want to be your lover—I'm still young, so don't charge me much.'"

"Godfather," said Foma, dark and menacing, "I won't listen to such things. If it were anybody else—"

"Who else is going to stand up for you? Good heavens!" wailed Mayakin, beating the air with his hands. "Has she really led you by the nose all the winter? What a nose! And what a harpy!"

The old man was indignant; anger, chagrin, even tears sounded in his voice. Never before had Foma seen him in such a state and he kept silence in spite of himself.

"She'll ruin you! Ugh, the Babylonian whore!"

Mayakin's eyes blinked rapidly and his lips twitched as he launched into an obscene tirade against Sophia Pavlovna, interrupting it with little shrieks of rage.

Foma sensed that the old man was telling the truth. A weight lay heavy on his heart.

"Very well, godfather, that's enough," he murmured miserably, turning away.

"What you need is to get married, and as quickly as possible," cried the old man.

"For God's sake, stop it!" implored Foma.

Mayakin glanced at his godson and said nothing. Foma's face was haggard and unspeakable pain could be read in his parted lips and anguished expression.

On the right and left stretched fields wearing tattered remnants of their winter garments. Rooks were hopping busily over dark patches of thawed ground. Water gurgled under the runners of the old sleigh and dirty snow came flying up from under the horses' hoofs.

"What an ass a man is in his youth!" exclaimed Mayakin under his breath. "Looks at a log, takes it for a hog. Oh, heavens!"

"Don't speak in riddles," said Foma surlily.

"What's there to say? Everything's clear: girls are cream, women are whey; you can catch the women, the girls slip away. In other words, go to Sonya, if you can't live without her, and tell her straight out, so-and-so and so-and-so. What are you sulking about, you fool? What are you pouting for?"

"You don't understand," said Foma quietly.

"What don't I understand? I understand everything."

"The heart; a person has a heart."

Mayakin narrowed his eyes.

"Then he hasn't got a brain," he said.

VI

AN aching, vengeful fury seized upon Foma when he got home. He had a fierce longing to insult and humiliate Sophia Pavlovna. For hours at a time he paced the empty rooms of his house, a scowl on his face, his teeth set, his hands deep in his pockets, his head held high. Resentment filled his heart to bursting. With slow regularity he pounded the floor with his feet, as if they were hammers forging his wrath.

"The slut . . . disguised as an angel."

Sometimes hope would lift a feeble voice:

"Perhaps it's all slander?"

But on recalling the force and the reckless assurance of his godfather's words, he set his teeth more firmly and held his head higher.

By casting a slur on Sophia Pavlovna, Mayakin had made her accessible to his godson and Foma soon came to appreciate this. For several days he was plunged in work connected with the opening of navigation and this served to cool his temper. His contempt for her as a woman was modified by his sorrow for her as a human being, and the thought of her accessibility whetted his desire. By imperceptible degrees he arrived at the conclusion that he ought to go to Sophia Pavlovna and tell her exactly what he wanted of her, without making any bones about it.

Sophia Pavlovna's maid was used to his visits.

"Go into the parlour, if you please," she said when he asked if her mistress was at home.

His courage left him for a moment, but on catching sight of himself in a mirror (his fine figure in the well-cut coat, his serious face framed by a curly black beard, his large dark eyes) he squared his shoulders and strode confidently through the drawing-room.

The music of strings floated to his ears—strange sounds, as if someone were laughing quietly and cheerlessly, pleading in tones that went straight to the heart, imploring for attention with little hope of getting it. Foma did not like to listen to music; it always saddened him. When the musical-box at the tavern ground out some melancholy tune, it depressed him so that he would ask them to turn it off, or else he himself would go away, unable to bear its wordless pleading, full of tears and grief. And now he involuntarily halted at the door of the parlour.

A curtain of strings of vari-coloured beads, which formed an exotic flower pattern, hung over the door. They stirred slightly, giving the impression that the air was filled with pale ghosts of flowers. Through the transparency of the curtain he saw inside the room. Sophia Pavlovna was sitting on her favourite sofa playing the mandoline. A Japanese parasol hanging on the wall formed a colourful canopy above her tiny dark figure, which was bathed in the warm glow shed by a tall bronze lamp with a red shade. The soft notes of the strings trembled in the fragrant twilight that filled the little room. Now she dropped the mandoline on her knee and touched the strings absent-mindedly as she gazed into space.

As Foma watched her, he saw that she was not as beautiful when alone as when among people—her face was graver and looked older, an expression of boredom took the place of the shy and tender expression in her eyes and her attitude was weary, as if she wished to get up but lacked the strength.

Foma gave a little cough. The woman started.

"Who's there?" she asked. The strings let out a little cry of alarm.

"It's I," said Foma, pushing aside the beads.

"Oh. But how softly you came! I'm glad to see you. Sit down. Why have you been away so long?"

She held one hand out to him and pointed to a small armchair beside her with the other. Her eyes gave him a happy smile.

"I was on the creek inspecting the boats," said Foma, with exaggerated ease as he pulled the armchair closer to the sofa.

"Is there much snow left on the fields?"

"Quite a lot. But it's melting fast. The roads are full of puddles."

He looked at her and smiled. She must have noted the informaltiy of his manner and something new in his smile, for she rearranged the folds of her skirt and edged away from him. Their eyes met. Sophia Pavlovna dropped hers.

"So it's melting," she murmured, looking at a ring on her little finger.

"Yes. Rivulets everywhere." Foma studied the toes of his boots.

"That's good. It means spring's coming."

"Well on its way."

"Spring's coming," repeated Sophia Pavlovna softly, as if testing the sound of the syllables.

"Time for people to start falling in love," laughed Foma, rubbing his hands together briskly.

"Are you about to?" asked Sophia Pavlovna dryly.

"Oh, no! I did that long ago. I'm in love for the rest of my life."

She darted a swift glance at him.

"How fortunate you are to be just starting out in life," she mused, beginning to play again. "To have a strong heart, with no shadows lurking in it—"

"Sophia Pavlovna!" cried Foma softly.

She stopped him with a gentle gesture.

"Wait, dear boy. Today I want to tell you something. Something nice. There are moments when a person who has seen much of life glances into his heart and unexpectedly finds things long forgotten, things that have lain for years in the depths but have not lost the fragrance of youth in all that time. And when memory lights upon them, it is as if the person had taken a deep draught of the refreshing air of morning—the morning of life."

The strings sobbed and trembled under her fingers. The sounds they made and the intonation of her voice played upon his feelings. He listened patiently without understanding a word of what she said.

Speak on, but I don't believe anything you say any more, he thought, firm in his decision.

This exasperated him. He was sorry he could not listen to her as trustingly as he once had.

"Do you ever think about how you ought to live?" she asked.

"Sometimes I think about it. But not for long. I have no time," said Foma with a little laugh. "And, besides, what's there to think about? Just look and see how others live and follow their example."

"Oh, don't do that! Be kinder to yourself. You're such a— such a fine person! There's something different about you. I don't know what it is, but I feel it. I'm afraid you're going to find it very hard to live in this world. I'm certain you won't go the usual way of people of your class. It's impossible that you should be satisfied with a life given up wholly to the making of money. Oh, no! There's something else you want, isn't there?"

She spoke rapidly, and there was a look of alarm in her eyes.

"What is she driving at?" thought Foma as he looked at her.

She moved closer to him and gazed into his face.

"Build your life after some other pattern," she urged him seriously. "You're young and strong and—good."

"If I'm good, then others ought to be good to me," cried Foma, aware of his growing agitation and the pounding of his heart.

"Good people are always treated worse than bad ones in this world," said Sophia Pavlovna sadly.

The trembling notes leaped out from under her fingers again. Foma knew that if he did not come out at once with what he had to say, he would not do it later.

God help me! he said to himself, and then, with a tight feeling in his chest, took the plunge.

"Sophia Pavlovna! Enough of this! I've got to talk to you. I came specially to say: Enough of this! You've got to be honest with me—frank and honest. First you did everything you could to make me like you, and now you cut yourself off from me. I don't understand what you say—mine is a dull mind. But I feel that you want to hide from me, and I see that you know what I've come for."

His eyes were flashing and with every word his tone grew louder and more fervent.

"Oh, don't go on," she said in a voice of alarm, giving a sudden lurch forward.

"Oh, no! Now that I've started, I'm going to speak!"

"I know what you are going to say."

"You don't know everything," said Foma threateningly, getting up. "But I know everything about you! Everything!"

"Do you? So much the better for me," said Sophia Pavlovna unperturbed.

She, too, got up, as if about to go away, but after a moment's deliberation she sat down again. Her face was grave, her lips compressed, and her eyes were lowered, so that Foma could not see their expression. He had thought that when he said: "I know everything about you!" she would be frightened and ashamed, and in her confusion she would ask his forgiveness for having trifled with him. And he would take her in his arms and forgive her. But this did not happen. He was the one who was confused at the sight of her imperturbability, and he stood staring at her and seeking for words he could not find.

"So much the better," she repeated firmly, dryly. "So you know all, do you? Naturally you think ill of me. I understand. I have done you wrong. But—no, I shall not try to justify myself."

She fell silent, then suddenly clutched her head, and—arranged the pins in her hair.

Foma gave a deep sigh. Sophia Pavlovna's last words killed the hope that had risen in him—a hope he recognized only when it was dead. He shook his head and said bitterly:

"How often have I looked at you and thought to myself: she's as gentle and pretty as a dove. And yet here you are admitting that you've done me wrong. Ugh!"

He broke off abruptly.

"How charming you are! And how amusing!" said the woman with a little smile.

He realized as he looked at her that he was disarmed by the gentleness of her words and the sadness of her smile. The icy things he had harboured in his breast melted in the warm light of her eyes. She looked as tiny and defenceless as a child. She kept on smiling and speaking in that gentle, persuasive way, but he did not listen to what she said.

"I came here resolved to show you no pity," he interrupted. "I'll tell her just what I think, I said to myself. But I haven't told you anything. And I don't want to. I haven't the heart. You cast some kind of spell over me. Oh, why did I ever meet you? What are you to me? I can see it would be better for me to go away."

"Wait, don't go away yet," said the woman hurriedly, holding out her hand. "Why should you be so—so harsh? Don't be angry with me. I'm not the person for you. You need another sort of woman—someone as simple and wholesome as you are yourself. A woman who is gay and courageous. I'm old already. All I do is sit and mope; my life is so boring and empty, so terribly empty. It's a dreadful thing when a person who is used to living a gay live finds nothing to be gay about any more. Then it is not he who laughs, but life that laughs at him. As for people . . . Oh, listen to me as if I were your mother: I warn you,

I beg and implore you not to obey anything but the dictates of your own heart! Live by its promptings. People don't know anything, they cannot give you any true advice. Don't listen to them!"

Agitated by the effort to speak as clearly and simply as possible, her words rushed out in a swift incoherent stream. And all the time that plaintive smile kept flitting over her lips.

"Life is stern: it insists that people submit to its demands and only the strong can defy it with impunity. And can even they? Oh, if you only knew how hard it is to live in this world! Man is driven to fear his very self. He becomes a dual personality, a judge and a criminal, forever accusing and defending himself. And to escape being alone with himself he is willing to spend his time, day and night, with people whom he despises, who are repugnant to him."

Foma raised his head and there was surprise and incredulity in his voice as he said:

"I can't understand what makes you talk like this! And Lyuba says the same thing."

"Who is Lyuba? And what does she say?"

"My godsister. The same thing—she's always complaining about life. Says it's impossible to go on living."

"What happiness that she, too, should speak of these things!"

"Happiness? A fine sort of happiness that makes a person moan and complain!"

"Listen to what she says. There is great wisdom in complaint. Wisdom is . . . pain."

As Foma listened, he glanced about him in perplexity. The familiar room looked different today, though it was filled with the same profusion of furniture, hung with the same pictures and shelves, ornamented with the same bright and pretty objects. The reddish glow of the lamp was sombre and disturbing. Everything was enveloped in gloom, with here and there the glitter of a gold frame, the glint of china. Heavy draperies hung motionless over the doors. Foma was oppressed by it all and felt himself lost in a maze. He was sorry for this woman, but she also irritated him.

"Are you listening to me? I should like to be a sister, a mother to you. I've never felt so kindly towards anyone before. And yet you look at me with such antagonism. Do you believe me or not?"

"I don't know," he said with a sigh, "I once believed you."

"And now?" she asked quickly.

"Now," he said, "it's best that I go. I don't understand anything. I don't even understand myself. I knew what I meant to say when I came here. But now everything is confused. You stirred me up, goaded me on. And now you say you want to be a mother to me. In other words: clear out."

"But can't you see I feel sorry for you?" exclaimed the woman softly.

Foma's exasperation with her increased and the more he spoke, the more mocking he sounded. He kept jerking his shoulders, as if trying to throw off invisible bonds.

"Sorry? I don't want you to feel sorry for me. If only I knew how to express myself! Then I'd tell you what I thought. You haven't played fair with me. Why did you have to stir up my feelings? Do you take me for a toy?"

"I wanted to have you near me," said the woman simply, guiltily.

But he did not hear what she said.

"When it came to the point, you got frightened and put a barrier between us. You began to be sorry. Said that life was to blame. But why should you put the blame on life? What is life? People—they're life, and outside them there is no life. But you invent some sort of bogy. That's just to deceive others and justify yourself. You take your pleasure, get tangled up in all sorts of deceptions, and then start groaning: it's a bad life! a cruel life! Who made it bad, if not you? And by hiding your guilt behind these complaints, you confuse others. Because you have gone wrong, why should you try to lead me astray? In revenge or what? 'If I have to suffer, you must too!' Is that how it is? For shame! God made you as beautiful as an angel, but where's your heart?"

He stood facing her, trembling all over and sweeping her from head to foot with an accusing glance. Now the words came pouring freely out of his mouth; he spoke softly but forcefully, and took pleasure in it. The woman raised her head and stared at him with wide-open eyes. Her lips twitched and deep lines formed at the corners of her mouth.

"A beautiful person ought to live beautifully, but what do people say about you? . . . " He broke off with a little wave of his hand, and ended abruptly: "Goodbye."

"Goodbye," said Sophia Pavlovna quietly.

117

Without giving her his hand he turned on his heel and walked away. But when he got to the door a stab of pity made him look back over his shoulder. She was standing alone in the corner, her head drooping, her hands hanging limply at her sides.

He realized he could not leave her like that, without another word, and he murmured in embarrassment, but without humbling himself:

"Forgive me if I've hurt your feelings. After all, I . . . I love you." He sighed, and the woman gave a queer little laugh.

"No, you haven't hurt my feelings," she said.

"Goodbye then," said Foma still more softly.

"Goodbye," murmured the woman.

Foma pushed the beads aside; they rustled and brushed against his cheek. He started at their cold touch, and went away with a heavy heart that fluttered as if it had been caught in some soft but inescapable net.

It was night by this time. The moon was shining and frost covered the puddles with a silvery crust of ice. As he walked along the pavement, Foma struck the ice with his walking-stick, making it crackle mournfully. The houses threw black squares of shadow across the road, the trees made fantastic patterns like thin fingers clutching at the earth.

"I wonder what she's doing now," thought Foma, seeing in his mind's eye the woman standing alone in the reddish gloom of that over-filled room.

"The best thing for me is to forget her," he resolved. But it was impossible to forget her; she intruded herself upon his memory, exciting now pity, now exasperation, even anger. So vivid was her image, so heavy the burden of his thoughts, that it was as though he were carrying her bodily within his breast. A cab came towards him, its wheels breaking the silence of the night as they clattered over the cobble-stones and crunched over the ice. The driver and his passenger lurched and swayed with the movement of the cab. Both of them were bending forward, and together with the horse formed a single big black smudge on the night. The street was mottled with light and shadow, but in the distance the darkness was as dense as if a solid black wall rose from earth to heaven. It seemed to Foma that the driver and his passenger had no idea where they were going. Nor did he know where he was going. He thought of his house with its six big rooms. Aunt Anfisa had gone to a convent and might die there without ever coming back. The only inhabitants were Ivan, the yard porter; Sekletea, an old maid who served as cook and housekeeper and a shaggy black dog with a blunt nose. The dog, too, was old.

"I suppose I ought to get married," thought Foma with a sigh.

He was disconcerted, even amused, by the realization of how easily he could get married. If tomorrow he told his godfather to find him a wife, within a month some girl would be sharing his house with him, would be near him day and night. He would say: "Let's go for a walk", and she would go; he would say: "Let's go to bed", and she would go. If she felt like kissing him, she would do it even though he did not want her to. If he told her to go away, that he didn't want her kisses, she would be hurt. What would he talk to her about? In his mind he went over all the girls of his acquaintance. Some of them were pretty and any one of them would be only too glad to marry him. But he did not want any of them as his wife. . . . What did young people say to each other when they found themselves alone in the bedroom after the wedding? Foma tried to imagine what he would say but could not, and only laughed in embarrassment. He thought of Lyuba Mayakina: she, surely, would not be at a loss, but her words would be false and borrowed. He was under the impression that all her ideas were borrowed and he found them unbecoming in a girl of her age, appearance and upbringing.

At this point he began to think of Lyuba's complaints. He slowed his steps, struck by the fact that everyone with whom he was intimate enough to exchange confidences invariably talked about life. His father, his aunt, his godfather, Lyuba, Sophia Pavlovna—all of them either complained of life or tried to teach him to understand it. He recalled what he had overheard the old man on the boat say about Fate and this brought to mind all the other remarks, criticisms and bitter complaints he had heard.

"I wonder why?" he thought. "What is life, if not people? Yet people always speak as if not they, but something outside themselves kept spoiling life for them."

Cold fear gripped his heart; he shuddered and glanced about him. The street was quiet and empty; the black windows of the houses stared into the darkness of the night and Foma's shadow glided stealthily behind him along the walls and fences.

"Driver!" he called out, walking more quickly. His shadow started and crept timidly at his heels, black and soundless.

VII

FOR a week after his talk with Sophia Pavlovna her image haunted him day and night, causing him untold heartache. He wanted to go and see her, he was sick with the desire to be near her, but, determined not to surrender to the desire, he set his teeth and threw himself heart and soul into his business, mentally fanning the flames of resentment against her. He felt that if he went to see her now he would find her changed—something would have happened to her after their talk, and she would not be as gentle to him as she had been, would not turn upon him that bright smile which always aroused wonderful thoughts and dreams. It was the fear of this that made him stubbornly resist temptation and endure his suffering.

His work and his longing for the woman did not keep him from pondering life. He did not attempt to solve its enigma, which kept him in a constant state of anxiety—he was not able to. But he began to listen attentively to everything people said about life. Instead of clarifying things for him, they merely increased his perplexity and made him suspicious. He could see that people were sly, cunning, clever. It was always necessary to be on one's guard with them. He had learned by this time that in important matters they never said what they thought. And the more he studied them, the less credence he gave to their groans and complaints. Silently, sceptically, he took in everything that went on about him and gradually a fine little line appeared on his forehead.

"Shchurov's arrived," his godfather said to him one morning on the exchange. "He wants to speak to you. Go and see him tonight, but mind you keep a tight hold on your tongue—he'll try to loosen it to pump you about your business. A sly old fox, Anani: he'll roll his eyes up to heaven while he slips a paw inside your breast pocket to steal your purse. Be on your guard."

"Do we owe him money?" asked Foma.

"Aye, we haven't paid him for that barge, and we've had a couple of hundred cords of wood from him besides. But if he asks you for the whole sum at once, don't give it to him. The rouble's a sticky thing—the longer you hold on to it, the more kopeks it collects."

"But how can we refuse to pay him if he asks for it?"

"Let him weep and beg; you sob and hold tight."

Anani Savvich Shchurov, a thriving timber merchant, owned a large sawmill, built barges, drove rafts down the river. He had had dealings with Ignat, and Foma had often seen him—a tall old man, straight as a pine, with a big white beard and long arms. His handsome figure, open face and clear glance had always inspired Foma with awe and respect, even though he had heard people say it was not honest labour that had brought "the woodsman" his wealth and that he lived an equivocal life in a remote village in the forest. From his father Foma had heard that Shchurov had been a poor peasant in his youth and that he had kept an escaped convict locked up in his bath-house where he had made counterfeit money for him. That was how he had started to grow rich. One day the bath-house had burned down, and in the ashes was found the charred body of a man with a broken skull. It was rumoured in the village that Shchurov had murdered his workman and burned the body. Such things were said about many a rich man in the town—all of them, it seemed, had accumulated their millions by killing, stealing or, more often, by making counterfeit money. From earliest childhood Foma had heard such stories and had never stopped to consider whether they were true or not.

He also knew that Shchurov had outlived two wives. One of them had died in his embrace on their wedding night. After that he had taken his own son's wife. His son had almost drunk himself to death with grief, but had been saved by going to live in a hermitage on the Irgiz river. When this woman died, Shchurov began to live with a deaf-and-dumb beggar girl; he was still living with her and she had borne him a dead child. On his way to the hotel to see Shchurov that night Foma recalled these stories of his father and others, and they imparted a strange fascination to the old man.

When Foma opened the door of the little hotel room whose only window looked out on the rusty roof of the adjoining house, he saw that Shchurov had just woken up and was sitting on the side of the bed gripping it with his hands and bending so far over that his white beard swept his knees. Even doubled up in this way he was enormous.

"Who's there?" asked Shchurov irascibly, without looking up.

"It's I. How do you do, Anani Savvich."

Slowly the old man raised his head and turned narrowed eyes upon Foma.

"Ignat's son?"

"Yes."

"Go and sit down by the window. Let's see what you're like. Have some tea?"

"I don't mind."

"Waiter!" called Shchurov; then, taking his beard in his hand, he began a careful scrutiny of Foma, who returned his gaze unflinchingly.

The old man's high forehead was deeply furrowed; curly white locks fell over his temples and pointed ears; a pair of calm blue eyes lent an expression of wisdom, even of nobility, to the upper part of his face, but his lips were thick and red and did not go with his other features. His long thin nose curved abruptly at the end, as if to hide itself in the white moustache, and when the old man moved his lips sharp yellow teeth gleamed. He was wearing a pink cotton tunic with a silk girdle round the waist, and his wide black trousers were tucked into high boots. One glance at the old man's lips convinced Foma that he was just what people said he was.

"You looked more like your father when you were a youngster," Shchurov said suddenly, adding: "Do you remember your father? Do you pray for him? You must pray for him," he urged when Foma had given his brief answers. "Ignat was a great sinner, and he died without repenting. All of a sudden. A great sinner."

"No more of a sinner than others," said Foma, offended by this manner of speaking of his father.

"Who, for instance?" asked Shchurov sternly.

"There are plenty of sinners."

"There's only one man in this world who's a greater sinner than the late Ignat, and that's your godfather Yakov, the damned hypocrite," said Shchurov emphatically.

"You're quite sure of that?" sneered Foma.

"I know it," said Shchurov with a shake of his head, his eyes suddenly growing dark. "I've got my own burden to bring before the Judgment Seat—a heavy burden of sin. The devil's had his way with me. But I believe in the grace of God. Yakov doesn't believe in heaven or hell or witches; he doesn't even believe in God, Yakov doesn't. And for that he'll be punished on this earth."

"And you're sure of that, too?" asked Foma.

"Yes, I am. I see you're laughing at me—'A prophet!' you're thinking. But a man who's sinned as much as I have grows wise. Sin's a great teacher. That's why Yakov Mayakin's the cleverest of us all."

As Foma listened to the hoarse, self-confident voice, he thought: he has smelt death already.

The waiter, a small, pale creature with a blurred face, brought in the samovar and trotted hastily out of the room. Shchurov busied himself with some bundles on the windowsill.

"You're bold," he said without looking at Foma, "and it's a dark look you turn on people. In former years people's eyes were light. And their souls were light. In former years everything was simpler—people were simpler, and their sins were simpler. Nowadays everything's very complicated."

He made the tea and sat down opposite Foma.

"At your age, your father (a bailer he was in the old days, and once his barge was anchored near our village)—at your age, I say, he was as clear as crystal; you could tell at a glance what sort of person he was. But when I look at you I can't see what you are like. And you yourself don't know. That's why you'll suffer. Everybody nowadays must suffer because they don't know themselves. Life's a wood, and you've got to find the path through it. People lose their way, to the delight of the devil. Are you married?"

"Not yet," said Foma.

"You see? You're not married, but you probably defiled yourself long ago. Do you give much time to your business?"

"I have to give some. I'm still working with my godfather."

"Working! What sort of work is it nowadays?" said the old man with a shake of his head, the light in his eyes now flaring up and now dying down. "That's not work! In former years merchants drove their horses about the countryside. In snowstorms, at dead of night—nothing stopped them. Robbers lay in wait on the roads to kill them. They died the death of martyrs, expiating their sins with their blood. Nowadays they ride in trains and send their agents. Or have you heard the latest? A man sits in his office and his voice can be heard five versts away. Satan's had a hand in that, you can be sure. It's the sitting and doing nothing and feeling bored that makes a man sin. Machines do his work for him nowadays. He sits idle, and idleness is a man's ruin. He provides himself with machines and thinks it's good. But machines are Satan's trap. When a man works he has no time to sin, but with machines he's free to do as he likes. Freedom kills a man off as surely as the sun kills off worms that live in the bowels of the earth. It's freedom brings a man to his ruin."

Having pronounced these words very distinctly, old Shchurov struck the table four times with his finger. His face shone with sinister triumph, his chest heaved, the silver hairs of his beard stirred on his chest. It made Foma's flesh creep to listen to him. His words rang with an unshakable faith that disturbed the youth. He had already forgotten the gossip about the old man which he had believed so recently.

Shchurov stared at him in a strange way, as if beyond him he saw someone else who was frightened and pained by his words, and whose fear and pain gave him pleasure.

"And all you people of today will perish through freedom. Satan has caught you; he has robbed you of labour and put machines and agents in its place. What makes the sons worse than their fathers? Freedom. It's freedom that has led them to drink and to loose living."

"Oh, but people drank just as much and lived just as loosely in the past," Foma put in quietly.

"Hold your tongue!" cried Shchurov, his eyes flashing fiercely. "Then people were stronger. They sinned according to their strength. Then people were mighty oaks. And God will judge them according to their strength. Their bodies will be weighed and angels will take the measure of their blood. And the angels will see that their sins do not outweigh their bodies and blood. The Lord will not call a wolf to account for devouring a lamb, but if a miserable rat should set its teeth upon a lamb, the Lord would call the rat to account."

"What can we know of how the Lord will pass judgment?" asked Foma thoughtfully. "We need a court of justice that all can see—"

"Why should they see it?"

"So that they will understand."

"Who but the Lord is capable of judging me?"

A glance at the old man made Foma lower his head and fall silent. He thought of the runaway convict Shchurov was said to have murdered and burned in the bath-house and his belief in this story was renewed. And the women—his wives and mistresses—undoubtedly the old man had suffocated them with his kisses, had crushed them under his bony chest, had sucked their blood with his thick lips, which were still red, as if the blood of the women who had died in his sinewy arms had not yet dried on them. And now, in anticipation of imminent death, he was taking account of his sins, passing judgment on others and saying that none but the Lord was capable of judging him.

"I wonder if he's afraid?" thought Foma to himself as he gazed at the old man from under his brows.

"Think about it, young man," said Shchurov, shaking his head, "think about how you ought to live. I've lived in this world a long, long time—ah, how long! Trees have grown up and been cut down and houses have been built of them and the houses have grown old and ramshackle, and I have seen it all, and still I go on living. When I look back on my life, I think: is it possible one man could have done so much? Is it really I who have lived through all this?" The old man gazed sternly at Foma, shook his head again and fell to dreaming.

It was quiet in the room. Something crackled on the roof, the rattle of cart wheels and the muffled sound of voices reached them from the street; the samovar on the table hummed a sad tune. Shchurov sat staring at his glass of tea and stroking his beard and Foma could hear something bubble in the old man's chest when he breathed.

"It must be hard for you without your father, isn't it?" Shchurov said at last.

"I'm getting used to it," said Foma.

"You're rich. And when Yakov dies you'll be richer still; he'll leave you everything. He's only got one daughter. And you'd better take that daughter. It doesn't matter that she's your god-sister and foster-sister. It's high time you got married—how can you go on without being married? I suppose you go wenching?"

"No."

"Really!" scoffed the old man. "Ah, yes—the merchant class is dying out. A forester once told me—maybe it's true, maybe it isn't—that all dogs were once wolves and they dwindled into dogs. So it is with us. Soon we'll all dwindle into dogs. We get learning, slap fancy hats on our heads and do all sorts of things to make ourselves look like other people. Soon you won't be able to tell a merchant from anybody else. It's the custom now to send all children to the *gymnasium*. They're all to be painted the same colour—merchants' children, noblemen's children or artisans' children—all the same. Put them all into grey uniforms and teach them all the same things. Grow people like trees. Why? Nobody knows. You can tell one log from another by the knots in it, but they want to plane down people until they're all exactly alike. Well, the day for us old folk is nearly over. Perhaps fifty years from now nobody will believe I ever lived on this earth—I, Anani, son of Savva, with the surname of Shchurov—or that I, Anani, feared no one but the Lord. And that in my youth I was a peasant with only two and a quarter dessiatins of land, and that by the time I reached old age I had eleven thousand dessiatins, all of them covered with forest. And something like two million roubles besides."

"Money—everybody talks about money," said Foma irritably. "What joy does money bring a man?"

"H'm," murmured Shchurov. "A poor merchant you'll make if you don't understand the power of money."

"Who does understand it?" asked Foma.

"I do," said Shchurov with conviction. "And so does every clever man. Yakov understands it. Money? Money's everything, my lad. Spread it out in front of you and try to see what it stands for. Then you'll know that money is power. Money is brains. Thousands of people have poured their lives into that money of yours. And you can throw it into the stove and watch it burn if you want to. And if you do, won't that give you a feeling of power!"

"But nobody does that."

"Because money never falls into the hands of fools. Money is set to work. And by this work the people get their daily bread. And you're the master of all these people. Why did God create people? So that they would pray to Him. In the beginning He was alone and He was lonely. He wanted power. And since it's written that man was made in the likeness and image of God, man, too, wants power. And what but money can give power? That's how it is, young man. . . . By the way, have you brought me my money?"

126

"No," said Foma. His head felt heavy and dizzy with the effort of listening to the old man and he was glad the talk had turned to business.

"Why not?" said Shchurov frowning. "The term's up—time to pay."

"I'll pay you half tomorrow."

"Half? I want it all."

"We're badly in need of money at present."

"And you haven't got it? Well, I'm in need of it too."

"You'll have to wait."

"Oh, no, I won't, friend. You're not your father. There's no trusting you young whipper-snappers. You can run your business to ground in a month's time and I'll be the loser. If you don't pay me the whole sum tomorrow I'll protest your note. I wouldn't think twice about it."

Foma marvelled as he looked at Shchurov. Could this be the same man who had just been expounding on Satan in the tones of a seer? The face was different and so were the eyes. Now his glance was hard and cruel, and the muscles on either side of his nostrils were twitching greedily. Foma realized that if he did not meet his note, Shchurov would not hesitate to bring disgrace on the firm by protesting it.

"So things are bad, are they?" grunted Shchurov. "Well, out with it—what have you squandered your father's money on?"

Foma had a sudden desire to put the old man to a test.

"Things *are* bad," he said with a frown. "No orders, no advance payments, and so money's tight."

"And you want me to give you a helping hand?"

"If you would extend the term of the note . . ." said Foma, dropping his eyes meekly.

"H'm. For your father's sake, eh? Well, I might."

"For how long?" asked Foma.

"For six months."

"I'm very grateful."

"For nothing. You owe me eleven thousand six hundred. So this is what we'll do: you'll write me a new note for fifteen thousand and pay me my interest on it in advance, and as security I'll take a mortgage on two of your barges."

Foma got up.

"Send me the note tomorrow," he laughed. "I'll pay you in full."

Shchurov's eyes did not waver under Foma's mocking glance. He pulled himself heavily to his feet and calmly scratched his chest.

"That's even better," he said.

"Thank you for your—kindness."

"I'd like to be kind to you, but you won't let me," grinned the old man.

"God help anyone who falls into your clutches."

"I'd make it pleasant for him."

"You'd make it hot for him."

"Enough of this, young man!" said Shchurov severely. "It's too soon for you to be patting yourself on the back. The game's a draw. Time enough to dance when you win. Goodbye. Have the money ready tomorrow."

"I will. Goodbye."

As Foma closed the door he heard the old man give a prolonged yawn and begin chanting in a deep, husky voice:

"Holy Virgin, Mother of God, open wide the gates of heaven."

Foma carried away with him two distinct feelings: he liked the old man and at the same time despised him.

As he recalled what Shchurov had said about sin and the strength of his faith in the mercy of God, he felt both respect and repulsion.

"He, too, talks about life. And he admits his sins without crying or complaining. 'I've sinned and I'm ready to take the consequences'. But she . . ." At the thought of Sophia Pavlovna Foma was miserable again. "She repents . . . and it's hard to tell whether she means it or just pretends."

Foma almost envied the old man, but on recalling how he had tried to fleece him, he was repelled. Unable to reconcile these conflicting emotions, he gave a puzzled little laugh.

"Well, I've been to see Shchurov," he announced as he sat down in the dining-room of Mayakin's house.

Mayakin, in a grease-stained dressing-gown and with an abacus in his hands, wriggled impatiently in his leather armchair.

"Pour him out a glass of tea, Lyuba. Tell us all about it, Foma," he said eagerly, "and do it quickly, for I have to be at the council at nine o'clock."

Foma told him laughingly how Shchurov had tried to get him to sign another note.

Mayakin clicked his tongue with a doleful shake of his head. 'You've spoiled the mass for me this time, lad. As if a person

128

could come straight out with things like that when he's doing business! Bah! Why in the world did I ever send you? I ought to have gone myself. I'd have wound him round my little finger!"

"I'm not so sure of that. He says he's as strong as an oak."

"An oak? Then I'm a saw. The oak's a fine tree, but its fruit's only good for the pigs. And it's solid wood, the oak is."

"But we'd have to pay anyway.

"Clever people are never in a hurry to do that. But as for you—you always come running with the money. A fine merchant!"

Mayakin was exceedingly displeased with his godson. He screwed up the wrinkles of his face and turned abruptly to his daughter, who was pouring out the tea.

"Pass the sugar," he said tetchily. "Can't you see it's out of my reach?"

Lyuba was pale, her eyes were dull, her hands moved slowly and clumsily.

Meek as a lamb when she's with her father, thought Foma.

"What did he talk to you about?" asked Mayakin.

"About sin."

"Ah, yes. People always like to talk about their speciality. He runs a sin-factory. He should have been in jail long ago. And they're crying for him in Hell—can't wait till he gets there."

"There's weight to what he says," said Foma pensively as he stirred his tea.

"Did he rail at me?" asked Mayakin with a sly grin.

"He did."

"And you?"

"I listened."

"H'm. What did you hear?"

"The strong are forgiven their sins, he says, but there's no forgiving the weak."

"Pooh! Even a flea knows that!"

For some reason Foma was annoyed by his godfather's contempt for Shchurov.

"He wastes no love on you," he laughed, looking straight at Mayakin.

"Nobody wastes love on me," said Mayakin proudly. "And there's no reason why they should—I'm not a pretty girl. But everybody respects me. And people only respect those they fear."

The old man winked at his godson boastfully.

"There's weight to what he says," repeated Foma. "He complained that the merchant class is dying out, that everyone's being taught the same things, so that soon you won't be able to tell one person from another—they'll all be the same."

"And he doesn't like that? The fool!" said Mayakin scathingly.

"Do you?" asked Foma, glancing dubiously as his godfather.

"It's a very clever thing to herd people of different kinds together in one place and teach them to have one opinion, for what is a person from the point of view of the State? Nothing but a brick, an ordinary brick, and bricks have got to be the same size and shape. Once people are all the same size and shape, you can build whatever you like with them."

"It's not very pleasant to think of yourself as a brick," said Foma glumly.

"Perhaps not, but it's a fact. You can't wipe out everybody's face, but hard hammering turns some people into gold. And if they crack under the blows, it can't be helped—that means they were weak to begin with."

"And he talked about work—said people were getting spoiled because machines did their work for them."

"There he goes again!" scoffed Mayakin with a contemptuous wave of his hand. "It's a marvel the way you lap up that balderdash! Machines! Has he ever stopped to think what machines are made of, the old idiot? Of steel! In other words, you don't have to waste any sentiment on them—wind them up and off they go, turning out roubles for you without any fuss or talk—just set them in motion and watch the wheels go round. But a workman, he's always wretched and dissatisfied—very wretched at times— moans and groans, sighs and cries, and gets drunk. There's a lot in a workman I could easily do without. But a machine's like a yardstick—it's got just what's needed and no more. . . . But it's time for me to go and get dressed."

He got up and went out, shuffling across the floor noisily in his house slippers.

"The devil himself couldn't make head or tail of it," muttered Foma with a frown as he watched him go. "One says this, another that—"

"It's the same with books," said Lyuba softly.

Foma looked at her and smiled good-naturedly. She gave him a hesitant smile in return. There was a sad, tired look in her eyes.

"Reading as much as ever?" asked Foma.

"Yes," she said cheerlessly.

"And moping?"

"Horribly. Because I'm all alone. I haven't a soul to talk to."

"That's bad."

She made no reply, merely dropped her head and began to finger the lace edging of the cloth.

"You ought to get married," said Foma, genuinely sorry for her.

"Oh, stop it," she said, wrinkling her brow in an unlovely way.

"Stop what? You *will* get married some day."

"Perhaps," she sighed. "I, too, think I ought to. But how can I? I feel as if—as if there was a fog between me and other people —a dense fog."

"That's the books," said Foma with conviction.

"Wait. I don't understand anything any more. It's all so hateful; nothing's as it should be, nothing at all. I can see that, but I can't tell you what's wrong or why."

"Not as it should be," murmured Foma. "It's the books, I tell you. But even I can see things aren't as they should be. Perhaps it's just because we're so young."

"At first," went on Lyuba, ignoring his remark, "I thought books would help me understand things."

"Forget those books of yours!" said Foma contemptuously.

"What are you saying? As if one could forget them! You wouldn't believe how many different ideas there are in the world! Some of them are terrific. In one book, for instance, it says that there is reason behind everything on earth."

"Behind everything?"

"Everything. And in another it says just the opposite."

"Look, can't you see that's nonsense?"

"What are you talking about?" came the voice of Mayakin from the doorway, where he was standing in a long frock-coat with medals round his neck and on his chest.

"Nothing special," said Lyuba glumly.

"About books," said Foma.

"What books?"

"The ones she reads. One of them says there's reason behind everything on earth."

"Well?"

"And I say it's all lies."

"H'm." Mayakin screwed up his eyes and plucked at his beard as he considered the matter.

131

"What book said that?" he asked his daughter after a pause.

"A little yellow one," she said reluctantly.

"Put it on my desk. People don't write things like that for nothing. H'm . . . reason behind everything. Somebody was very clever to think of that. Even put it well. And if it wasn't for the fools in this world, a person might believe it. But seeing that fools don't fit anywhere, it's quite impossible to say there's reason behind everything. Well, good-bye, Foma. Are you staying, or shall I drive you home?"

"I'll stay a little longer."

Once more Foma and Lyuba were alone together.

"A queer creature," said Foma, nodding after his godfather.

"Why?"

"He has his own opinion about everything, his own word for everything."

"He's clever. But he doesn't understand why I'm so unhappy," said Lyuba mournfully.

"Neither do I. You imagine things."

"What, for instance?" said the girl irritably.

"Oh, everything. They're not your ideas—they're other people's."

"Other people's, other people's!"

She was about to say something cutting, but held back. As Foma looked at her, he could not help comparing her with Sophia Pavlovna.

How different people are, he thought sadly. Women, too. And each of them makes you feel different.

It was growing dark outside and in the room as well. The wind was blowing through the boughs of the lime-trees, whose twigs scratched at the walls of the house as if they were cold and wanted to be let in.

"Lyuba," said Foma softly.

She raised her head and looked at him.

"Did you know I had quarrelled with Sophia Pavlovna?"

"Why?" asked Lyuba, brightening.

"Nothing in particular. She cheated me."

"Well, I'm glad you've quarrelled," said the girl. "She'd have wound you round her little finger. She's a vile flirt. It you only knew what I know about her!"

"She's not vile at all," said Foma sullenly. "And you don't know anything about her. They're all lies."

132

"Oh no, they're not!"

"Listen, Lyuba," pleaded Foma softly, "don't talk against her to me. I know everything, honestly I do. She told me herself."

"She did?" said Lyuba in astonishment. "What a strange creature she is! What did she tell you?"

"She said she was—was guilty," said Foma with a crooked little smile.

"Is that all?" The note of disappointment in the question raised Foma's hopes.

"Isn't that enough?" he said.

"Do you love her very much?"

Foma looked out of the window for a minute without replying.

"I don't know," he said at last. "Sometimes I think I love her more now than I ever did."

"I simply can't understand how you can love such a woman," said Lyuba with a shrug of her shoulders.

"Oh, it's not hard!"

"I can't understand it. It's just because you've never seen anyone better."

"I haven't," agreed Foma; then, after a moment's pause: "Perhaps there are none better. I need her terribly," he mused. "I'm afraid of her—that is, I don't want her to have a bad opinion of me. Sometimes I'm so disgusted with it all I feel like drinking myself silly. But then I think of her and can't do it. It's like that with everything: whenever I think of her and of what she'd say, I grow faint-hearted."

"Then you really do love her," said Lyuba pensively. "I'd be like that, too, if I loved somebody. I'd always think of him and what he'd say."

"Everything about her is—different," said Foma. "She speaks differently from everybody else, and God, how pretty she is! So tiny. Like a child."

"What happened between you?" asked Lyuba.

Foma drew his chair closer to hers and, leaning over, began to speak in a low voice. He told her everything, and as he recalled the words he had spoken to Sophia Pavlovna, the feelings that had prompted them were revived.

"I said to her: for shame! why did you have to play with me?"

His voice was full of angry protest, and Lyuba, flushed with excitement, nodded her approval and encouragement.

"Good for you! And what did she say to that?"

"Nothing," said Foma miserably, with a little shrug of his shoulders. "That is, she said something or other, but what difference does it make?"

He grew silent. Lyuba, too, said nothing as she sat toying with her plait. The samovar had grown cold. Darkness was thickening in the room, and the windows had become opaque blotches.

"Why not light the lamp?" suggested Foma.

"How unhappy we are, you and I!" sighed Lyuba.

Foma did not like this.

"I'm not unhappy," he objected firmly. "I just haven't got used to life yet."

"A person is unhappy if he doesn't know what he is to do tomorrow," said Lyuba sadly. "I don't know, and you don't either. My heart is never at ease; it's always stirred by some inexplicable longing."

"Oh, I have that too," said Foma. "Well, I must be off to the club."

"Don't go," said Lyuba.

"I've got to; somebody's waiting for me. Goodbye."

"Goodbye," She held out her hand and gazed sadly into his eyes.

"Are you going to bed?" asked Foma as he gave her hand a tight squeeze.

"I'll read a bit first."

"Books are to you what vodka is to the drunkard," he said disapprovingly.

"Can you suggest something better?"

As he went along the street he glanced up at the window and caught a glimpse of Lyuba's face, as vague as her thoughts and her longings. He nodded to her, thinking to himself: She's as lost as the other one.

The idea made him quicken his steps and toss his head, as if to shake off thoughts of Sophia Pavlovna.

Gusts of cold wind swept the street, blowing dust into the faces of the passers-by. People were scurrying through the darkness. Foma screwed up his face and half closed his eyes.

"If I meet a woman first," he thought, "it means Sophia Pavlovna will receive me as kindly as before, and I'll go and see her tomorrow. But if it's a man, I won't go tomorrow; I'll wait."

But it was a dog, and this exasperated him so much that he felt like kicking the animal.

He was met in the club bar by the jovial Uhtishchev, who had been standing near the door talking to a fat man with whiskers. On catching sight of Foma he came towards him.

"Hullo, you modest millionaire!" he said with a smile.

Foma liked him for his geniality and was always glad to see him. He shook his hand cordially.

"What makes you think I'm modest?" he asked.

"Anybody can see that: a chap who lives like a hermit, doesn't drink, doesn't play cards, doesn't chase women—oh, by the way, did you know that our incomparable patroness is going abroad tomorrow for the whole summer?"

"Sophia Pavlovna?" said Foma slowly.

"Yes. The sun of my life (and maybe of yours, too?) is setting."

He made a droll face and glanced slyly into Foma's eyes. Foma stood there, conscious that his head was drooping, but unable to pull himself together.

"So Sonya's leaving, is she?" came an unctuous bass voice. "Excellent. I'm very glad."

"Come, now; why should you say that?" exclaimed Uhtishchev.

Foma smiled foolishly and turned a puzzled look on Uhtishchev's bewhiskered companion. The latter stroked his moustache pompously and squirted thick, oily words over Foma.

"Because there will be one less *cocotte* in town."

"Oh, fie, Martyn Nikitich!" remonstrated Uhtishchev with a grimace.

"How do you know she's a coquette?" said Foma grimly, taking a step towards the bewhiskered gentleman, who merely swept him with a supercilious glance and turned away.

"I did not say 'co-quette'," he drawled, the muscles of the calf of his leg twitching.

"You mustn't say such things about a woman who—" began Uhtishchev vehemently, but Foma interrupted him.

"Just a minute!" he said. "I should like to ask this gentleman what he meant. What was the word he used?"

Foma spoke calmly and distinctly, thrusting his hands deep into his pockets and expanding his chest in a way that made him look very belligerent. The bewhiskered gentleman threw another glance in his direction and gave a mocking smile.

"Gentlemen!" protested Uhtishchev under his breath.

"I said *'cocotte'*." The bewhiskered gentleman seemed to smack his lips over the word. "If you don't know what that means, I can explain it to you."

"Yes," said Foma, taking a deep breath and holding the man with his eyes, "please explain it."

Uhtishchev rolled up his eyes and darted to a safe distance.

" *'Cocotte'*, for your edification, means a prostitute," said the bewhiskered gentleman in a low voice, pushing his fat face close to Foma's.

Foma gave a soft growl, and before the other knew what had happened, he had caught him by his curly iron-grey hair and was shaking him convulsively with his right hand, waving his left in the air and chanting in time to the shaking:

"Don't call people names . . . behind their backs. Say it . . . to their faces. Say it straight . . . to their faces."

He got enormous satisfaction out of seeing how comically the man beat the air with his fat hands, how his knees collapsed with the shaking and his feet scraped across the floor. The man's gold watch leaped out of his pocket and dangled on its gold chain over his belly. Foma, madly exultant, drunk with a sense of his own strength, with the joy of his vengeance, and of the humiliation of this "respectable" citizen, roared with delight as he dragged him along the floor. At last he felt relieved of the awful burden on his heart that had made him sick with despondency for so long. Hands caught at his waist and shoulders and seized his fingers, bending them back. Somebody stepped on his toes, but his blood-shot eyes saw nothing but the dark heavy mass that was writhing and groaning in his clutch. At last he was torn away from his victim and held fast, and he saw, as through a red mist, the man he had trounced lying at his feet. Rumpled, dishevelled, he was making helpless little movements with his feet in the effort to rise. Two men in black were supporting him. His arms hung down like broken wings, and he shouted at Foma in a voice choking with sobs:

"You can't touch me! You can't! I've been decorated! You ruffian! You low ruffian! I have children! Everybody knows who I am! You wretch! You cannibal! A duel!"

"Come away—for God's sake come away," whispered Uhtishchev in Foma's ear.

"Wait a minute! I'll kick him in the teeth!", said Foma. But he was dragged away. His head reeled, his heart was pounding, but he felt relieved and happy. He took a deep breath of air when they got to the entrance of the club.

"He won't forget that in a hurry, will he?" he said to Uhtishchev with a bland smile.

"You must be mad!" gasped the gay little secretary. "Why, I've never witnessed anything like it in my life!"

"But, my dear fellow," said Foma amiably, "didn't he deserve a good shaking? Isn't he a bounder? How dared he say such a thing behind her back? Go and say it to her face—straight to her face."

"But, damn it all, you don't mean to say it was just on *her* account you gave him that drubbing?"

"What do you mean, on her account? What other reason?"

"How do I know? You must have had an old score to settle with him. Good Lord! What a scene! I won't forget it to the end of my days!"

"That fellow—who is he?" asked Foma; then, bursting out laughing: "The way he roared, the jackass!"

Uhtishchev stared at him intently for a moment before he asked:

"Listen, don't you really know who he is? And did you really do it purely on account of Sophia Pavlovna?"

"I swear it," said Foma.

"Of all the damn foolishnesss!" Uhtishchev halted, shrugged his shoulders incredulously, gave a little wave of his hand, and set off down the pavement again. "You'll pay for this, Foma Ignatiyevich," he said, glancing at Foma out of the corner of his eye.

"What will he do, take me to court?"

"You'll be lucky if that's all he does. He's the vice-governor's son-in-law."

"Wha-a-at?" gasped Foma. His face dropped.

"Yes. To tell you the truth, he *is* a rascal and a swindler; from which one can deduce that he deserved the drubbing. But considering that the lady to whose defence you came is also—"

"Listen," said Foma firmly, putting his hand on Uhtishchev's shoulder, "I've always liked you. And you left them to come away with me—I understand and appreciate that. But there's one thing I ask of you: don't speak slightingly of her to me. Whatever she is to you, to me she's—she's very dear. There's nobody like her for me. And so I'm telling you straight to your face: since you've come with me, don't speak of her. If I find her good, let's leave it at that."

Foma spoke with such feeling that Uhtishchev glanced at him in wonder.

"Well, you are an interesting chap, no doubt about that," he said.

"I'm a simple sort. Savage, I suppose. I wiped the floor with that fellow, and now I feel wonderful. I don't care what happens."

"And plenty may happen, I fear. To tell you the truth, I like you too, although I find you . . . er . . . dangerous. You may get another fit of chivalry for all I know and wipe the floor with *me*."

"Oh, come; I don't do that every day. In fact I've never done it before," said Foma uncomfortably. Uhtishchev laughed.

"A monster if ever there was one! But listen, fighting is savage: it's low, if you'll forgive my saying so, although in the present case I must admit you made a happy choice of victim. He's a louse, a lecher, a sponger; a man who stole the very shirt off his nephews' back and went scot-free."

"Glad to hear it," said Foma with relish, "At least I've given him a little punishment."

"A little? Very well, let's assume it was only a little. But listen to me, my boy—a word of advice from a clerk of the court. He's a rascal, true, but you can't wipe the floor even with rascals, for they, too, are members of society and enjoy the protection of the law. They are not to be touched until they overstep the line drawn by our legal code, and even then not you, but we, their official judges, will mete out punishment. So if you don't mind, try to be patient."

"Will it take long for him to fall into your hands?" asked Foma innocently.

"It's hard to say. Inasmuch as the gentleman in question is not stupid, the probabilities are that he'll never fall into our hands, and that to the end of his days the law will recognize him to be as worthy a citizen as you or me. Oh, my God! What am I saying?" and Uhtishchev sighed comically.

"Giving away secrets?" laughed Foma.

"Not exactly secrets, but it's scarcely fitting for me to be so light-minded. Damn it all! This business has quite stirred me up. Nemesis, it seems, can fulfil her function by just kicking like a horse."

138

Foma suddenly came to a halt, as if he had run up against some obstacle in his path.

"And it all began with your saying Sophia Pavlovna was going away," he said slowly, in a flat voice.

"She is. What of it?"

He stood opposite Foma and looked at him with a twinkle in his eye. Foma was silent, with hanging head, poking his walking-stick between the paving stones.

"Come along."

Foma went. "Well, let her go," he muttered indifferently.

Uhtishchev twirled his walking-stick and whistled a tune as he watched his companion out of the corner of his eye.

"As if I couldn't go on living without her!" said Foma, his eyes fixed on some point ahead of him; then, after a pause, softly and irresolutely: "I can, of course."

"Listen, here's a good piece of advice: be yourself," said Uhtishchev. "A person should always be himself. Yours is the epic temperament, to to speak; lyricism doesn't become you. It's not your *genre*."

"Use simpler words when you speak to me, friend," said Foma, who had tried to understand.

"Very well, what I wanted to say was: drop that lady. She's poison for such as you."

"That's just what *she* said," remarked Foma unhappily.

"Did she? H'm. Well, shall we go somewhere for supper?"

"Let's," agreed Foma. "And if we go, we'll go in fine style!" he roared savagely, shaking his fists in the air. "What a spree I'll have! After all that's happened, I'll break loose and there'll be no holding me!"

"But why? Just a modest little supper."

"Tell me, what is it?" said Foma despondently, taking him by the shoulder. "Am I worse than other people? They seem to enjoy life—always hurrying here and there, going after something or other. But—I'm bored to death. They're all pleased with themselves—the complaints they make are mere pretence, the scoundrels. Just putting on airs. But I don't know how to put on airs. I'm a simpleton, I don't understand anything, and I don't know how to think things out. It's sickening. One says this, another that . . . and as for her—oh, if you only knew! I had put all my hopes in her. I expected her to . . . to . . . what did I expect? I don't even know. But I know there's nobody that can come up

139

to her. And I was so sure that some day she would tell me something—something very special. She has such wonderful eyes. God, a man's afraid to look into them! I wasn't just in love with her, I gave my whole soul to her. I thought it would make a man of me just to be near someone so beautiful."

Uhtishchev listened to the incoherent words pouring from his mouth, saw the muscles of his face twitching with the effort to express his thoughts, perceived the profound grief behind this farrago. There was something deeply touching in the helplessness of this strong, savage young man who suddenly set off down the street with big uneven strides. As Uhtishchev hopped after him on his short legs, he felt in duty bound to comfort him in some way. All that Foma had said and done that evening had excited his interest and he was, in addition, flattered by having received the confidences of the wealthy Gordeyev. He was crushed by the weight of these confidences, he was confounded by their overwhelming force, and although, despite his youth, he had stock phrases ready for every eventuality in life, he had difficulty in recalling them in the present instance.

"Good heavens, man," he said, as he slipped his arm through Foma's affectionately, "you can't go on like this. You're philosophizing when you've hardly entered upon life. You really can't, you know. Life was given us to live. In other words, live and let live. That's the whole of philosophy. As for that woman—Heavens! the sun doesn't rise and set with her! If you want me to, I'll introduce you to a woman so intoxicating you'll forget all about your philosophy the minute you lay eyes on her! A most delectable lady! *She* knows how to make the best use of life! She, like you, has the epic temperament. And she's beautiful—a very Helen. Just the person for you! A brilliant idea. I'll certainly introduce you to her. One poison as an antidote for another."

"I have a conscience," said Foma dismally. "As long as Sophia Pavlovna's alive I can't even look at a woman."

"What? A hale and hearty fellow like you? Ho, ho!" and Uhtishchev launched on a didactic exposition of the necessity of giving vent to one's feelings in carousing.

"The very thing, just what you need, take my word for it. As for your conscience—excuse me, but you're mistaken on that point: it's not your conscience that holds you back, but your shyness. You're not used to mixing with people, and so you feel self-conscious and embarrassed in their presence. You sense this vaguely, and take it for the voice of conscience. But there can be no talk of conscience here—what has conscience to say, since it's natural for a man to enjoy himself? Since it's his right and his necessity?"

Foma stared straight ahead of him as he walked along, adapting his step to that of his companion. The street with its rows of buildings on either side was like an enormous ditch filled with darkness. It seemed as if there were no end to it, and as if an inexhaustible stream of something black and suffocating were flowing sluggishly along it. Uhtishchev's gentle, persuasive voice went on monotonously and, while Foma did not listen to the words, he was aware of a tenaciousness that made them cling to his memory in spite of himself. And though he had a companion at his side, it was as if he were alone, lost in the darkness that wrapped itself about him and drew him steadily onward. He knew he was being lured somewhere, but lacked all power of resistance. Weariness kept him from thinking; he did not wish to resist what Uhtishchev said—why should he?

"We only live once," went on Uhtishchev, admiring his own sagacity, "and therefore we mustn't lose any time. Take my word for it. But why waste words? Let me jolt you out of this. Come with me to a certain house where two sisters live—and *how* they live! Do come, will you?"

"Why not?" said Foma with a yawn of indifference. "But isn't it too late?" he asked, glancing up at the cloudy sky.

"It's never too late to go and see *them!*" cried Uhtishchev gaily.

VIII

THREE days after the incident in the club Foma found himself on the timber wharf of the merchant Zvantsev, seven versts outside the town, in the company of Uhtishchev, Zvantsev's son, an imposing bald-headed, red-nosed gentleman with side whiskers, and four women. Young Zvantsev was pale and thin and wore pince-nez; the muscles of his calves twitched when he stood still as if they hated having to support his emaciated body topped by a ridiculously small head in a jockey cap that was worn with a long checked coat with a hood. The gentleman with the side whiskers called him Jean, pronouncing it as if he had a chronic cold in the nose. Jean's girl was tall and full-breasted, her head looked as if it had been compressed on both sides, her low forehead receded sharply, her long nose gave her a bird-like look. No part of this ugly face ever moved, except the small, cold, round eyes, which kept screwing up in a cunning smile. Uhtishchev's girl was named Vera. She was tall and pale and had such thick auburn hair that it looked like an enormous hat coming down over her ears, her cheeks, her high forehead and the pair of big blue eyes that gazed out languorously from under it.

The gentleman with the side whiskers was sitting next to a plump, fresh-looking young girl who kept giggling at something he whispered in her ear as he bent over her shoulder.

Foma's girl was a brunette with a handsome figure, dressed all in black. Dark-complexioned, with wavy hair, she held her head so high and looked upon everything with such a haughty air that one could easily see she considered herself superior to her companions.

The party had disposed itself upon the last of a string of rafts that stretched far out into the quiet, empty river. Boards had been laid on the raft, and in the middle stood a rough table. Food hampers, empty bottles, bon-bon papers and orange peelings were scattered everywhere. Earth was piled on one corner of the raft and on top of it was a camp-fire beside which a peasant in a sheepskin was crouching, warming his hands and casting side-long glances at his betters. They had just finished eating some fish soup, and the table in front of them was now laden with wine and fruit.

The dinner, in addition to two days of debauchery, had left them spiritless. They sat gazing into the river and talking, but their conversation kept petering out. The young spring day was clear and invigorating, as spring days are. A bright cold sky stretched majestically above the turbid river in spate. The hills of the far shore were enveloped in bluish mists, and on their summits the crosses of the churches glistened like huge stars. Over on the hilly side the river was lively: steamers travelled up and down, the sound of their chugging coming in heavy sighs to this, the meadow side, where the quiet flow of water filled the air with little lapping sounds. A string of big barges labouring against the current looked like monstrous pigs churning up the water with their snouts. Black smoke poured fitfully from funnels and dissolved slowly in the clear air. Occasionally a ship's siren sounded; it was like the roar of some huge animal, enraged by toil. All was quiet and still on the water-meadows. The trees that here and there thrust out of the flood were spangled with bright green leaves. The water, hiding their trunks and reflecting their tops, turned them into airy green balls of magical beauty, that the slightest breeze, it seemed, would send rolling over the glossy surface of the water.

The auburn-haired woman began to sing quietly and sadly as she gazed into the distance:

> *Soft a boat goes floating,*
> *Down the Volga tide. . . .*

The brunette narrowed her big eyes contemptuously.

"It's dreary enough without that," she said, turning away.

"Don't stop her, let her sing," said Foma, glancing good-naturedly into his girl's face. He was very pale, fires smouldered in his eyes, a vague, indolent smile hovered about his lips.

"Let's all sing," proposed the gentleman with the side whiskers.

"No, just the two of them," put in Uhtishchev quickly. "Vera sing that—you know—'I'll go at dawn'. Sing, Pavlenka."

The giggling girl glanced at the brunette. "May I sing, Sasha?" she asked humbly.

"I'm going to sing myself," said Sasha, Foma's companion; then, turning to the girl with the bird-like face, who happened to be her sister: "Sing, Vassa."

Vassa ran a hand over her throat and fixed her eyes on her sister's face. Sasha got up, leaned on the table with one hand, threw back her head, and began to sing in a voice that was as strong and deep as a man's:

> *He alone can happy be*
> *Whose restive heart is not bowed down*
> *By care . . .*

Her sister gave a toss of her head and sang in a high contralto, plaintively, drawing out the notes:

> *Ah, the heart of this poor maid . . .*

Sasha's eyes flashed on her sister as she responded in deep tones:

> *Is withered like a leaf.*

The two voices mingled and floated out over the water in rich, full tones that trembled from an excess of force. One of them complained of a suffering that was beyond endurance and it thirstily lapped up the poison of complaint, sobbing inconsolably. The other voice, deep and courageous, poured out tears to quench the fires of torment and rang with resentment as it rose mightily into the air. Clearly enunciating the syllables, it flowed out in a deep stream, each word a threat of vengeance.

> *And pay he shall. . . .*

wailed Vassa, closing her eyes, while Sasha sang a warning, tossing her words into the air with grim determination:

> *I shall scathe him, I shall sear him. . . .*

Suddenly she shifted key and rhythm, exultantly pouring out maledictions in a voice as long-drawn as her sister's:

> *Dry as wind, as desert wind,*
> *Dry as grass that scythe has cut,*
> *That scythe has cut, that sun has scorched. . . .*

Foma, his elbows on the table, gazed into the girl's face—into her dark, half-closed eyes. They were staring into space, and so vindictive was their gleam that the velvety voice pouring from her throat seemed to him as dark and glistening as her eyes. As he recalled her caresses, he thought to himself: What could have made her like this? There's something frightening about her.

Uhtishchev had nestled close to his girl and was listening to the song with a blissful look on his face. Zvantsev and the gentleman with the side whiskers were drinking wine and whispering together. The auburn-haired girl was holding Uhtishchev's hand and studying it thoughtfully. A solemn look had come over the face of the giggling girl, who was listening to the music with drooping head, without stirring, as if under a spell. The peasant left the fire and tiptoed cautiously over the boards, his hands behind his back and his broad, bearded face wearing a smile of wonder and innocent joy.

Ah, take pity, kindly lad!

sang Vassa, shaking her head mournfully. Her sister, lifting her chin even higher, ended the song:

Such are the pangs of love!

When it was finished, she cast a proud look about her, then sank down next to Foma and put a strong arm round his neck.

"A nice song?"

"Lovely," said Foma, smiling at her.

"Bravo, bravo, Sasha!" cried Uhtishchev, and everyone clapped. She paid no attention to them.

"Give me a present for the song," she said to Foma, embracing him possessively.

"Indeed I will," said Foma.

"What?"

"Anything you like."

"When we get to town. Oh, the love I'll show you if you give me what I ask for!"

"Only for that reason?" said Foma with a dubious little laugh. "Can't you love me for my own sake?"

She gazed at him calmly, and after a moment's reflection said:

"It's too soon to say. I'm not one to lie; I tell you frankly: I love for money, or for presents. Oh, I know a person can love without them. But it's too soon. When I get to know you better, perhaps I'll love you free of charge. But meanwhile—don't judge me harshly. A person who leads my life needs money, lots of money."

Foma listened to her, smiled and trembled at the touch of her body. He was conscious of Zvantsev saying in a high, cracked voice that jarred his nerves:

"I don't know why everybody raves about the beauty of Russian songs. What's so beautiful about them? The howling of a pack of hungry wolves—wild and hungry. Or better—a pack of dogs. No gaiety, no *chic*! You ought to hear the French sing. Or the Italians."

"Oh, come, Ivan Nikolayevich," protested Uhtishchev indignantly.

The gentleman with side whiskers sipping his wine said:

"I agree with him—Russian songs are gloomy and monotonous."

The sun was setting. It dappled the dark water with pink and gold as it sank somewhere far beyond the water-meadows. As Foma stood watching the glow and the tremulous play of colour on the glistening surface of the river, he fancied that the snatches of talk that drifted to him were dark moths fluttering aimlessly. Sasha put her head on his shoulder and whispered words into his ear that made him blush and want to take her in his arms and kiss her ardently, endlessly. She was the only one of the party who interested him in the least. Zvantsev and the gentleman with the side whiskers disgusted him.

"What are you staring at?" Uhtishchev shouted suddenly.

His shout was directed at the peasant, who snatched the cap off his head, slapped it against his knee, and said with a smile:

"I—I wanted to listen to the lady's singing."

"Do you like it?"

"Who could help liking it!" he replied, looking rapturously at Sasha. "There's a lot of power in that breast of hers."

His words brought a laugh from the women and suggestive comments from the men.

"Do you sing?" Sasha asked the peasant.

"If you call it singing," he said disparagingly.

"What songs do you know?"

"Oh, all sorts; I love singing." He smiled apologetically.

"Come, let's sing together, you and I."

"I'm no partner for you, miss."

"You begin."

"Isn't this jolly!" said Zvantsev, making a wry face.

"If you don't like it, you can drown yourself," and Sasha's eyes flashed as she looked at him.

Zvantsev winced.

"The water's too cold," he said.

"The time's ripe: the river's in flood—you couldn't poison all the water with that putrid body of yours."

"Ha, you're not at all funny," said the youth, adding contemptuously: "In Russia, even the *cocottes* are coarse."

He turned to his neighbour, who gave him an inebriated smile. Uhtishchev, too, was drunk. His bleary eyes were fixed on his girl's face as he muttered to her incoherently. The girl with the bird-like face was pecking at a chocolate, holding the box under her very nose. Pavlenka had withdrawn to the edge of the raft and was throwing orange peel into the water.

"This is the rummest party I've ever known," complained Zvantsev to his neighbour.

Foma watched him with a mocking smile, glad that he was bored and that Sasha had given him a piece of her mind. He glanced at Sasha affectionately—he liked her brusqueness, and the proud way she carried herself, as if she were a gentlewoman.

"Miss," said the peasant, who was standing next to her, "will you give me a drop of something to liven my spirits?"

"Pour him out a glass, Foma."

The peasant gulped it down and smacked his lips.

"Now begin," ordered Sasha.

Pulling down one corner of his mouth, the man sang in a high tenor:

I cannot eat, I cannot drink. . . .

And the girl took it up:

My soul will have no more of wine. . . .

The peasant smiled blissfully, shook his head, closed his eyes, and poured out a stream of high, quavering notes:

The time has come when I must leave. . . .

The girl seemed to be weeping:

Must leave my home, my kith and kin. . . .

147

Lowering his voice, the peasant half-sang, half-spoke, in a passion of grief:

And hie me to an unknown land. . . .

As the two voices sobbed in the chill silence of the evening, everything about them seemed to grow warm and benevolent. Everything seemed to wear a smile of compassion for this poor soul whom dark forces were tearing away from hearth and home and driving off to a strange land, there to pour out his life in hard toil. Not in sound, not in song, did the complaint find utterance, but in human tears gushing from a bleeding heart. The very air seemed moistened by these tears. The suffering of a soul exhausted by struggle, the pain of wounds dealt by the iron hand of need—this is what was expressed in the crude words and inexpressibly mournful melody that floated up into the empty, distant sky, where there was no echo.

Foma recoiled from the singers and watched them with a feeling akin to fear. Like seething waters the song poured into his breast, flooding his heart with the wild force of its grief. He felt that he was about to burst into tears. His throat contracted and the muscles of his face twitched. He caught a hazy vision of Sasha's black eyes—fixed, enormous eyes, that seemed to be growing bigger every minute. And he fancied that not two people, but everything about him was singing and sobbing and trembling in the torments of grief and that all living things were clinging to each other in despair.

When the song came to an end a shudder of excitement passed over him, and he smiled at the two, his face wet with tears.

"Did it move you so?" asked Sasha. She was pale with exhaustion and her breath came quickly. Foma glanced at the peasant: he was wiping the sweat off his brow and looking about him in a daze, as if he did not understand what had happened.

Not a sound was to be heard. Everyone was silent and motionless.

"God!" breathed Foma, pulling himself to his feet; then, almost shouting: 'Sasha! And you, you peasant! Who are you?"

"Stepan," replied the peasant, smiling apologetically.

"How you sing!" Foma was shifting excitedly from foot to foot.

"Ah, Your Honour," sighed the peasant, "it's misery that makes us—misery enough to turn a bull into a nightingale. But as for the young lady here—none but the Lord can tell what makes her sing as she does. A man would gladly lie down and die, once he'd heard her. She's a gem, she is."

"A very good performance," said Uhtishchev in a drunken drawl.

"Damn it all!" cried Zvantsev irritably, almost tearfully, as he jumped up from the table. "I came here for a good time, to enjoy myself, not to have a dirge sung over me! Outrageous, I call it! I can't stand it. I'm leaving!"

"I'll go with you, Jean," said the gentleman with the side whiskers.

"Vassa," cried Zvantsev, "put on your things,"

"Yes, it's time to go," the girl with the auburn hair said calmly to Uhtishchev. "It's getting cold, and it'll be dark soon."

"Clear things up, Stepan," ordered Vassa.

Everyone began to talk and move about. Foma watched them uncomprehendingly, still shuddering from time to time. Pale and spent, they were staggering about the raft, saying foolish, disconnected things to each other. Sasha jostled unceremoniously as she gathered up her things.

"Stepan! Call for the horses!"

"I'm having another cognac. Who wants to join me?" drawled the gentleman with the side whiskers, waving a bottle in the air.

Vassa wound a scarf about Zvantsev's neck. He was standing in front of her pouting like a sulky child, looking very crumpled, the muscles of his calves twitching nervously. The sight of him filled Foma with such aversion that he stepped on to the next raft. He marvelled that these people could behave as if they had not heard the song. It went on sounding in his heart, evoking a restless desire to do or to say something.

The sun had gone down by this time and the horizon was veiled in blue mist. Foma glanced at it and turned away. He did not want to go back to town with these people. They were still moving about the raft on unsteady legs, swaying from side to side and muttering incoherently. The women were more sober than the men, but it was some time before the auburn-haired girl could struggle to her feet.

"Well, I *am* drunk," she said when she stood upright at last.

Foma sat down on a chopping block, picked up the axe with which the peasant had chopped wood, and began tossing it into the air and catching it.

"How vulgar!" whined Zvantsev.

149

Foma hated the man violently—hated him and everybody else except Sasha, who filled him with awe and kept him in constant fear that she might do something unexpected and calamitous.

"You scum!" screeched Zvantsev, and Foma saw him give the peasant a push. The peasant snatched off his cap and slunk away.

"Blockhead!" shouted Zvantsev, gesturing wildly as he went after the man.

"Stop! Don't dare touch him!" warned Foma.

"What?" cried Zvantsev, turning round.

Foma hunched his shoulders and strode towards him. And suddenly a bright idea flashed into his mind. With an exultant laugh, he whispered to the peasant:

"Is the raft fastened in three places?"

"It is."

"Cut the ropes."

"But—the people?"

"Sh-h. Cut them, I say."

"But if . . ."

"Cut them! And do it so that nobody sees you."

The peasant took the axe and walked unhurriedly over to the edge of the raft where the fastenings were. He struck the ropes a few times and came back to Foma.

"I don't want to answer for this, Your Honour," he said.

"Have no fear."

"It's drifting away," gasped the peasant in horror, crossing himself swiftly. Foma chuckled to himself, but he had a ghastly feeling in the pit of his stomach—a prickly, burning sensation, caused by a fear he had never known before, but which he found sweet.

The people were still walking about the raft, bumping into each other, helping one another on with their coats, laughing and talking, while the raft drifted slowly, haltingly, away from the others.

"If they run head-on into a string of barges, they'll get smashed to pieces," whispered the peasant.

"Hold your tongue! Take a boat and follow them."

"Yes, yes. After all, they're human beings."

Smiling contentedly, the peasant jumped from raft to raft until he reached shore. Foma stood gazing out over the water, longing to shout, but restraining himself until the raft had had time to float off far enough to prevent his drunken companions jumping to safety. He found it pleasant and soothing to watch the soft rocking of the raft as it was carried further and further away. It was as if all the dark thoughts that had weighed down upon him of late were drifting away with the raft. He inhaled the fresh air deeply—wholesome air that cleared his head. Sasha was standing with her back to him on the very edge of the drifting raft. The sight of her handsome figure reminded him of Sophia Pavlovna. Only Sophia Pavlovna was smaller . . .

Stabbed by his memories, he cried out in a mocking voice:

"Farewell! Happy journey!"

Suddenly, simultaneously, the dark figures made a movement towards him, and crowded together in the centre of the raft. But by this time six feet of cold water glistened between them and Foma. There was silence for a few seconds.

Then there came a storm of shrieks and screams and horrid wails of sheer animal fright. More shrill and repulsive than all the others was the thin, chattering cry of Zvantsev:

"He-e-e-lp!"

"He's drowning us! He's drowning live people!" roared a bass voice, probably that of the gentleman with the side whiskers.

"Do you call yourselves people?" shouted Foma, to whom the cries were as irritating as insect bites.

The people plunged about on the raft in panic; it rocked more violently and this made it drift faster. The water could be heard splashing over it and gurgling under it. Cries rent the air, people leapt about waving their arms. Sasha alone remained standing where she was, silent and motionless.

"Give my regards to the crabs!" called out Foma. The further away the raft drifted, the lighter grew his heart.

"Foma Ignatiyevich," said Uhtishchev in a sober but trembling voice, "think what you're doing. This is dangerous. I shall file a complaint."

"When you're dead? Go ahead and file it!" laughed Foma.

"Murderer!" sobbed Zvantsev. But at that moment there was a splash that sounded as if the water were gasping in fright or surprise. Foma gave a start and froze to the spot. The women set up a wild howl, the men shouted in horror and everyone stood rooted to the spot. Foma gazed at the water as if transfixed. Something black was moving towards him.

Instinctively Foma threw himself down on the raft and hung with outstretched hand far out over the water. The next few seconds were an eternity. At last his hand was seized in cold, wet fingers and he caught a glimpse of shining black eyes.

The fear that had filled his heart was replaced by joy. He grasped the girl, pulled her out of the water, clasped her to his breast and gazed wonderingly into her eyes, not knowing what to say. She smiled at him tenderly.

"It's cold," she said at last, a tremor passing over her.

The sound of her voice made Foma laugh with delight. He picked her up in his arms and almost ran down the rafts to the shore. She was as cold and wet as a fish, but her breath was hot; it burned his cheek and filled his heart with wild joy.

"So you wanted to drown me, did you?" she said, pressing closer to him.

"How clever of you to have jumped off!" said Foma as he ran.

"What you did was rather clever too. I wouldn't have thought you had it in you."

"Listen to them; they're still roaring."

"The devil take them! If they drown, you and I will go to Siberia," she said. She began to shiver. Foma felt it and quickened his pace.

From the river behind them came shouts and cries for help. There on the placid waters a tiny island with dark human figures running about drifted through the twilight, further and further from the shore, out towards the main current of the river.

Night was closing in on them.

IX

ONE Sunday afternoon Yakov Mayakin was having tea in his garden. He was sitting on a bench under a green canopy of cherry boughs, his shirt collar open, a towel round his neck, wiping the sweat off his face and gesticulating vigorously as his tongue rattled on without pause.

"He who lets his belly rule his mind is a fool and a scoundrel."

There was an angry glitter in the old man's eye, his lips twisted contemptuously, and the wrinkles on his lowering face quivered.

"If Foma was my blood son, I'd teach him a thing or two!"

Lyuba sat playing idly with a twig of acacia, studying her father's indignant, agitated face curiously, but without comment. Although she was not aware of it, her attitude towards him was becoming less cold and distrustful as time went on. For all his cleverness and ceaseless activity, he was always alone. Lyuba perceived his loneliness and knew how hard it was to bear, and this made her feel more kindly towards him. At times she brought herself to argue with him. He was always contemptuous of any objection she raised and was sure to ridicule her, yet each time they argued he listened more attentively and tolerantly.

"If the late Ignat could read what the papers say about his son, he'd kill him," said Mayakin, striking the table with his fist. "The things they've written! A disgrace!"

"He deserved it," said Lyuba.

"I don't say he didn't. There's no smoke without fire. But who wrote that masterpiece?"

"What difference does it make?" asked Lyuba.

"It would be interesting to know. The scoundrel gave a very rich description of Foma's behaviour. He must have been one of the company and seen all that debauchery with his own eyes."

"He'd never go drinking with Foma," said Lyuba definitely and blushed under her father's searching look.

"H'm! Nice friends you have, Lyuba!" drawled Mayakin caustically. "Well, who wrote it?"

She did not wish to tell him, but he insisted with growing asperity.

"Promise you won't do him any harm?" she asked at last.

"Harm? I'll bite his head off! You simpleton! What harm could I do him? They're not fools, those writers. They're a force, curse them. And I'm not the governor. Even if I were, I couldn't break their arms or tie their tongues. They're like rats—you can't stop their gnawing. Come, now, who wrote it?"

"Do you remember that *gymnasium* student called Yezhov who used to come and see me when I was still at school? A dark-haired lad."

"I do. So it was he, was it? A rat all right! Even in those days you could see nothing good would ever come of him. I should have taken him in hand then. I might have made a man of him."

Lyuba shrugged her shoulders as she glanced at her father and asked defiantly:

"Why, aren't they men—those people who write for the papers?"

Mayakin did not answer immediately; he sat drumming on the table and studying his reflection in the brightly polished brass of the samovar.

"No, they're not men; they're sores," he declared at last, lifting his head and narrowing his eyes. "Russia's blood has gone bad, and it's this bad blood that breeds the book-writers, the news-writers—all sorts of raving Pharisees. They've broken out all over her body, and the infection is spreading. And why has her blood gone bad? Because she moves too slowly. It's swamps that breed mosquitoes; all sorts of vermin are bred in stagnant water. The same holds true when life gets stagnant."

"I don't think you're right, Father," said Lyuba gently.

"What's that?"

"I don't. Writers are the most disinterested people in the world. They're to be respected. They want nothing for themselves: nothing but justice, nothing but the truth. They aren't mosquitoes, they're—"

Lyuba could not suppress her agitation as she sang the praises of those she admired so deeply. A flush dyed her cheeks and the eyes she turned to her father implored him to believe her even though she was incapable of convincing him in words.

The old man interrupted her.

"Dear, oh. dear!" he sighed. "You read too much, Lyuba. Tell me this: who are they? Nobody knows. Take that Yezhov—who is he? A pimple in the eyes of God. They want nothing but the truth, you say. Hear, hear! Very modest, eh? But what if the truth's the dearest thing in the world? And what if everybody is searching for it in his own way? Believe me, there's no such thing as an unselfish person. Nobody's willing to fight for what belongs to other people, or at least if he is, he's a fool, and no good will come of it—neither for him nor anybody else. If a man's to succeed, he's got to know how to stand up for his *own* rights, for what belongs to *him*. The truth? For almost forty years I've been reading the same newspaper, and this is what I've learned: look at this face of mine—here it is, staring straight at you; and there it is again, in the samovar—the same face, but different. Well, it's that samovar face the newspapers show you. They don't even see the real one. And you take it for the genuine thing. As for me, I know my face is distorted on the samovar."

"But, Father, books and newspapers fight for the common good, defend the interests of everybody," protested Lyuba unhappily.

"Show me the paper where it says that you're bored with life and ought to have got married long ago. That's how they defend *your* interests! They don't defend mine either, and how can they? Who knows what I want? Who but myself knows what my interests are?"

"Oh, but Father, that's all wrong! I don't know how to put it, but I feel that it's all wrong," protested Lyuba in despair.

"It's all *right*," said the old man determinedly. "Russia has lost her head, there's nothing solid any more, everything's unstable. People live lopsided and walk crooked and everything is twisted out of shape. There's a great clamour of voices, but nobody knows what anyone else wants. A fog lies over everything and people breathe this fog and it spoils their blood. That's where the sores come from. A man is given freedom to think as he likes, but he isn't allowed to do anything, and so instead of living a full life, he just rots away and stinks."

"What's to be done about it?" asked Lyuba, putting her elbows on the table and leaning towards her father.

"Done? Everything's to be done!" cried the old man. "Each of us has to do what he can. But first of all you've got to give

155

people free rein. If the time's come when every little jackanapes fancies he can do wonders and was created for the sole purpose of ordering life as he sees fit, give him the reins, damn it all! Go ahead, you scum, show us what you can do! And then the comedy begins. As soon as he feels the bridle's off, he leaps up higher than his head and darts hither and thither, puffed up with conceit, believing himself a miracle worker."

Mayakin paused for a second; then, smiling cunningly, resumed in a low voice:

"But there's only the merest mite of breath in your miracle worker, no more than enough to keep him puffed up for a day or two. Very soon he feels the wind going out of him, poor thing, for he's rotten at the core. And this is the moment when he'll be caught by the genuine people, the capable people, whose right it is to order life as they see fit and who will not rule by rod and pen but by hand and brain. 'What?' they'll say, 'is the heat too much for you?'" Here the old man assumed a loud, imperious tone: "'Well, then, you so-and-so and so-and-so, hold your tongue! Not a squeak out of you or we'll sweep you off the earth like ants off the doorstep. Not a squeak!' That's how it'll be, Lyuba. He, he, he!"

The old man was enjoying himself. His wrinkles quivered, he twitched all over with the joy of expressing himself, he closed his eyes and smacked his lips as if savouring his own wisdom.

"And then those who took the helm when all was confusion will build life in their own way, a sensible way. And there will be no more of this turmoil; life will proceed in a well-ordered fashion like the notes of a song. But I won't live to see it, that's the pity."

Her father's words fell about Lyuba like the meshes of a strong net in which she was becoming entangled. Unable to free herself, she sat listening in stunned silence, intently scanning his face, searching for moral support in his words, discovering in them something similar to the things she had read in books and had thought to be the truth. But her father's gloating laughter lacerated her heart and the wrinkles that crept like worms over his face made her afraid of him. She felt that he was turning her away from the aims that had seemed so simple and desirable in her dreams.

"Father'" she said impulsively, "Father, what do you think Taras is like?"

Mayakin started. His eyebrows beetled angrily and he fixed his daughter with a sharp eye as he remarked dryly:

"What makes you ask a thing like that?"

"Why, mayn't we speak of him?" asked Lyuba softly.

"I don't want to speak of him, and I don't advise you to." The old man shook his finger at his daughter, glowered at her, then dropped his head. But he must have misunderstood himself when he said he did not want to speak of his son, for a minute later he said irascibly:

"Taras is one of the sores. Life sends all sorts of smells to the noses of you young whipper-snappers, and since you can't tell the good from the bad, you breathe them all in and they cloud your minds. Taras, the old snout-face . . . he must be thirty years old by now . . . and for me, he's—he's dead."

"What did he do?" asked Lyuba, eagerly drinking in her father's every word.

"Who knows? I don't suppose he knows himself; not if he's got any brains by this time, and he ought to have: he was born of a clever father and he's seen enough of life. They're too soft with them, with those nihilists. If I had my way, I'd show them! 'Into the wilderness with you, into the desert—forward, march! Here you are, bright lads, here's your chance to mould life according to your taste! Show us what you can do!' And I'd put some sturdy peasants over them. 'Come now, we've fed you, we've clothed you, we've taught you—what is it you've learned? Time to repay us for all our care'. Not a kopek would I waste on the likes of them, and I'd squeeze every drop of juice out of their flesh—make them pay and pay! You can't throw away human beings—can't just put them in jail. 'So you broke the law, did you, and yet live like gentlemen? Oh, no, you don't! We'll get some work out of you!' A single grain of corn puts forth a whole ear, and are we to let a single man be lost without reaping any benefit from him? A careful carpenter finds use for every little chip; in just such a way must a man be used up to the last drop. The vilest vermin has its place in life, and a man is not to be compared to vermin. Ah, but it's a sad thing to find strength without sense; and just as sad to find sense without strength. Take Foma, for instance . . . But who's that coming? Have a look, Lyuba."

Lyuba turned round and saw Yefim, captain of the *Yermak*, coming down the path, bowing respectfully to her, clutching his cap in his hand. He wore an expression of guilty despair and seemed, in general, to be completely crushed.

"What's happened?" called out Mayakin as soon as he saw who it was.

"I decided to—to come to you," said Yefim, making a low bow.

"I can see that well enough. What's the matter? Where's the boat?"

"The boat's there," said Yefim, waving his hand in an uncertain direction and shifting heavily from one foot to the other.

"Where, damn you? Speak up! What's happened?" shouted the old man angrily.

Yefim took a deep breath before he announced:

"Barge No. 9 is smashed. One man was hurt and another is missing—drowned, I'm afraid."

"Hm," said Mayakin, measuring the captain with a wrathful eye. "Well, Yefim, I'll flay you for this."

"It wasn't me," put in Yefim quickly.

"Not you?" cried the old man, trembling all over. "Then who was it?"

"The master himself."

"Foma? And you? What about you?"

"I . . . I was lying in the hold."

"Lying down, were you?"

"I was bound."

"Wha-at?" shrieked the old man.

"Here, I'll tell you everything as it happened. He'd had a drop too much, the master had, and he shouted: 'Get out of here! I'll do the commanding.' And I said: 'I can't do that,' I said. 'How can I, when I'm the captain?' 'Bind him hand and foot!' he said, and they bound me and put me down in the hold with the boat-hands. And as he'd had a drop too much, he wanted to have some fun, and so when he sees six empty barges towed by the *Chernogorets* coming down stream—he blocks their way. They blew their whistle, blew it more than once; they did blow it, it's only fair to say that."

"Well?"

"Well, there was nothing they could do. The two front ones crashed into us—straight into our port side and smashed us to bits. And they were smashed too, but we got the worst of it."

158

Mayakin jumped up from his chair and gave a frightful cackle. Yefim hunched his shoulders.

"He has a very violent character. When he's sober, he doesn't speak, just goes about as if he had something on his mind, but the minute he oils his springs with drink he breaks out, and then he's no longer master of himself or his business, but is his own worst enemy, begging your pardon for saying it. I want to leave the job, Yakov Tarasovich. I can't go on without a real master; I can't get used to it."

"Enough of that," said Mayakin sternly. "Where's Foma?"

"Out there where it happened. It brought him to his senses at once, and he sent for the workmen straight away. They're going to raise the barge, they must have begun by this time."

"Is he alone there?" asked Mayakin, hanging his head.

"Not . . . er . . . quite," murmured Yefim with a sidelong glance at Lyuba. "He has a young lady with him—dark-haired she is, and out of her wits if you ask me: she sings all the time, sings very beautifully—a big temptation," said Yefim with a sigh.

"I didn't ask about her," shouted Mayakin, beside himself. The wrinkles on his face deepened as if he were in pain, and Lyuba was afraid he was going to cry.

"Calm yourself, Father," she said gently. "Perhaps the loss isn't very great."

"Not very great?" cried Mayakin. "What do you know about it, you fool? Do you think it's a barge that's lost? It's a man that's lost, that's what it is. And a man that I need, that I *need*, you confounded fools!"

With a wrathful toss of his head, the old man made for the house.

While this was taking place, Foma was in a village hut on the bank of the Volga some four hundred versts away. He had just woken up and was lying on a heap of fresh hay in the middle of the floor gazing sullenly through the window at a sky covered with tattered grey clouds.

He lay without moving his head, which was heavy with drink, and he fancied that the same sort of grey clouds were floating through his breast, floating on and on in an endless stream, effusing a damp and blighting chill. There was something feeble, something craven about the slow-moving clouds; and he felt the same within himself. He let his memories of the last few months drift across his mind without reflecting on them.

It was as though he had fallen into a hot and turbid stream that caught him up in its dark waters; and as though these waters, moving like clouds in the sky, were carrying him away. Through the noise and the darkness about him he could vaguely perceive that he was not alone, but that others were being borne along with him, and that these others kept changing from day to day, but that all of them were pitiable and revolting. Drunken, boisterous, greedy, they circled round him, caroused at his expense, cursed him, fought with each other, shouted, even wept. He struck them. He remembered hitting one man in the face, snatching the coat off another and throwing him into the water. Someone kissed his hands with lips as cold and clammy as a frog, tearfully imploring him not to kill him. Faces, words, fragments of sound flashed through his mind. A woman in a yellow silk blouse, wide open at the breast, sang in a loud, sobbing voice:

Today let us live and be merry,
Let the morrow take care of itself. . . .

All these people were caught up in the same dark wave that had caught him, and they, like him, were being carried away as if they were so much refuse. Not one of them dared to look ahead and see where the wild stream was taking them, and so, drowning their fears in wine, they howled and splashed and capered and clowned, without knowing what it meant to be truly gay. He did just as they did. And now it seemed to him that he did it merely to get through this bad stretch of life as quickly as possible.

Sasha alone remained calm and serene amid the mad whirl of debauchery, among people who were swept along by raging passions and were half crazed by the longing to forget. She never got drunk, always spoke in a firm, commanding tone and all her movements were as full of confidence as if, instead of being caught up in this wild stream, it was she who directed it. She seemed to Foma the cleverest of all those who surrounded him and the most eager for noise and revelry. She ordered everyone about, was always inventing some new form of entertainment and treated everyone the same; for the driver, the lackey and the boat-hand she used the same tone and the same words as for her friends and for Foma. She was younger and prettier than Pelagea, but her caresses were cold and given in silence. It seemed to Foma that she was hiding some dreadful secret in the depths of her heart and that she would never love anybody or reveal herself completely. He was attracted to her by this secretiveness, this mystery; it aroused his curiosity and made him want to plumb the depths of her impassive soul, which was as dark as her eyes.

Foma once said to her:

"What a lot of money you and I have thrown to the winds."

"What else should we do with it?" she asked.

Yes, what else? thought Foma, surprised by her casualness.

"Who are you?" he asked her on another occasion.

"Why, have you forgotten my name?"

"Hardly."

"Then what else do you want to know?"

"I was wondering where you came from."

"Oh, that? I'm from Uglich, in the province of Yaroslavl. I was a harpist by profession. Do you like me any better, now that you know who I am?"

"Do I know?" asked Foma with a little laugh.

"So that's not enough for you? Well, I won't tell you anything more. Why should I? We all spring from the same source—people and animals alike. All this talk about origin is nonsense. But let's think about something more important: how shall we spend the day?"

They spent it on a river boat with a band on board, and they drank champagne until all of them were drunk. Sasha sang a song that was particularly mournful and made Foma weep like a child. After that he and she did a Russian dance, and finally, exhausted, he threw himself overboard and was almost drowned.

Now as he lay on the floor with these and many other memories drifting through his mind, he felt ashamed of himself and displeased with Sasha. He glanced at her lovely body, listened to her even breathing and knew that he did not love her and did not need her. Drab, depressing thoughts began to take shape in his aching head. It seemed as if everything he had lived through during this time was reduced to a hard, moist ball of wool that went rolling about inside him, gradually unwinding and entangling him in its thin grey threads.

What's happening to me? he thought. Who am I?

The question startled him, and he pondered it, trying to discover why he could not live quietly and contentedly, as other people did. This thought made him more ashamed than ever. He tossed on the hay and gave Sasha an impatient push with his elbow.

"Careful," she murmured, half-asleep.

"That's all right, you're not such a great lady," he retorted.

"What?"

"Nothing."

She turned her back on him and yawned.

"I dreamt I was playing the harp again," she said sleepily. "Playing and singing a solo, and there was a big dog standing in front of me baring its teeth and waiting for me to finish. I was terrified; I knew it would spring at me the moment I stopped singing, and so I sang on and on, until I felt my voice giving out. Horrible! There it stood, gnashing its teeth. What do you suppose a dream like that means?"

"Wait a minute," said Foma in hollow tones. "First tell me this: what do you know about me?"

"That you've just woken up," she said without turning over.

"Yes, I've just woken up," mused Foma, putting his hands behind his head. "Which is precisely why I asked you what sort of a person you think I am."

"A drunken one," yawned Sasha.

"Listen," said Foma imploringly, "stop talking nonsense, Sasha, and tell me honestly what you think of me."

"I don't think of you at all," she replied.

He gave a deep sigh and fell silent. Both of them lay for a minute or so without speaking, then:

"A fine thing!" said Sasha in her usual indifferent voice. "Expecting me to waste my thoughts on all sorts of people! Why, I haven't even time to think about myself—or perhaps I don't want to."

Foma laughed mirthlessly.

"If only *I* didn't want to!" he said.

The girl lifted her head for a moment to glance into his face.

"You think too much," she said. "Look out. No good will come of it. I can't tell you anything about yourself. The only thing I can say is that you're better than others. But what do you care?"

"Why better?" asked Foma pensively.

"Oh, I don't know. If I sing a sad song, you weep; if a man's a blackguard, you knock him down. You're straightforward with women—don't take advantage of them. And you know how to make love to them too."

None of this satisfied Foma.

"You haven't understood me," he said quietly.

162

"I can't guess what goes on inside your head. They're raising the barge now. What shall we do?"

"What do you mean?" asked Foma.

"Shall we go to Nizhni-Novgorod or Kazan?"

"What for?"

"On a spree."

"I've had enough of sprees."

For a long time they both lay without speaking or looking at each other.

"You're a hard person to get on with," said Sasha at last. "Boring."

"I don't intend to drink any more," said Foma firmly.

"I don't believe you," said the imperturbable Sasha.

"You'll see. Do you think it's right to live the way we do?"

"Time will tell."

"Come, do you think it's right?"

"What's better?"

Foma glanced at her out of the corner of his eye.

"Ugh, it's disgusting to hear you!" he said testily.

"So you don't like the way I talk either?" laughed Sasha.

"People like you!" snorted Foma. "The way you live! Rushing ahead, you don't know where. Even a cockroach knows where it's crawling. But you? Where are you crawling?"

"What business is it of yours what I do? "Sasha interrupted calmly. "Take what you want of me, but don't try to peer into my soul."

"Soul!" scoffed Foma. "Have you got a soul?"

She rose and began gathering up her scattered garments. Foma watched her, vexed that even what he had said about her soul could not ruffle her. She wore her usual expression of indifference, but he wanted to see her angry or offended—anything that would make her more human.

"Soul!" he went on. "As if a person with a soul could live the life you live! A soul has fire in it, shame in it!"

She was sitting on a bench pulling on her stockings, but his words made her lift her head and stare at him with hard eyes.

"What are you looking at?" said Foma.

"Why did you say that?" she said without dropping her eyes. There was a threat in the question, and Foma shrank.

"Why shouldn't I?" he said in a voice that had lost its bravado.

"You're a fine one!" she sighed and resumed her dressing.

163

"What's so fine about me?"

"Oh, nothing. It's as if you had been born of two fathers. Do you know what I've noticed about people?"

"What?"

"If a person can't answer for what he does, he's afraid of himself, and that means he's not worth his salt."

"Do you mean me?" he asked after a pause.

She threw a flowing pink dressing-gown over her shoulders and stood looking down at the man lying at her feet.

"Don't you dare speak about my soul," she said presently, in a deep, soft voice. "It's no business of yours. I'm the only one who can speak about that. If I wanted to, oh! I'd give the whole lot of you a piece of my mind! I have a lot of words I could use for you—words like trip-hammers. I'd strike you over the head with them until you went out of your mind. But words can't cure you. You need to be burnt pure, as frying pans are burnt over the fire on the first Monday of Lent."

With an impulsive gesture she let down her hair, which fell in heavy black tresses over her shoulders.

"It doesn't matter that I'm a loose woman," she said with a disdainful toss of her head. "Some people are cleaner in their filth than those who wear silks and fine linen. If you only knew what I think of you gay sparks—all the hatred that's stored up in me! But hatred makes me keep my mouth shut for fear that if I speak my mind, I'd be empty and unable to go on living."

Now he liked her again. Her words harmonized with his mood. He gave a little laugh, and his face and his voice reflected his satisfaction as he said:

"I, too, feel that something is coming to a head inside me, and when it does, I, too, will have my say."

"Against whom?"

"Against everybody!" exclaimed Foma, leaping to his feet. "Against sham! I'll ask—"

"Ask if the samovar has boiled," Sasha interrupted coolly.

Foma shot her a swift glance.

"Go to the devil!" he shouted. "Ask yourself."

"What are you bawling about?"—and she went out of the hut.

The wind was blowing in violent gusts down the river, and the waves, crested with foam and spitting spume, heaved angrily up at it. Down to the earth bent the willow wands, trembling

164

under the blows of the wind. The air was filled with whistling and howling and gasping sounds as if from dozens of human throats.

"There she goes! There she goes! There she goes!" "One, two—heave! One, two—heave!"

Two empty barges lay anchored near the high bank of the river, their tall masts describing an invisible pattern on the sky as they rocked from side to side. Heavy timber scaffolding had been erected on these barges; there were pulleys everywhere, ropes and cables swung in the air. There was a faint clanking of chains. Men in red and blue shirts were dragging an enormous beam across the deck, shuffling noisily and chanting as they worked:

"One, two—heave! One, two—heave! One, two—heave!"

Red and blue dots were to be seen on the scaffolding, too. The wind distorted the men's forms by blowing out their shirts and trousers, so that now they looked hunch-backed, now inflated like toy balloons. Bare hands and arms flashed on decks and scaffolding—making fast, chopping, sawing, drilling, hammering. The wind carried the lively sound of their activity across the river: saws bit into wood with vicious delight; logs grunted hoarsely under the blows of axes; boards splintered with a shriek of pain; planes gave out sly little chuckles. The clang of chains and the screech of pulleys merged with the roar of the waves, and the wind let out a howl as it drove the clouds across the sky.

"At it, men! Come, now!"

"One more pull! One more pull!" urged someone in a high voice.

Foma, looking very tall and handsome in his short woollen jacket and high boots, stood leaning against a mast tugging at his beard with trembling fingers as he gazed in admiration at the labourers. The noise all about him made him want to cry out, to join the men in their work, to hew wood, carry heavy loads, order people about—in a word, to become the centre of attention, so that everyone should see how strong, quick and energetic he was. But he restrained himself and stood there without speaking or moving. He was embarrassed by the fact that he was the master of these men, and if he joined them in their work, not one of them would believe he was doing it for his own satisfaction; all would think he was trying to get more work out of them by setting an example.

A fair, curly-headed lad with his shirt open at the neck kept passing him, now with a plank over his shoulder, now with an axe in his hand. He jumped about as lightly as a goat, joking, laughing, swearing and working indefatigably, helping this one and that, running nimbly up and down the cluttered deck. Foma, who scarcely took his eye off him, was filled with envy.

"He must be happy," he thought, and the thought provoked in him a desire to injure the lad, to humiliate him in some way. All these men were caught up in the excitement of this urgent work. In complete accord they were putting up the scaffolding, mounting the pulleys, getting everything ready to raise the sunken barge from the bottom of the river. They were all gay and light-hearted; all were living life to the full at this moment, and here was he, standing apart, wondering what he should do, not knowing how to do anything, feeling that he was extraneous to this great effort, that nobody needed him. It was painful to realize that he was superfluous, and the longer he watched the men, the more painful it became. The thought that all this was being done for him and yet he had nothing to do with it was like a knife in his heart.

"Where is my place?" he thought gloomily. "What is my job?"

The contractor, a short man with a pointed grey beard and little slits of eyes in a wrinkled, colourless face, came over to him.

"Everything's ready, Foma Ignatiyevich," he said in a low voice, pronouncing his words very precisely. "We're all set. With your blessing, we'll begin."

"Begin," said Foma brusquely, turning away to avoid the penetrating glance of those narrow eyes.

"God be praised!" said the contractor, buttoning up his coat unhurriedly and squaring his shoulders. Slowly turning his head, he examined the scaffolding on the barges, then called out:

"To your places, lads!"

The workmen quickly gathered in little groups on deck and at the windlasses, and their talk ceased. Some climbed the scaffolding nimbly from where they gazed out over the scene.

"Have a last look at everything, lads," came the contractor's calm voice. "Everything tight? When the woman's time is on her, it's too late to make the baby's dress. Ready? Then let's say a prayer."

The contractor flung his cap down on deck, lifted his face to the sky, and crossed himself again and again. All the workmen lifted their faces in the same way and made the sign of the cross on their breasts. Some of them prayed aloud, their murmur mingling with the noise of the waves.

"Thy blessings, Lord . . . and the Holy Virgin . . . and Nikolai the Humble. . . ."

Foma stood listening, and the words fell like weights on his soul. All heads were uncovered; he alone had forgotten to take off his cap, and the contractor, when he had finished praying, turned to him and said reprovingly:

"Don't you think you ought—?"

"Mind your own business; don't teach me," snapped Foma, throwing him an angry glance. The further matters went, the sharper grew the sting of feeling himself superfluous among these workmen who, confident of their own strength, were getting ready to raise a weight of many tons from the bottom of the river on his account. He hoped they would fail. He wanted them to be humiliated.

"Perhaps the chains will snap," was the thought that flashed through his mind.

"At-tention!" called out the contractor; then, raising his arms in signal: "Heave!"

The workmen took up the cry, shouting in tense, excited voices: "Heave ho! Heave!"

Pulleys creaked and screeched, chains rattled as they took the strain, men shouted as they set their chests to the cross-bars of the windlasses and tramped round and round in circles. The water surged between the barges as if unwilling to sur-render its prize to these humans. Taut chains and cables were quivering all round Foma: they slid over the deck at his feet like enormous grey snakes; they climbed upwards, link by link; they dropped back with a crash. But the deafening shouts of the workmen drowned everything else.

"Here she comes! Here she comes! Here she comes!" they chanted exultantly, while the clear voice of the contractor cut into the solid wave of sound as a knife cuts into butter:

"All together, boys! All together!" he called.

Foma was strangely moved. He longed with all his heart to be a part of that chant flowing out like a broad and mighty river, to identify himself with the clang and screech of metal and the roar of the waves. The intensity of his longing made his forehead sweat and drained the colour from his face. All of a sudden he

167

tore himself away from the mast and made for one of the wind-lasses.

"All together! All together!" he shouted wildly.

He ran full speed into the cross-bar of the windlass, but he did not feel the pain of the impact on his chest. Joining his voice to the voices of the workmen, he began to go round and round with them, stamping powerfully with his feet. Something came pouring into his chest in a hot stream replacing the energy he expended on the windlass. Inexpressible joy seethed within him and forced its way out in excited cries. He felt as if he alone were turning the windlass and raising this enormous weight, and that his strength increased with every turn. With lowered head and arched body he lunged forward like a bull to meet this great weight, which, though it kept throwing him back, was forced to yield to him. His excitement grew with every step, and his expended energy was instantly made up for by a tempestuous rush of pride. He was dizzy, his eyes were bloodshot, he saw nothing. The only thing he knew was that he was winning, getting the upper hand, overthrowing with the strength of his muscles some colossal force standing in his way—overthrowing it, conquering it and, as soon as this was done, he would breathe freely and easily, filled with proud joy. For the first time in his life he felt a sense of creation and his hungry soul seized on it, grew drunk with it, and poured out its ecstasy in wild shouts uttered in time to the chant-ing of the workmen:

"Here she comes! Here she comes!"

"Stop! Hold fast! Stop, boys!"

Foma was thrown back by a blow on the chest.

"Congratulations, Foma Ignatiyevich," said the contractor, the wrinkles of his face radiating satisfaction. "God be praised! Are you tired?"

A cold wind blew in Foma's face. All about him he could hear a happy, boastful murmur. Cheery workmen were crowding round him, swearing good-naturedly, smiling and wiping the sweat off their brows. He, too, smiled in a dazed way; he was still too much excited to realize what had happened and why everyone was so pleased and happy.

"One hundred and seventy thousand poods pulled up by the roots, like a turnip!"

From where he was standing on a coil of cable, Foma looked over the workmen's heads and saw another barge standing between the original two—a black one, covered with slime and bound with chains. It was warped and bloated as if by some horrible disease; there it stood, weak and ugly, leaning on its two companions for support. Its broken mast stood out mournfully, streams of rusty water flowed like blood over its deck and it was still freighted with rusty iron and sodden timber.

"She's raised?" asked Foma, unable to think of anything else to say as he looked at the hideous mass. Was it, he thought resentfully, to save this crippled and befouled monster he had become so excited, so overjoyed?

"Well, is she—?" he murmured vaguely to the contractor.

"She's all right. We'll unload her and put twenty or thirty carpenters to work on her and she'll be ship-shape in no time," said the contractor comfortingly.

The fair-haired lad grinned at Foma.

"How about a drink?" he said.

"Plenty of time for that," said the contractor brusquely. "Can't you see the man's tired?"

The workmen supported him:

"Of course he's tired."

"Not an easy job, that."

"Anybody'd get tired who wasn't used to it."

"Get tired eating porridge if you're not used to it."

"I'm not tired," said Foma sharply. The men pressed closer about him, offering their observations as a mark of respect.

"Work's a pleasant thing if your heart's in it."

"Like a game."

"Or a woman."

But the fair-haired lad was not to be side-tracked.

"Come, master, just one pailful," he coaxed with an engaging smile.

As Foma looked at the bearded men in front of him he had a sudden impulse to say something insulting. But his head was foggy. no ideas came to him, and at last he blurted out:

"All you think of is drink! You don't give a damn about anything else. When you do a thing, you ought to stop and think why? What for? You ought to try to understand."

A puzzled look came over the bearded faces. The men in the blue and red shirts began to sigh, scratch their heads, and shift from foot to foot. Some of them shot a hopeless glance at Foma and turned away.

"Quite right," murmured the contractor. "A very good thing—understanding. Wise words, well spoken."

"The likes of us aren't expected to understand," said the fair-haired lad with a shake of his head. He had lost interest in Foma and was rather angry with him, for he suspected him of not wanting to stand the men drinks.

"Oh, but you are," said Foma instructively, pleased by what he thought was the deference the boy showed him, and unaware of the mocking glances cast in his direction. "When a person understands, he realizes he must do his job so that it will last to the end of time."

"To the glory of God," explained the contractor to the men, adding with a pious sigh: "True, oh, how true!"

Foma felt an urge to utter right and weighty words that would make the men change their attitude towards him. He was displeased to find that all of them except the fair-haired lad had grown silent and were looking at him with surly, hostile eyes.

"You want," he said with a lift of the eyebrows, "to do a job that people will see a thousand years from now and say: that was done by the men from Bogorodsk."

The fair-haired lad looked at Foma in astonishment.

"What sort of a job? Drink the Volga dry?" he said, adding with a snort and a shake of the head: "We can't do that, you know; we'd burst."

His words confounded Foma, who glanced round to find the men smiling mirthlessly and superciliously. Their smiles pricked him like needles.

A serious-looking greybread who had kept his mouth shut so far, opened it now, stepped forward, and said slowly:

"If we was to drink the Volga dry and take a bite out of that hill besides, it'd all be forgotten anyway, master. Everything gets forgotten—life's long, you know. It's not for us to do deeds that will stand out above all others."

So saying, he spat on the ground and sauntered away, digging into the crowd as a wedge digs into wood. What he had said was the last straw for Foma. He felt that the men found him stupid and absurd. In the hope of saving himself in their eyes and reviving their flagging attention, he threw out his chest and puffed out his cheeks ridiculously as he said:

"I'll stand you three pails of vodka!"

Short speeches are always the most effective. The men withdrew respectfully, bowed low and, with happy smiles on their faces, thanked Foma in chorus.

"Row me to shore," said Foma, aware that the new wave of excitement that had swept over him would not last long. Restiveness was gnawing at his heart.

"I'm sick of everything," he said on entering the hut where Sasha, in a pretty red dress, was putting food and wine on the table. "Sasha, can't you do something about it?"

She studied him intently for a moment, then sat down beside him on the bench.

"If you're sick of everything, you need a change. What would you like?" she asked.

"I don't know," he said with a sad shake of his head.

"Think it over."

"I can't think."

"You infant!" she said softly and contemptuously, edging away from him. "What you have a head for is more than I can say."

Foma did not notice her tone nor her movement of withdrawal. He was leaning forward gripping the bench with his hands and staring hard at the floor.

"Sometimes I think day and night—think so many thoughts that they smear me all over, like tar. And all of a sudden everything seems to go out of me, just vanishes into thin air, and then it's as dark as the grave in my soul. Frightening. As if I wasn't a human being at all—nothing but a gaping hole."

Sasha threw him a sidelong glance and began to sing in a soft voice,

> *Ah, the wind, the wind is blowing,*
> *Mist is rising from the sea. . . .*

"I've had enough of this wild life—always the same thing: the same people, the same amusements, the same wine. It gets my blood up, makes me want to fight everybody. I don't like these people. What are they living for? I can't make it out."

Sasha went on singing, her eyes fixed on the wall:

> *What is life, my love, without you?*
> *Empty as a wilderness.*

"But they go on living and enjoying themselves. I'm the only one who just stands blinking my eyes. Perhaps I have this apathy from my mother. My godfather says she was cold as ice—and always longing to be somewhere else. I feel like going and saying to people: help me, brothers, I don't know how to live! But when I look round me, there's no one to say it to. They're all scoundrels.'

Foma uttered an obscene oath that made Sasha break off in the middle of her song and edge further away from him. The wind was hurling handfuls of dust against the window-pane. Cockroaches could be heard crawling among the tinder in the stove. A calf was making plaintive little sounds out in the yard.

"Hear your brother-in-misery crying out there?" said Sasha, looking at him mockingly. "Go and join him; you and he can sing a duet." She put her hand on his curly head and gave it a playful push. "What are you moaning about? If you're sick of this life, go back to your business."

"God, if only I could make you understand me! If only I could!" In exasperation he fairly shouted at her: "Business? That's what they call it, business, but if you look close you'll see it's nothing but a waste of time. What's the good of it? To make money? I've got plenty of money as it is. I could smother you with it, bury you from head to foot in it. Business is nothing but a big fraud. I've seen lots of business men; they throw themselves into the whirl of business to keep themselves from seeing what they're really like. They hide from themselves, the ostriches. What would happen to them if they ever got off the roundabout? They'd stumble like blind men and go out of their minds. Do you think business makes a man happy? Oh, no, that's not the whole of it. Rivers flow so that people can sail on them, a tree grows so that man can make use of it, even a dog has its purpose —to guard the house. There's a use for everything on earth except men, and they're like cockroaches—good for nothing. Everything exists for them, but what do they exist for? What use are they?"

Foma was triumphant. He felt he had discovered something that would help him and hurt others. He gave a loud laugh.

"Does your head ache?" asked Sasha, gazing at him searchingly.

"No, my soul aches," exclaimed Foma defiantly. "My soul aches because it's not willing to accept things. It's got to know the answers. How to live? To what purpose? Take my godfather —there's a clever man for you. He says: make of life what you want. But everybody else says: life eats us up!"

"Listen," said Sasha gravely. "If you ask me, what you want, quite simply, is to get married."

"Why should I?" asked Foma with a shrug of his shoulders.

"You need to be put in harness, and—"

"Oh, nonsense! I'm living with you, aren't I? And all of you are alike—one's no sweeter than another. Before I was with you I had another of the same kind. Not quite—she did it because she wanted to. She took a liking to me. She was a good sort. But otherwise, it was just the same, exactly as it is with you, except that you're prettier than she was. But there was another—a lady, a gentlewoman of noble birth. They said she was loose. She was clever, educated; she lived in the grand style. I used to think I'd get a taste of the real thing from her. But she was too good for me. If she hadn't been, perhaps everything would have been different. I wanted her terribly. And now I drown out thoughts of her in wine. I try to forget. That's no good either. Ugh, what a beast man is!"

Foma became lost in thought while Sasha walked up and down, biting her lip.

"Listen to me," she said at last, coming to a halt in front of him and clasping her hands behind her head, "I'm leaving you."

"Where are you going?" asked Foma without so much as looking up.

"I don't know. It doesn't matter. You talk too much. You bore me."

Foma raised his head.

"Really, do you mean it?" he said with a dismal little laugh.

"I'm like you. When the time comes, I'll begin thinking about things, too, and that will be the end of me. But it's too soon yet. I'll have a good time first, and then—come what may!"

"Will it be the end of me, too?" asked Foma indifferently, worn out by the effort of talking.

"It will," said Sasha with calm conviction. "People like us always come to a bad end."

They looked at each other without speaking for a minute or two.

"What ought we to do?" asked Foma.

"Have dinner."

"I mean, in general. Later."

"I—don't know."

"So you're leaving me?"

"Yes. Let's have a real fling before we part. Let's go to Kazan and have a spree, make things hum! We'll drink your cares away."

"All right," said Foma. "We really ought to in parting. God damn this rotten life! Listen, Sasha, they say women of your kind are greedy for money, that they even steal it."

"They can say what they like," said Sasha unperturbed.

"Aren't you insulted?" asked Foma curiously. "Nobody can say you're greedy. It's to your interest to stay with me because I'm rich, yet here you are leaving me. In other words, you're not greedy."

"Me?" Sasha reflected a moment, then gave a little wave of her hand: "Perhaps I'm not, but what of it? I'm not the lowest street-walker. And as for being insulted—who can insult me? Let them say whatever they please. People like to talk, but I know what it's worth, coming from them. If I was a judge, the only people I'd acquit would be the dead." She gave an ugly laugh. "Well, let's change the subject. Let's have dinner."

The next morning Foma and Sasha were standing beside each other on the deck of a boat that was approaching Ustye. Sasha's enormous black hat, which was turned up rakishly and trimmed with big white feathers attracted everyone's attention. Foma felt uncomfortable standing there beside her while these inquisitive eyes crawled over his face. With a hiss and a shudder the boat struck the landing, where a crowd of people in bright clothes had gathered. Among all these strange faces, Foma thought he saw a familiar one that kept hiding behind other people's backs but never took its eyes off him.

"Let's go into the cabin," he said to Sasha uneasily.

"Don't try to hide your sins," she laughed. "Have you seen somebody you know?"

"Somebody's watching me."

He looked into the crowd again, and suddenly a change came over his face.

"It's my godfather," he said under his breath.

At the edge of the landing, squeezed between two fat women, stood Mayakin. His icon-like face was lifted to Foma and he was waving his cap with a politeness that had a touch of venom in it. His beard quivered, his bald pate glistened and his eyes bored into Foma like drills.

174

"The old vulture," muttered Foma as he took off his cap and bowed to him.

The bow seemed to delight Mayakin, for he began to wriggle and hop and smile maliciously.

"It looks as if my little boy were in for it," chaffed Sasha.

This remark and Mayakin's smile kindled fire in Foma's breast.

"We'll see about that!" he hissed between his teeth, but the next minute he became stonily calm. As soon as the boat was moored the passengers rushed on to the landing. Mayakin was swept away for a moment, but presently he bobbed up again, wearing a smile of triumph. Foma stared at him intently from under knitted brows as he strode down the gang-plank. His irritation was increased by the pushing, squeezing and jostling of the crowd. At last he came face to face with the old man, who greeted him with an elegant bow.

"And where may you be going, Foma Ignatiyevich?" he asked.

"I'm here on personal business," Foma declared, without bothering to greet his godfather.

"Very commendable," beamed Mayakin. "And who might the young lady in the feathers be?"

"My mistress," said Foma in a loud voice, his eyes holding steady under Mayakin's piercing gaze.

Sasha was standing just behind him, calmly studying the little old man whose head did not come up to Foma's chin. Foma's loud voice had attracted the attention of the people about him and they were all staring at him in expectation of a scene. Mayakin, too, expected it, for he had perceived Foma's aggressive mood. He put his wrinkles in play and chewed his lips for a moment before saying in a mollifying tone:

"I'd like to have a word with you. Shall we go to an inn?"

"Very well. But not for long."

"No time, eh? In a hurry to wreck another barge?" said the old man, unable to contain himself any longer.

"Why not wreck them if they're wreckable?" retorted Foma.

"Why not, indeed? It wasn't you who bought them, so what do you care? Well, come along. Couldn't you . . . er . . . drown the young lady for an hour or so?" whispered Mayakin.

"Go into town and take a room at the Siberia, Sasha. I won't be long," said Foma; then, to Mayakin jauntily: "Let's go!"

175

They walked to the inn without a word. Noticing that his godfather had to run to keep up with him, Foma intentionally lengthened his stride. The old man's inability to keep step with him heightened the protest that was seething within him and threatening to break out any minute.

"Bring me a bottle of cranberry juice, lad," said Mayakin amiably to the waiter as they entered the dining-room and made for a table in a far corner.

"And me a bottle of cognac," said Foma.

"That's the way," laughed Mayakin. "When your cards are bad, always lead a trump."

"You don't know how I play," said Foma as he sat down.

"Oh, don't I? Lots of people play like that."

"I play so that I smash either my head or the wall," said Foma, bringing his fist down hard on the table.

"Haven't you got over your last drink yet?" asked Mayakin with a faint smile.

Foma settled himself in his chair.

"You're a clever man, godfather," he said with a distorted face. "I respect you for your brains——"

"Thank you for that, son," said Mayakin, half-rising to make a little bow.

"What I wanted to say was, I'm not twenty any longer; I'm not a baby."

"Of course not," agreed Mayakin. "Many a winter has passed over that hoary head of yours. If a mosquito had lived as long it would be as big as a chicken."

"Keep your joking for later," said Foma in a voice so steady that Mayakin was taken aback and the wrinkles in his face began to quiver anxiously.

"What made you come here?" asked Foma.

"You've been . . . er . . . misbehaving. I thought I'd come and see what the damage was. I happen to be a sort of relative. The only one you've got."

"You shouldn't have bothered. Listen, godfather, do one of two things: either leave me strictly alone, or take over the business—the whole of it—to the last rouble."

Foma was as surprised by his own words as Mayakin; the idea had not occurred to him before. But as soon as he had said it he felt that if Mayakin were to relieve him of all his possessions he would be a free man, would be able to go wherever he liked and do whatever he pleased. He had always been fettered, though he did not know what his fetters were or how to get rid of them; and now here they were, falling off of their own accord, very simply and painlessly. A spark of hope was kindled in his heart. This filled him with joy and excitement and he began to murmur incoherently:

"That would be best; take everything, and be done with it. I'll go where I please. I can't go on living like this. It's as if I was wearing a ball and chain. I want to be free, to find out things for myself. I want to make my own way. As it is, what am I? A prisoner. Take everything—go the devil with it! I'll never make a merchant. I hate it all. If you take it, I'd go away somewhere—find myself some kind of work. As things are I just drink. And I've got myself tied up with that woman—"

Mayakin watched and listened with a face as hard and cold as stone. The low hum of the inn was all about them, people passed them by and Mayakin kept bowing without seeing whom he bowed to, for all his attention was concentrated on the face of his godson, which was wearing a dazed, happy, pitiful smile.

"A very tart little berry you are," Mayakin sighed at last. "You've lost your bearings. Talking nonsense. What I'd like to know is whether it's the cognac, or just your foolishness."

"Godfather!" expostulated Foma. "People used to do that—give up everything and go away!"

"Not in my day. Nobody I ever knew," said Mayakin severely. "If they had, I'd have shown them!"

"Lots of them went away and became hermits."

"They wouldn't have if *I'd* had anything to say about it. But why try to talk seriously to you? Bah!"

"But why *not*, godfather?" cried Foma with feeling.

"Listen: if you're a chimney-sweep, climb roofs, damn you! If you're a fireman, stand on the watch-tower! All kinds of people live all kinds of lives. Calves aren't expected to roar like bears. Be what you were born to be, and don't look enviously into other people's orchards. Live your own life in your own way."

The sure, confident words Foma had heard so often came pouring out of the dark cavity of the old man's mouth in a sparkling stream. So absorbed was Foma in dreams of freedom (now so easily to be achieved, it seemed), that he did not listen. His mind was given over completely to his dreams, and his heart grew firm in its resolution to break with this empty and turbid existence, with his godfather, the boats, the orgies and everything else that made life so stifling.

The old man's voice came to him as if from afar, blended with the clatter of dishes, the bawling of drunkards and the scraping of the waiters' feet along the floor.

"And all this nonsense has come into your head because you're too full of youthful spirits," said Mayakin, striking the table with his hand. "Your recklessness is stupid; your ideas are worthless. What do you think of doing—going into a monastery?"

Foma listened without comment. The noise of the inn seemed to be receding little by little. He fancied he was in the midst of a vast, restless mass of people with eyes starting out of their heads, who, without knowing why, were shouting, pushing, falling down and pressing forward but not getting anywhere. He was oppressed by his inability to understand what they wanted or believe what they said. If he could only break free and view them from a distance, surely he would see what was happening and find his own place among them.

"I understand," said Mayakin, adopting a softer tone on seeing Foma so distracted. "You want to find happiness. But that's not easy. You have to search for it as you would for a mushroom in the forest; you have to break your back over it, and when you think you've found it, it may turn out to be a toadstool."

"Well, will you give me my freedom?" said Foma, lifting his head suddenly. Mayakin turned away to avoid his burning eyes. "Give me a breathing-space, give me a chance to get away from everything! Once I've had a look at things from the outside, perhaps I'll . . . But if I don't get away, I'll drink myself to death."

"Stop talking nonsense! Be sensible!" cried Mayakin angrily.

"Very well," was Foma's calm rejoinder. "You won't? Then that's the end. I'll throw everything to the winds. We have nothing else to say to each other, you and I. Goodbye. I'll do things properly, this time—you'll see the sparks fly."

Foma was composed and his voice was steady; he was sure that, having made up his mind, there was nothing his godfather could do to stop him. But Mayakin straightened up and said in a voice as steady as his own:

"Are you aware of the measures I can take?"

"Any you like," said Foma with a wave of his hand.

"Very well. And this is what I like: I shall go back to town and take measures to have you declared insane and put into an asylum."

"Is that possible?" asked Foma incredulously, a note of fear in his voice.

"Everything's possible with me, young fellow."

Foma glared at his godfather, thinking with a shudder: he'll do it—he's ruthless enough.

"If you're seriously determined to make a fool of yourself, I'll have to take serious measures to stop it. I promised your father I'd put you on your feet, and I intend to do it. If you won't stand up, I'll put you in irons. You'll stand up then all right. I know this all comes of too much drinking. But if I see you squandering your father's hard-earned money out of wantonness I'll salt my soup with you, I'll run you into a mole hole. I'm not a comfortable person to play with, young man."

The wrinkles on Mayakin's cheeks gathered together under his eyes, which were smiling coldly, mockingly, out of dark sockets. The lines in his forehead made a strange pattern below his bald skull. The expression of his face was cruel and implacable.

"In other words, there's no way out for me?" asked Foma hopelessly. "You're cutting off every way of escape?"

"There's one way open to you. Take it, and I'll guide you. It will bring you out at the right place."

His godfather's complacency, his unshakable conceit, drove Foma to a frenzy. Thrusting his hands into his pockets to keep from striking the old man, he sat up straight in his chair and hissed through clenched teeth:

"What makes you so boastful? What have you to boast of? Your son? Where is he? Your daughter? What have you made of her? A fine one you are to teach others how to live! You're clever—you know everything; tell me this: what are you living for? Don't you expect to die? What have you ever done that was worth doing? For what will you be remembered?"

Mayakin's wrinkles quivered and drooped, giving his face a sickly, lugubrious expression. He opened his mouth, but no words came out of it; he just sat there looking at his godson in surprise, almost in fear.

"Hold your tongue, you puppy," he muttered at last.

Foma got up, threw his cap on to his head, and stood looking down at the old man with hatred.

"I'm going on a spree. To spend everything I've got."

"Very well. We'll see what comes of it."

"Goodbye, Sage," scoffed Foma.

"Until we meet again," said Mayakin softly and as if out of breath.

Yakov Mayakin was left alone in the inn. He went on sitting at the table and, bending over it, made patterns on the tray, dipping his trembling finger in the spilt kvass. His pointed head kept falling lower, as if he were trying to make out what he had drawn on the tray with his bony finger.

Drops of sweat stood out on his bald crown, and the wrinkles in his cheeks were quivering anxiously, as they often did.

At last he called the waiter.

"What do I owe you?" he asked, with peculiar intensity.

X

BEFORE his quarrel with Mayakin, Foma had caroused half-heartedly, because he was bored with life. But now he did it with a vengeance—viciously, desperately, in defiance of everybody. At times he himself was shocked by this defiance. He observed that sober, the people he met were stupid and miserable and, when drunk, they were repulsive and even more stupid. He was not interested in any of his companions, did not bother to ask their names, forgot when and where he had made their acquaintance and always felt an urge to insult them. In expensive, fashionable restaurants he was surrounded by ne'er-do-wells, rhymesters, conjurers, actors and landowners who had squandered their property in riotous living. At first these people assumed a patronizing attitude towards him boasting to him of their discriminating tastes and their knowledge of wines and food; later they became obsequious and borrowed money from him that he himself got by signing promissory notes. Barbers, billiard-scorers, clerks and choristers hovered about him like vultures when he went to cheap taverns. He felt more at home with these people. They were less corrupt and less of a riddle to him; at times they evinced strong and wholesome emotions, and they were always more human. But they were just as greedy for money and just as shameless about taking it as the "respectable" people. He saw it and jeered at them.

And, of course, there were women. Being a healthy man, Foma bought them: cheap ones, expensive ones, pretty ones, ugly ones. He made them presents of big sums of money, changed them almost every week and respected them, on the whole, more than he did the men. He made fun of them and would say shameful, offensive things to them, but never, even when he was drunk, could he overcome the shyness he felt in their presence. He felt that all of them, even the most brazen, were as defenceless as little children. And he, who was always ready to pick a fight with a man, never laid a hand on women, although when irritated he sometimes abused them foully. He felt that he was immeasurably stronger than any woman, and immeasurably more fortunate. Those who vaunted their depravity and revelled in lewdness filled him with shame and made him feel shy and embarrassed. One day a drunken woman of this sort struck Foma on the cheek with a melon rind at the supper table. Foma, who was half drunk, turned white, got up, put his hands in his pockets, and said savagely, his voice trembling with rage:

"Get out of here, you bitch! Anyone else would have broken your skull for this, but you know I wouldn't lift a finger against you. Throw her out of here!"

When they had been in Kazan only a few days, Sasha went to live with a brewer's son.

"Goodbye, darling," she said to Foma, as she was leaving for a trip up the Kama with her new lover. "Perhaps we'll meet again some time: we're both going the same way. Don't give too much rein to your feelings; enjoy yourself without any backward glances, and when the dish is empty, smash it. Goodbye."

She gave him a long, hard kiss on the lips, and when she drew away her eyes had become darker than ever.

Foma was glad she was leaving him; he was tired of her and frightened by her cold indifference. But at this moment he felt a pang of regret and turned away.

"If you don't enjoy your life with him, come back to me," he murmured.

"Thanks," she said, breaking into a hoarse laugh that sounded quite unlike her.

And so Foma went on living from day to day, nurturing the faint hope of escaping to the edge of life, out of the tumult and confusion. At night, when he was alone, he would shut his eyes tightly and see a throng of people, frightening in its vastness. Crowded together in an enormous crater filled with clouds of dust, going round and round on the same spot like grain in a flour mill, and it was as if invisible millstones under their feet were grinding them, and the people rose and fell in waves, some striving to reach the depths to be crushed and annihilated as quickly as possible, others struggling to keep on top and escape the merciless millstone.

Foma recognized familiar faces in the crowd: there was his father pressing forward, pushing aside and shouldering everyone out of his way as, laughing thunderously, he disappeared, trampled under the feet of the crowd. There, wriggling like a snake, leaping on to people's shoulders and gliding between their feet, his godfather was working his lean, sinewy body. Here was Lyuba, crying and struggling as she made to follow her father, now forging ahead, now falling back. Pelagea moved swiftly forward in a straight line. Sophia Pavlovna was standing with her hands hanging limply by her sides, as she had stood in her drawing-room when he had seen her for the last time. Her large eyes were filled with terror. Sasha, imperturbable, indifferent to the jostling of the crowd, was making her way into its very centre, her dark eyes gazing serenely into the distance. Foma heard uproar, howls, laughter, drunken shouts, shrill disputes; songs and wailings hung over the heaving mass of human bodies crowded into the pit as they jumped, fell, crawled, crushed one another, leapt on to each other's shoulders, stumbling and groping as if blind, fighting, falling, struggling and disappearing from sight. Money rustled, soaring like bats over the heads of the people who greedily stretched out their hands to snatch it; gold and silver jingled, bottles clattered, corks popped, there was a drunken sobbing and a mournful woman's voice sang:

> Today let us live and be merry,
> Let the morrow take care of itself.

Foma could not free himself from this wild image which grew larger and more vivid each time it arose in his mind, exciting a mixed feeling into which flowed, like streams into a river, fear and a sense of outrage, compassion and wrath. These feelings seethed in his breast boiling up into a desire so intense that it choked him, brought tears to his eyes, made him want to shout, to howl like a wolf, to frighten the people. Made him want to stop their senseless turmoil, to pour into the tumult something of himself: to utter loud words, full of meaning, to guide them all in one direction and not against one another. He wanted to seize them and tear them apart, to thrash some, to caress others, to rebuke them all and to illumine them with some great fire.

But there was nothing in him: neither words nor fire. Only the desire, clear but impossible of fulfilment. He pictured himself standing above the pit in which the people struggled, firm and resolute, but speechless. He might of course cry out: "What sort of lives are you living? Aren't you ashamed?" But what if, on

hearing his voice, they should ask: "And how ought we to live?"?
He knew that if that question were put he would come hurtling
down from his height, down under the feet of the throng, on to the
millstone. And laughter would accompany him to his destruction.

At times he thought he was going mad from drinking too
much, and that was why his mind was possessed by the vision,
the horror. And then he would stamp it out by an act of will,
but the minute he was left to himself and was not too drunk, the
delirium came back, crushing him under its weight. The longing
for freedom grew and strengthened in him. But he was unable to
cast off the fetters of his wealth.

Mayakin, whom he had given the legal right to conduct his
business, let not a day pass without forcing upon him a consciousness of his responsibilities. Creditors were sent to him to collect
their bills, contractors to sign freight agreements, clerks to discuss
matters they had formerly decided themselves. They sought him
out in taverns to ask what they should do and how they should do
it, and he would tell them, often doubting the correctness of his
advice. He noticed the scepticism with which they received it
and saw that instead of doing as he said, they did things in their
own way, which was better. He knew that his godfather was
behind all this, that it was Mayakin's way of bringing pressure
to bear on him, so that he would be turned into the path he had
chosen for him. And he also knew that he was not really the head
of his business, but a mere accessory to it, and an unimportant
one at that. The annoyance of this increased his aversion to the
old man and made him more anxious than ever to get rid of the
business, even if it meant ruin. He began to squander money at a
furious rate in taverns and brothels, but this did not last long:
Mayakin closed his bank accounts. Soon Foma realized that
people were not lending him money as willingly as before. This
was a blow to his pride. But the real blow, an infuriating and
frightening one, came when he heard that his godfather was
spreading rumours of his insanity, hinting that it would be
necessary to appoint a legal guardian over him. Foma did not
know just how far his godfather would go and hesitated to consult
anyone on the matter. He believed that Mayakin was a figure
of sufficient importance in the world of trade to do whatever he
chose. At first he was terrified by the strong hand of his godfather,
but soon he got used to it and went on with his wanton life, taking
interest in nothing but people. With every day he became more

convinced that the men about him were worse than he was and lived lives that were even more meaningless. They were not the masters of life but its slaves, and it was ordering them about, bending and twisting them at its will.

And so he went on living as if he were walking in a bog that threatened to suck him down at every step, while his godfather twisted up above him like a vine growing on firm dry ground and kept a sharp eye on him from a distance.

After the quarrel with Foma, Mayakin went home very glum and thoughtful. There was a dry glitter in his eye and he held himself as straight as a taut string. His wrinkles were deeper and his face seemed to have shrunk and grown darker, so that when Lyuba saw him she thought he must be seriously ill. He paced the floor nervously, spitting out hard, dry words in answer to his daughter's questions and at last shouting at her impatiently:

"Leave me alone! I have no time for you!"

She was moved to pity by the sight of the dull misery in his green eyes, and when he sat down to dinner she went over to him impulsively and put her hands on his shoulders. "Aren't you well, Father?" she asked, looking at him tenderly.

She rarely showed him affection, and so each little demonstration touched him deeply. And while he never returned it, he appreciated it. This time he shrugged her hands off his shoulders and said:

"Come, come, sit down. What's the matter with you?"

But Lyuba did not sit down; she went on looking into his face.

"Why do you always talk to me like that, Father, as if I were a child, or very stupid?" she said in hurt tones.

"Because you're grown-up but not very clever. That's why. Sit down and eat your dinner."

She took her place opposite him in silence and with tight lips. He spent more time over his meal than usual, playing with his spoon and staring absent-mindedly at his soup.

"If only that cluttered head of yours could understand your father's thoughts!" he said suddenly, giving a wheezing sigh.

Lyuba threw down her spoon.

"Why are you always hurting my feelings, Father?" she said on the verge of tears. "Can't you see how lonely I am, how very lonely? Surely you understand how hard it is for me to go on

185

living like this, and yet you never say a kind word to me. But you're lonely, too, and it's hard for you—"

"Braying like Balaam's ass!" said the old man with a short laugh. "Well, what else have you to say?"

"You are too proud of your cleverness."

"Anything else?"

"You oughtn't to be. Any why do you keep repulsing me? After all, I have nobody in the world but you."

Tears welled up in her eyes, and brought a startled look to his face.

"If only you weren't a girl!" he exclaimed. "Or if you had a mind like, say, Marfa Posadnitsa. Oh, then I'd snap my fingers at the world, Lyuba—at Foma and everybody else! Come now, don't cry."

"What's Foma doing?" she asked, wiping her eyes.

"Rearing and kicking. He says: here, take everything I own and let me go free. He wants to find salvation—in a tavern. That's what our Foma has got into his head."

"But why?" asked Lyuba hesitantly.

"Why?" said Mayakin, twitching with excitement. "It's either from drink, or, God help him! from his mother—from the Old Faith. If this leaven rises in him I'll have to struggle hard with him. He's declared open war on me—shown great arrogance. But he's young. There's no cunning in him. He says he'll drink up everything. Oh, he will, will he? I'll show him!" Mayakin shook his fist menacingly. "How dare you? Who founded your business? Who built it up? You? No, your father. Forty years of labour he put into it, and you want to throw it all to the winds. We've got to move forward in a body, we merchants—all together in the open, single file up the cliffs—forward in a body until we reach our destined place. It's we, the merchants, the tradesmen, who have carried Russia on our shoulders generation after generation, and we're still carrying her. Peter the Great had God-given wisdom—he knew our worth. What did he do to support us? Printed books for us, teaching us our business. I've got one of the books printed at his order, a book by Polidor Virgil Urbinsky about inventors. Printed in the year 1720. Think of that! He gave us a start. Now we stand on our own feet but we want to move unhampered. We've laid the foundations of life, we've put our very lives in the earth along with the bricks. And now that the time's come for us to build up the storeys, be so

186

kind as to give us freedom of action. That's the line we merchants have got to follow; that's the task ahead of us. Foma doesn't see it. But he must see it, he must carry on the work. He has his father's means, and when I die he'll get mine as well. Go on, work, young man! But instead, he gets up on his hind legs and makes a big noise. Oh, just you wait, you young puppy, I'll put you in your place!"

The old man was choking with rage, and his eyes flashed as though Foma were in her place. Lyuba was frightened.

"The path has been cleared by your fathers, and it's up to you to take it. For fifty years I've been slaving away, and what for? My children? Where are my children?" The old man's voice broke off and he dropped his head. The next time he spoke it was in a voice as hollow as if it came from his bowels:

"One's lost . . . another's drunk . . . and a daughter . . . Who is to carry on when I die? If I had a son-in-law, now . . . If that Foma would sow his wild oats and settle down, then I'd give him your hand and all my possessions as well. But Foma won't do. And I don't see anyone else. People aren't what they used to be. They used to be like iron. There's no resistance in them nowadays. Why is it? What's the reason?"

Mayakin looked at his daughter with alarm, but she made no answer.

"Tell me this: what do you want of life?" he said. "How do you think people ought to live? You've been to school and read a lot of books. What do you want?"

The suddenness with which the questions were put flustered her. She was glad her father had asked them, but she was afraid to answer lest she lower herself in his estimation. And so, summoning all her strength as if about to leap over the table, she said in a trembling, irresolute voice:

"I want everybody to be happy. And contented. And all people to be equal. Everybody needs freedom, everybody . . . as they need air. And equality in everything."

"Just as I thought—a hopeless fool!" her father drawled contemptuously.

Lyuba drooped, but the next moment she threw back her head and exclaimed protestingly:

"But you yourself said that freedom . . ."

"Hold your tongue! You can't even see what is written on every man's face. How can all people be happy and equal when

187

each wants to get ahead of the other? Even a beggar has his pride and is sure to find something to boast of to his fellows. Even the smallest child wants to be first in his games. And you'll never get people to give in to each other—only fools believe that. Each man has a soul of his own, and the only people who will let you whittle them down to the same pattern are those who have no love for their own souls. Bah! You've read too much—swallowed all sorts of rubbish. . . ."

There was bitter rebuke, withering scorn in the old man's eyes. Pushing his chair back noisily, he got up, clasped his hands behind his back and began pacing the floor quickly, darting to and fro, shaking his head and muttering to himself in a wheezy voice. Lyuba, pale with shame and agitation and oppressed by a sense of her own helplessness and stupidity, listened to his whispered words with palpitating heart.

"Left all alone . . . like Job. Oh, God, what am I to do? Am I not clever? Am I not cunning?"

The girl's heart went out to him; she had a passionate longing to help him, to be needed by him. With burning eyes she followed his every movement and suddenly she said in a low voice:

"Don't grieve so, Father: after all, Taras is still alive. Perhaps he—"

Mayakin halted as abruptly as if he had been struck, and slowly raised his head.

"If a tree grows crooked when still young, how is it to brave the storm when it's older? And yet it's true—Taras is a straw for me to clutch at, though he can scarcely be worth more than Foma. Foma at least has character. He has his father's daring. He could do great things if he had a mind to. But Taras . . . Taras . . . you did well to remind me of him."

And the old man, who a moment before had been rushing about the room like a squirrel in a cage, now walked calmly over to the table, replaced his chair very precisely, and sat down.

"I must try to find out something about Taras," he said with a grave face. "He's living in Usolye, at a factory there. I was told this by some merchants. A soda works, I believe. I'll try to find out something."

"Father, would you let me write to him?" asked Lyuba softly, flushing and trembling with joy.

"You?" said Mayakin, throwing her a swift glance; then, after a moment's reflection: "Perhaps that would be even better.

188

Yes, write to him. Ask him if he's married, how he's getting on, what his views are—but I'll tell you what to write when the time comes."

"Let's do it soon, Father," said Lyuba.

"The thing we've got to do soon is get you married. I have my eye on a certain red-haired fellow—seems to be a bright lad—with European trimmings, by the way."

"Is it Smolin, Father?" asked Lyuba eagerly.

"Well, what if it is?" said Mayakin in a matter-of-fact tone.

"Nothing. I don't know him," said Lyuba non-committally.

"You'll get to know him. High time, Lyuba, high time. We can't count on Foma—although I don't intend to let him have his way."

"I wasn't counting on him."

"A pity. If you had shown more sense, perhaps he would never have gone astray. When I saw you together, I used to think: the lad will make a home for my Lyuba. But I was wrong."

As she listened to him she fell into a reverie. She was a strong, healthy girl, and of late she had thought a great deal about marriage. She saw no other way out of her loneliness. She had long since got over her desire to leave her father and go away to study and work, as she had got over many other desires just as superficial. The many books she had read had left in her mind a muddy sediment that was alive only in the sense that protoplasm is alive. It made her discontented with life and anxious to be independent, to be free of her father's strict supervision, but it could not effect her emancipation or even show how it could be effected. Meanwhile nature ran its course, and whenever she saw young mothers with infants in their arms she was filled with envy and longing. Sometimes she would stand before the mirror gazing at her fresh young face with the dark circles under the eyes and she felt sorry for herself. Life was passing her by, pushing her aside. Now, as she sat listening to her father, she tried to imagine what Smolin was like. She had seen him when he was still a *gymnasium* student. Then he had been a freckled, snub-nosed, neat, well-behaved little bore, a clumsy dancer and un-interesting companion. But that was a long time ago. Since then he had travelled and studied abroad. What was he like now? Her thoughts jumped from Smolin to her brother and, with a sinking heart, she wondered how he would answer her letter. Her brother as she pictured him in her imagination was of infinitely more importance to her than either her father or Smolin, and she had made up her mind that she would not agree to get married until she had seen Taras, when her father startled her out of her reverie by shouting:

"Wake up, Lyuba! What are you dreaming about?"

"Oh, I was just thinking how quickly it passes."

"What passes?"

"Everything. Last week you forbade me to mention Taras's name, and now—"

"It's need drives me to it. Need is a great force, child; it will even bend steel into a spring, and steel is strong. Taras? We shall see. A man proves his worth by the resistance he offers to life; if he bends it to his will instead of being bent by it, he has my respect. Ah, me! A pity I'm so old. Things move at a brisk pace these days. Every year life gets more interesting, has more spice to it. I should like to go on living forever."

The old man smacked his lips and rubbed his hands and his eyes sparkled.

"But you young folk—it's thin blood you've got in your veins. You rot before you're ripe and get as spongy as an old radish. You don't even see how good life is growing. For sixty-seven years I've lived on this earth and now as I stand on the brink of the grave I see that in my youth there were fewer flowers in the world, and poorer ones, than there are today. Everything is getting better. Look at the handsome buildings we have now! And the implements—implements of trade! The ships! All the brains that have gone into them! It makes you want to say when you look at them: Well done, people! Everything is good, everything is gladdening—everything but our sons and heirs, who haven't a spark of life in them. The lowest charlatan from among the working folk has more spirit in him than our young people have. Take that—what's his name?—Yezhov. A nobody, yet he has the spunk to judge the whole world. Has the courage of his convictions. And you? Bah! You live like beggars. You ought to be skinned alive and have salt sprinkled on your flesh—that would make you jump all right!"

Yakov Mayakin—little, shrivelled, bony, bald, with black stumps of teeth in his mouth, with skin as dark as it if had been smoked in the heat of life—Yakov Mayakin trembled with agitation as he poured his scathing words on his fair, plump daughter. She looked at him guiltily and smiled self-consciously and deep down in her heart grew a feeling of respect for this old man, her father, who pursued his desires with such dogged determination.

Foma went on with his riotous living. In one of the town's fashionable restaurants he found himself joyfully embraced by the brewer's son who had gone off with Sasha.

"What a surprise! For three days I've been pining away in loneliness. Not a decent person in town—I even took up with some journalists in despair. Not a bad lot. At first they were very superior, looked down their noses at me, but soon they were all dead drunk. I'll introduce you to them. One of them writes feature articles—the one who wrote about you—what's his name? An amusing chap, devil take him!"

"How's Sasha?" asked Foma, somewhat stunned by the effusiveness of this tall, unceremonious fellow in loud clothes.

"Ugh!" he said, making a face. "That Sasha of yours is no good. Something dark and mysterious about her. Very dull. And cold as a fish. I'm giving her up."

"She *is* cold," said Foma, growing thoughtful.

"Whatever a person does, he ought to do it to the best of his ability," said the brewer's son sententiously. "Once you agree to be a man's mistress, you ought to do your duty by him, that is, if you're an honest woman. Well, how about some vodka?"

They drank. And they got drunk.

That evening a big and noisy crowd gathered in the tavern and Foma said to them in a maudlin, thick-tongued voice:

"This is how I see it: some people are worms, others sparrows. The sparrows are the merchants. They eat the worms. That's what they're for. That's their purpose. But you and me—what are we for? No justification for us. Nobody wants us. And those others . . . and everybody else . . . what are they for? That's something to think about! Who wants me? Nobody wants me. Kill me! Kill me dead! I want to die!"

He wept copious tears. A strange little swarthy man came up to him, slobbered over him, whispered a word in his ear, threw himself on his breast, and shouted as he pounded the table with his knife:

"Silence! The elephants and mammoths of this disordered life have the floor! Listen to the sacred words of the raw Russian conscience! Roar out, Gordeyev! Roar with all your might!"

He clawed Foma's shoulders and fell on his breast again, and his round, black, close-cropped head kept twisting and turning under Foma's nose, so that the latter could not get a glimpse of the man's face and pushed him away irritably, saying:

"Keep off! Where's your face?"

Shouts of drunken laughter rose on all sides and, between paroxysms, the brewer's son gasped hoarsely to somebody:

"Come over here! Hundred roubles a month and board and lodging. Honest to goodness. To hell with the paper. I pay more."

Everything was rocking with a rhythmic motion; the crowd now receded, now drew near, the floor rose, the ceiling fell, and it seemed to Foma that the next moment he would be caught between them and crushed flat. Then he fancied he was sailing down a broad, swift river. He struggled to his feet and cried out in fright:

"Where are we going? Where's the captain?"

He was answered by shrill, drunken laughter and the harsh voice of the little dark man:

"Righto-o-o! Where's the captain?"

Foma awoke from his nightmare in a little room with two windows in it, and the first thing his eyes fell upon was a withered tree just outside one of the windows. Its thick trunk with the bark peeling off prevented the light entering the room, and its leafless boughs, black and twisted, groped the air, creaking plaintively when the wind blew. Rain was falling. Water streamed down the window-panes and could be heard falling off the roof on to the ground, making a weeping sound. To this was added the intermittent scratching of a pen on paper and little bursts of muttering.

With an effort Foma lifted his head off the pillow and saw the small dark man sitting at the desk writing energetically, nodding his approval from time to time, twisting his head from side to side, twitching his shoulders, keeping every bone and muscle of his puny body (clothed in nothing but pants and a night shirt) in a constant state of movement, as if he were sitting on hot coals and for some reason could not get up. With his skinny left arm he rubbed his forehead vigorously or made cabbalistic signs in the air; his bare feet scraped about on the floor, the cords on his neck quivered, even his ears twitched. When he turned his head Foma saw thin lips moving soundlessly, a sharp nose and a sparse moustache that jumped whenever he laughed. His face was so yellow and wrinkled that the lively black eyes seemed not to belong to it.

When Foma had looked his fill, he turned his eyes and slowly examined the room. The walls were studded with nails on which hung bunches of newspapers, forming ugly excrescences. The white paper pasted to the ceiling was blistered, the blisters had burst and now the paper hung down in dirty shreds. The floor was strewn with clothes, boots, books and scraps of paper. Altogether the room looked as if a tornado had passed through it.

The little man threw down his pen, bent over the writing table, drummed nervously on the edge of it with his fingers, and began to sing to himself in a high, thin voice:

> *Take up your drum without fear!*
> *On the sutler's lips press a kiss!*
> *That's the message of science and art,*
> *All philosophy's wisdom's in this.*

"I wish I had some soda-water," said Foma with a deep sigh.

"Ah!" exclaimed the little man and, bounding off his chair, sat down on the edge of Foma's couch. "Good morning, friend. Soda-water? With or without cognac?"

"Better with," said Foma, grasping the hot thin hand that was held out to him and looking hard at the little man's face.

"Yegorovna!" called the man, turning to the door; then, to Foma: "Don't you recognize me, Foma Ignatiyevich?"

"There's something familiar about you—we seem to have met before."

"For four years running, but that was a long time ago. Yezhov."

"Good Lord!" ejaculated Foma, raising himself on his elbows. "Is it really you?"

"I sometimes doubt it myself, friend, but doubts bounce off anything as hard as a fact."

Yezhov twisted up his face in a droll way and began to feel his chest.

"Lord!" gasped Foma, "how old you look! How old are you?"

"Thirty."

"You look fifty. All yellow and dried up. Life seems to have treated you badly."

Foma was sorry to see his once gay and lively schoolmate looking so worn and living in such a hole. He blinked sadly as he gazed at him, noticing the twitching of Yezhov's face and the irritable flash of his eyes. Yezhov was too busy opening the bottle of soda-water to speak; he held it between his knees and strained every muscle in his effort to pull the cork out. Foma was touched by his inability to cope with the cork.

"Life has sucked all the juice out of you," he mused. "And you once had a bent for learning."

"Here," said Yezhov, white from strain, as he held out a glass. Then he wiped his forehead and sat down beside Foma.

"Say no more about learning," he said. "Learning is a divine beverage, my friend, but, like raw spirits, it's not yet fit for use. It's not yet ready to bring men happiness, and anyone who has recourse to it is sure to get a headache. Like you and me at the moment. By the way, what makes you drink so much?"

"What else is there to do?" asked Foma with a little laugh.

Yezhov looked at him with narrowed eyes.

"By comparing this remark with the wisdom that came from your lips last night, I conclude that life has not been too good to you, either."

Foma sighed audibly and got up from the couch.

"Life?" he said bitterly. "Life is a mad-house. I'm always alone . . . wondering what it's all about. I'd be only too glad to spit on it all and disappear somewhere. Run away from everything. I can't bear it."

"Very curious," said Yezhov, rubbing his hands together and wriggling all over. "Very curious, if true, for it testifies to the fact that the holy spirit of discontent has penetrated into the bed-chambers of the merchant class, has sought out the dead souls of those drowned in fat soups, in seas of tea and other beverages. Tell me your story, friend, bit by bit, and I shall write a novel."

"I was told that you'd already written something about me," said Foma, studying the face of his boyhood friend again and wondering what such a poor wreck of a man could write.

"I have. Did you read it?"

"No, I didn't get a copy."

"What did they tell you?"

"That you had gone for me pretty hard."

"H'm. Aren't you interested in reading it?" asked Yezhov, looking fixedly at Foma.

"Oh, I'll read it all right," said Foma quickly, sensing that Yezhov was hurt by his indifference. "Of course I'm interested if it's written about me," he added, smiling good-naturedly.

This encounter with his old schoolmate evoked quiet, gentle feelings associated with childhood memories that flashed into his mind like tiny lights glimmering through the years.

Yezhov went over to the table on which the boiling samovar was standing and silently poured out two cups of tea as black as pitch.

"Come and have tea," he said, "and tell me everything."

"There's nothing to tell. It's an empty sort of life I live. I'd rather hear about you—you've seen more than I have."

Still wriggling his body and twisting his head from side to side, Yezhov became lost in thought. His face alone remained immobile as he reflected. The wrinkles gathered about his eyes like rays, and his eyes seemed to sink deeper under his brows.

"True enough, I've seen a thing or two, friend," he said, shaking his head. "And I suppose I know more than is good for me. It's just as bad for a man to know too much as to know too little. So you want me to tell you about myself? I'll try. I've never told anybody anything about myself because nobody has ever shown the least interest in me. It's hard to live in this world when not a soul has the least interest in you."

"I can see from your face and everything else that you've had a hard time of it," said Foma, getting a certain satisfaction out of the knowledge that this man, too, had found life difficult.

Yezhov gulped his tea, banged his glass down on the saucer, pulled his feet up to the edge of his chair, hugged his knees and rested his chin on them. In this pose, looking as small and flexible as a piece of india-rubber, he began to speak:

"Student Sachkov, once my tutor, now a doctor of medicine and an accomplished lickspittle, used to say to me whenever I recited my lessons well: 'Good for you, Kolya! You're a clever chap. Poor people like us, who have come in by the back door of life, have got to study hard if we mean to get ahead of everybody else. Russia is badly in need of men who are clever and honest. If you turn out to be such a man, you'll be master of your fate and a valuable member of society. It's on us, people who belong to no particular class, that the hopes of the country rest. We are the ones who have been called upon to bring light and truth to our people . . . 'and so on, and so on. I believed him,

195

the swine. Almost twenty years have passed since then. We people who belong to no particular class have grown up, but we've not given any sign of our cleverness, nor have we brought light into the darkness. Russia still suffers from her chronic complaint —a superabundance of scoundrels—and people of our sort are only too ready to swell their ranks. My former tutor, let me repeat, is a lackey, a nobody, who does whatever the mayor orders him to do. And I? I'm a clown in the service of society. I've won no little fame for myself in this town. When I walk down the street I see the drivers nudge each other and say: 'There goes Yezhov— he's got a terrible bark, the old devil!' Even a reputation like that has to be won, my friend."

Yezhov made a bitter face and laughed noiselessly, with his lips alone. Foma did not understand what he had said but, feeling that something was expected of him, he made the first remark that came into his head:

"So you haven't reached the mark you set yourself?" he said.

"No. I thought I'd be a person of more importance. And I would have been!" exclaimed Yezhov, jumping up 'from his chair and flinging up and down the room as he went on speaking in his shrill voice. "But one's got to have enormous resources to preserve oneself intact. I had them. I was clever, I was adaptable. But I spent all my resources on getting an education which is useless to me. I, and many others like me, robbed ourselves to build a fund we thought we would draw on in the future. In the hope of raising my value, I did all sorts of things that made me worthless—think of it! For six years on end I taught a pack of blockheads their letters and swallowed the insults their papas and mamas heaped on me, so that I could keep body and soul together while I studied. I earned my bread and meat, but I had no time to earn my boots, and so I applied to a charitable society for a loan. Oh, if only those charitable societies knew how much of a man's spirit they kill in preserving the life of his body! If only they realized that every rouble they give him for bread contains ninety-nine kopeks worth of poison for his spirit! May they burst with the pride and complacency with which their philanthropic activities inflate them! No creature on earth is more loathsome than he who gives alms; no creature is more miserable than he who takes them."

Yezhov was still darting about the room as if in a fit of madness. The papers on the floor rustled, were torn, flew out from under his feet. He gnashed his teeth, twisted his neck, flapped his arms like broken wings. Two feelings contended in Foma as he watched him: he pitied him, yet he derived pleasure from the sight of his suffering.

A little screeching sound, as of unoiled hinges, came from Yezhov's chest.

"Poisoned by humankindness, I was brought to ruin by the fatal tendency to accept the little in anticipation of the much, a tendency shown by every poor man who tries to rise in the world. Oh, more people die from underrating their own abilities than from consumption! And that, I presume, is why men who might be leaders of the masses become police inspectors."

"To hell with them!" said Foma with a wave of his hand. "Go on with your story."

"My story? Here it is, the whole of it," cried Yezhov, stopping in the middle of the room and beating himself on the breast. "I have accomplished all I am capable of accomplishing. I have risen to the position of public jester, and I can rise no higher."

"Just a minute," put in Foma quickly. "Tell me this: what must a person do to live in peace—that is, to be satisfied with himself?"

"Live a stormy life, and fear contentment like the plague."

The words held no meaning for Foma; they evoked no feeling in his heart, no ideas in his mind.

"A person must always strive after something beyond his reach. A man grows by stretching towards the unattainable." Yezhov's tone was more tranquil now that he had stopped talking about himself. His voice was firm and convincing, his face stern and grave. He stood in the middle of the room gesturing with one hand and speaking as if reading out of a book:

"The self-satisfied man is a tumour in the breast of society. He crams himself with paltry truths and scraps of musty wisdom, and is like a lumber-room where a stingy housewife keeps all sorts of trash that neither she nor anyone else can use. If you touch such a man, if you open the door leading into him, you are enveloped in fumes of decay—a stream of putrefaction comes pouring into the air you breathe. These miserable creatures are called strong men, men of principle and conviction. And no one cares to remark that their convictions are merely coverings for the nakedness of their souls. The words 'Temperance and

Tranquillity' are written on their low foreheads in shining letters. False words! Rub their foreheads with a firm hand, and you will see the true words: 'Narrowness and Stupidity.'

"How many people like that I've met!" cried Yezhov in horror and wrath. "They're like shops dealing in all sorts of things—tar, lozenges, cockroach poison, linen for shrouds—everything but what is fresh, wholesome and essential. You come to them sick at heart, worn out with loneliness, thirsting for a word of encouragement, and they offer you tepid ideas stolen from books and ruminated until they've gone stringy. And these chewed-over ideas are so poor that to give them expression it's necessary to use a vast number of high-sounding, empty words. When I hear such a man speak, I think to myself: here is a well-fed, well-drugged horse hung about with bells, whose job it is to cart the garbage out of town—and nothing could give it more pleasure, poor beast!"

"They, too, are superfluous people," said Foma.

Yezhov came to a halt in front of him and smiled sardonically.

"Oh, no, they are not superfluous," said he. "Their purpose in life is to serve as an example of what not to be. In point of fact, their place is in an anatomical museum, where all sorts of freaks, all sorts of deviations from the normal are on display. Nothing in life is superfluous, my friend. Even I have my uses. The only people who are superfluous are those who have grown an enormous festering abscess of self-love in place of their dead hearts. But they, too, are needed, if only to give me an object on which to vent my spleen."

All day long Yezhov ranted, pouring curses on the heads of those he hated. Foma was infected by his vengeful ardour, and the infection put him in a belligerent mood.

But later, there were moments when his faith in Yezhov wavered, and one day he said to him point-blank:

"Would you tell people such things to their faces?"

"I do whenever I have the chance—and every Sunday in the newspaper. Shall I read you what I write?"

Without waiting for Foma to reply he ripped a few papers off the nails and, still pacing the floor, began to read. He growled, yapped, bared his teeth, and was for all the world like a savage puppy tugging at its chains in impotent rage. Foma missed the meaning of the words, but he was aware of his friend's reckless daring, his biting ridicule, his burning indignation, and he enjoyed this as he enjoyed slapping his body with the besom in the steam bath.

"Well said!" he would cry out when some phrase went home. "You gave it to them that time!"

The names of eminent citizens and merchants of his acquaintance were repeated again and again as Yezhov reduced them to a ridicule that was now bold and unmasked, now as fine as a needle and couched in tones of respect.

Yezhov was encouraged by Foma's approval and by the pleasure shining in his eyes, and he yapped and howled all the louder, sometimes dropping exhausted on the couch, only to jump up again and rush over to Foma.

"Read what you wrote about me," cried Foma.

Yezhov rummaged in a heap of papers, then planted himself, feet wide apart, in front of his friend, who smiled up at him from the depths of a dilapidated armchair.

The article began with a description of the orgy on the raft and, as Yezhov read, Foma found that some of the words stung him like mosquitoes. His face lengthened, he dropped his head and grew sulky. The mosquito bites increased.

"Haven't you laid it on a little thick?" he said at last, angry and ashamed. "Disgracing people won't buy you into God's good graces."

"Hush! Wait," barked Yezhov, going on with his reading.

When he had shown in his article that no other class could compete with the merchants in brawling and carousing, he stopped to ask why this was so, and in answer he had written:

"It seems to me that this tendency to wild indulgence springs from a lack of cultivation added to an excess of energy and leisure. There can be no question but that our merchants, with few exceptions, are the most robust of our people, and at the same time they have the least to occupy themselves."

"There you have it!" exclaimed Foma, striking the table with his hand. "A truer word was never spoken. Take me: I have the strength of an ox and do the work of a sparrow."

"How is the merchant to use up his energy? The exchange takes very little of it, and so he squanders vast sums of muscular capital in the taverns, having no idea that it might be spent in ways that would bring benefit to society. He has not yet risen beyond the animal stage, and his life is a cage that is much too confining for one of his robust health and sweeping nature. Having no cultural interests, he resorts to debauchery. The debauchery of a merchant is the raving of a caged beast. This, unquestionably, is deplorable, but oh! how much worse it will be when this beast applies intelligence to the savage force that is in him and begins to make it serve his end! You can be sure he will not become less violent, but his acts of violence will become historical events. God help us then, for whatever he does will spring from a desire to take power into his own hands, to set his class above all others, and he will spare nobody and nothing to accomplish this."

"Am I right?" asked Yezhov, throwing down the paper when he had finished.

"I didn't understand the end," replied Foma, "but you were right as to his strength."

And in a burst of confidence he told Yezhov his own views on life and people, and described his moral tangle. When he had finished, he threw himself down on the couch and was silent.

"H'm," murmured Yezhov. "So that's the pass you've come to! And it's a very good thing. What's your attitude to books? Do you read?"

"No. I don't care about books. I never have read."

"That's why you don't care about them."

"I'm afraid to. I've seen what it's done to a certain person— a girl I know. Reading's worse than drink with her. And what's the good of it? The things you read are only made up. I've no objection if they're amusing. But it's absurd to think that books can teach a man how to live. After all, it's men, not God, who write these books, and what rules and laws can men lay down for themselves?"

"What about the Gospels? They were written by men."

"But they were apostles. There aren't any apostles today."

"True; the correct answer. There aren't any apostles today; there aren't anything but Judases left, and poor ones at that."

Foma was pleased that Yezhov listened to him so attentively. He seemed to be weighing every word he said. No one had ever done this before, and it was so encouraging that Foma confided his thoughts to his friend freely and boldly, without worrying about the words, sure that Yezhov would understand, because he wanted to understand him.

"You're a curious fellow," Yezhov said to him a few days after their talk. "Words come hard to you, but I see you have a valiant heart. If you had more knowledge of the ways of life, you'd have something to say, and you'd say it at the top of your voice, I'm sure of that."

"Words can't help a man free himself," observed Foma with a sigh. "You once spoke about people who pretend that they know everything and can do anything. I know such people—my godfather, for instance. If we could only do something about them—show them up! They're a wicked lot."

"I don't know how you're going to go on living with such a burden on your heart, Foma," said Yezhov reflectively.

He, too, drank—this undersized man whom life had battered so brutally. This is how his day began: at breakfast he would read the local papers, gleaning material for the feature he would write then and there at that table. Then he would rush off to the newspaper office, where he would take cuttings from country papers to make up "Scenes from Provincial Life". On Fridays he wrote his Sunday feature. For all these services he received one hundred roubles a month. He worked quickly and devoted all his spare time to "the observation and study of benevolent institutions"; that is, all night long he and Foma went from one club, restaurant and tavern to another, and in each of them he gathered material for his writings, which he called "brooms for sweeping the public conscience". He referred to censors as "supervising-managers in charge of the distribution of truth and justice". He called newspapers "procurers who introduce the public to dangerous ideas", and his work on the paper "the retail selling of my soul" or "a feeble attempt to thumb my nose at sacred institutions".

Foma had difficulty in telling when Yezhov was joking and when in earnest. He spoke about everything with great feeling and was relentless in the judgments he passed. Foma liked this in him. But sometimes he would reverse his views in the middle of a passionate tirade and show quite as much spirit in refuting what he had just said, reducing the whole thing to a joke. At such times Foma felt there was nothing this man really loved, nothing so deeply rooted in him that it governed his every action. Yezhov adopted quite a different tone when the talk concerned himself, and the more feelingly he spoke about himself, the more mercilessly he upbraided everyone and everything else. He was not consistent in his attitude towards Foma. At times he would encourage him, saying emphatically:

"Tear down and wipe out as much as you can. Remember that nothing is as valuable as a human being. Shout 'Freedom! Freedom!' at the top of your voice."

Yet when Foma, inflamed by his speeches, would consider how he was to wipe out the people who cramp life for the sake of their own private gain, Yezhov would break in with:

"Drop it! What can you do about it? Nobody needs people like you. Your day—the day of the strong but ignorant—is over. There's no place for you in this life of ours."

"Isn't there? That's a lie!" Foma cried, angered by his inconsistency.

"Very well, what *can* you do about it?"

"Kill you, that's what I can do!" Foma retorted, clenching his fist.

"Clown!" Yezhov said with a shrug of his shoulders. "What good will that do? I'm half dead as it is—" and then, in a sudden flash of fury and despair: "Fate has played a dirty trick on me. Why did I work like a slave for twelve years on end? So that I could study. Why did I study those twelve long years in the *gymnasium* and the university, swallowing a lot of dull, dry, contradictory nonsense that's quite useless to me? So that I could become a feature-writer, could give a daily performance to amuse the public, telling myself that they needed it and would benefit by it. I fired off all the explosives my soul was charged with at the rate of three kopeks a shot. And what do I believe in? Nothing. The only belief I have is that the world in its present form is worthless, and that everything in it must be torn down and razed to the ground. What do I love? Myself. Yet I realize that the object of my love is unworthy of it."

He was on the verge of tears and kept clawing at his throat and chest with thin, feeble fingers.

But there were times when he was caught up in a wave of hope, and then he spoke in a different vein.

"Oh, no, my song is not sung to the end!" he would say. "You'll hear from me yet! Just wait—one of these days I'll drop the newspaper and settle down to serious work. There's a little book I'm thinking of writing—'Swan Song' is what I shall call it. The song of the dying. And my book will be incense burnt at the deathbed of this society, damned with the damnation of its own impotence."

By following carefully what Yezhov said and comparing one of his speeches with another, Foma came to the conclusion that his friend was just as weak and muddled as he was. But Foma learnt to use words by listening to him and at times was delighted to notice that he was expressing himself in clear, forcible language.

On several occasions he had met people at Yezhov's who, it seemed to him, knew everything and understood everything, seeing falsehood and deceit everywhere. He watched them and listened to them in silence. He liked their audacity, but was embarrassed and repulsed by their condescending manner towards him. He was struck by the fact that when these people were in Yezhov's room they seemed more upright and clever than when he met them in taverns or the street. They had room-words, room-themes, room-gestures, which they exchanged for ordinary human ones the minute they left the room. Sometimes when they gathered at Yezhov's they flared up like a great bonfire, Yezhov burning brighter than any of the others. But this fire threw little light into the darkness of Foma's soul.

"We're going on a picnic," Yezhov said to him one day. "Our compositors have formed a co-operative society and are doing all the work for our newspaper by contract. In honour of the occasion they are having a blow-out and I'm invited (I'm the one who advised them to form the society). Do you want to come along? You might treat them."

"I may as well," said Foma. It made little difference to him how he spent the time that lay so heavily on his hands.

That evening Foma and Yezhov were sitting among some grey-faced men who had gathered at the edge of a wood outside the town. There were twelve compositors. They were decently dressed and treated Yezhov as their equal, a thing that surprised and even annoyed Foma, for in his eyes Yezhov was their superior and they were his subordinates. They paid no attention to Foma, though when Yezhov had introduced him they had shaken his hand and said they were glad to see him. He lay down under a hazel bush a little distance away and watched them, feeling very much out of things. Yezhov seemed to have purposely withdrawn and paid no more attention to him than the others did. Foma noticed that the little feature-writer was putting himself out to be accepted as one of these men. He helped them make the fire, opened beer bottles for them, laughed and swore in a loud voice and tried in every way to be like them. He was even dressed more simply than usual.

"It's grand to be with you, brothers," he said with a swaggering air. "I'm not much of a nob myself—just the son of a night watchman, non-commissioned officer Matvey Yezhov."

Why should he tell them that? wondered Foma. What do they care whose son he is? A man's respected for his brains, not for his father.

The sun was going down. The sky had its own enormous bonfire, staining the clouds blood-red. Silence and dampness came from the wood, at the edge of which dark human forms were moving about noisily. A thin, middle-sized man wearing a wide-brimmed straw hat was playing an accordion, while another, with a black moustache and a cap on the back of his head, was singing softly. Two others were testing their strength by pulling on the opposite ends of a stick. Several figures were bending over the hamper containing beer and food. A tall man with a grey beard was standing in a cloud of thick white smoke throwing sticks on the fire. The damp wood crackled and hissed as the flames caught it; the accordionist swung into a gay tune that was taken up by the falsetto voice of the singer.

Three young lads were lying on the edge of a small ravine and Yezhov was standing in front of them and saying in a loud voice:

"You are carrying the sacred banner of labour in your hands. I, too, am just a common soldier in the same army; all of us serve His Majesty the Press, and so we ought to be firm, fast friends."

Foma turned his attention from Yezhov to a conversation of more interest taking place nearby. Two men were talking. One of them was tall, consumptive, poorly dressed, and wore a sour look. The other was young, with fair hair and beard.

"If you ask me," the older man was saying between coughs, "it's foolishness? How can folk like us marry? There are bound to be children, and who's to keep them? A wife's got to be dressed. And who knows how she'll turn out?"

"My girl is a good sort," said the younger one shyly.

"I daresay she is now. A girl's one thing, a wife quite another. But that isn't the point. The point is: how are you going to support them? You'll work your fingers to the bone and wear her out too. Oh, no, marriage is not for us, mate! As if we could keep a family on what we make! Take me—I'm married . . . only four years . . . and I'm done for already."

He coughed—coughed long and hard, with a whistle at the end, and when the fit was over, he turned to his companion:

"Drop the idea. Nothing will come of it," he gasped.

The younger man hung his head unhappily, and Foma thought to himself: the old one's right.

It hurt him to be ignored in this way, yet he respected these men with their lead-stained faces for not toadying to him. They talked in a serious way, mostly about their jobs, using many unfamiliar words. None of them sought his favour or pressed themselves upon him like his tavern companions. He was pleased by this.

"What a proud lot they are!" he laughed to himself.

"Come, Nikolai Matveyevich," said someone in reproving tones, "you don't want to judge by what's written in books, but by what you see all around you."

"Very well, friends, what have you learned from the experience of your fellow-workers?"

Foma turned to look at Yezhov, who was waving his hat in the air as he made a fiery speech. But at that moment somebody said:

"Won't you move closer, Citizen Gordeyev?"

A stout lad wearing a workman's blouse and high boots was standing in front of him, smiling good-naturedly. Foma liked his round fat face with the fleshy nose, and he smiled back.

"With pleasure," he said. "But isn't it about time for us all to be moving closer to the cognac? I brought about a dozen bottles with me—just in case."

"Ho! There's a merchant for you! I'll report your message to headquarters."

The boy laughed loud and long at his own humour. Foma joined in, catching a whiff of warmth that came, perhaps from the lad, perhaps from the fire.

Slowly the sunset faded. It was as if an enormous purple curtain were being lowered in the West, revealing the unfathomable depths of the night sky shimmering with stars. An invisible hand had sprinkled lights over the black solidity of the distant town, but here the blackness of the woods was unrelieved. The moon had not risen yet and the fields were wrapped in warm shadow.

The men sat themselves in a big circle by the fire. Foma sat next to Yezhov with his back to the light, so that he could see the jolly, fire-lit faces. Light-hearted from drink, though not yet drunk, the men laughed, joked and sang snatches of song as they drank cognac and ate white bread, cucumbers and sausage. Everything tasted particularly good to Foma and, caught up in the general merriment, he grew bolder and felt an urge to say something to these men that would help them and make them like him. Yezhov, who was sitting beside him, kept wriggling about, knocking against him with his shoulder and shaking his head as he muttered unintelligibly.

"Brothers!" shouted the stout lad. "Let's have the student song. Come, now, one, two—"

Swift as the waves . . .

Someone joined in in a bass voice:

Roll the days of our life. . . .

"Comrades!" said Yezhov, struggling to his feet with his glass in his hand. He tottered and caught at Foma's head for support. The song broke off and all eyes were turned to him.

"Men of labour!" he said. "Allow me to say a few heartfelt words to you. I am happy to be in your company. I am contented when I am with you, because you are working men, men whose right to happiness cannot be denied, though it remains unrecognized. How good it is for a man who is lonely and embittered by life to find himself in the wholesome, ennobling company of such honest men!"

Yezhov's voice faltered and his head shook. A drop fell on Foma's hand, and he looked up to see his friend's distorted face. "I am not alone," Yezhov went on, trembling all over. "There are many of us who, like me, are sick, broken, hunted by fate. We are less fortunate than you workers because we are weaker in body and spirit, but we are stronger than you because we are armed with knowledge—which we cannot use. All of us would be only too glad to come and give ourselves wholly to you, that your lives might be made easier. There is nothing else for us to do. Without you, we have no ground to stand on; without us, you are without light. Comrades! We were made for each other!"

What does he want of them? wondered Foma. He looked at the faces of the compositors and saw that they, too, were surprised, perplexed and bored.

206

"The future is yours, my friends," said Yezhov irresolutely, with a sad shake of his head, as if he grudged them this future and was conceding them power against his will. "The future belongs to honest working men. A great task awaits you. The creating of a new form of civilization will fall upon your shoulders. I, the son of a humble soldier, am with you body and soul, and I propose a toast to the future that is yours! Hurrah!"

With his glass to his lips, Yezhov dropped heavily to the ground. The compositors caught up his broken cry, filling the air with a roar that shook the leaves on the trees.

"Now for a song!" said the stout lad again.

"A song!" came two or three approving voices. A hot argument arose as to what they should sing. As he listened to the babble, Yezhov twisted his head from side to side to get a better look at everybody.

"Comrades!" he cried out suddenly. "I want a reply! A reply to my toast!"

And again, though not at once, the men became silent and stared at him, some in curiosity, others hiding a smile, still others with ill-concealed displeasure on their faces. He got up and began to speak excitedly:

"There are two of us here whom life has rejected: our guest and me. Both of us long for the same thing: consideration, and the joy of feeling that we are needed. Comrades! This big and foolish fellow—"

"You have no right to insult our guest, Nikolai Matveyich," someone objected in a deep voice.

"No, you haven't," agreed the stout lad. "No slurs."

"We came here to rest and enjoy ourselves," someone else asserted very loudly and definitely.

"Fools!" sniggered Yezhov. "Good-hearted fools. Do you feel sorry for him? Do you know who he is? He's one of those who suck your blood."

"Enough of that, Nikolai Matveyich," the men called out, and they went back to their talk, completely ignoring Yezhov. Foma was too sorry for his friend to take offence at what he had said. He saw that the men who had sprung to his defence were deliberately snubbing the feature-writer, and he knew that if Yezhov saw this it would hurt him. And so, to distract his attention, he dug him in the ribs and said good-naturedly:

"Come, old boy, let's have a drink, shall we? Or is it time to go home?"

"Home? Where is home for one who has no place among men? Comrades!" he cried again.

But his cry, drowned out by the general babble, remained unanswered. Seeing this, he hung his head.

"Let's go," he said.

"If you wish, although I wouldn't mind staying. Very interesting. They're decent fellows, damn it all, the devils!"

"I can't stay any longer; I'm frozen."

Foma got up, took off his cap, and bowed to the compositors.

"Thank you for your food, gentlemen. Goodbye," he called out gaily.

He was instantly surrounded on all sides and urged to stay.

"Wait a little. Where are you going? We'll have a song."

"No, I must go. I can't let my friend go alone. Enjoy yourselves without us."

"Oh, don't go yet!" exclaimed the stout lad, adding under his breath: "We'll see him off."

"Do stay," urged the consumptive in a low tone. "We'll take him as far as the town, put him in a cab, and come back."

Foma wanted to stay, and at the same time he was afraid to. Yezhov struggled to his feet.

"Come on," he said, clutching Foma by the sleeve. "To hell with them!"

"Goodbye, gentlemen, I'm leaving," said Foma. And he went away followed by exclamations of regret.

"Ha, ha, ha!" laughed Yezhov when they had gone some twenty paces. "They see us off with tears in their eyes, but actually they're glad I've gone. I was in the way—prevented them making beasts of themselves."

"It's true you were in the way," said Foma. "Why did you have to make speeches? They came together to have a good time, not to be lectured. You bored them to death."

"Shut up! You don't know what you're talking about," said Yezhov harshly. "Think I'm drunk? It's my body that's drunk, but my soul's sober. It's always sober and feels everything. Oh, how much vileness, pettiness, senselessness there is in the world! And those stupid, miserable men!"

Yezhov came to a halt and stood swaying on his feet, holding his head in his hands.

"They're not a bit like other people," murmured Foma. "Very polite. Almost gentlemen. And they have sensible opinions. They know what they're talking about. Just simple working men."

In the darkness behind them rose a song in chorus. Faltering at first, it grew in volume until it poured, a mighty wave, into the fresh night air above the empty fields.

"God!" breathed Yezhov softly and mournfully. "What is there for the soul to cling to? What can quench its thirst for love, friendship, brotherhood, pure and holy labour?"

"The common folk," mused Foma, who was too absorbed in his own reflections to be aware of what his companion was saying, "they aren't bad, if you take a good look at them. They're even a . . . a curious lot. Peasants, working men . . . at first glance they seem to be nothing more than horses that go plodding on, puffing and snorting. . . ."

"They carry our whole life on their backs," interrupted Yezhov impatiently. "And they go plodding along like horses, thick-skulled, submissive. Their submissiveness is a misfortune—a curse."

For some time he staggered ahead in silence, and then, all of a sudden, he began to recite poetry in a choking voice, waving his hand in the air.

> *Bitterly life has deceived me,*
> *Deep is my sorrow, my pain. . . .*

"That was written for me, friend," he said, stopping and shaking his head sadly. "What's the rest? I've forgotten. . . ."

> *The dreams that lie buried within me,*
> *Will never rise again.*

"You're luckier than I am because you're—you're stupid."

"Stop snivelling," said Foma irritably. "Listen to them singing."

"I don't want to listen to other people's songs," said Yezhov. "I've got my own," and he broke into a loud wail:

> *The dreams that lie buried within me,*
> *Will never rise again.*
> *Many the dreams! . . .*

He whimpered and cried like a woman. Foma was touched, but he felt uncomfortable.

"Stop it," he said, giving his friend's shoulder an impatient tug. "You *are* a spineless creature."

Yezhov clutched his head, straightened up, and with great effort began his mournful wailing again:

> Many the dreams,
> And narrow their coffin,
> A shroud of soft rhymes do I sew,
> And many the songs that I sing them,
> Melodies mournful and low.

"Oh God!" breathed Foma in despair.

From far away, through the darkness and silence, came the song of the workers. Someone whistled in time to the refrain, and the high, shrill whistle rode the crest of the wave of strong voices. Foma looked back and saw the black wall of forest, the flames of the fire playing on it and the hazy forms of the men round the fire. The forest was a vast breast, the fire a gaping wound in it. Wrapped in mist, the men looked as small as children, and they, too, seemed to be flames, illuminated by the glow of the fire and waving their arms as they sang in loud, powerful voices.

Yezhov, who was standing beside Foma, cried out again in sobbing tones:

> Sung is my song, and my lute
> The last sad measure has played.
> Oh, Lord! Give repose to my spirit,
> Afflicted beyond mortal aid.
> Oh, Lord! Give repose to my spirit!

Foma started at the sound of his melancholy wail. The little feature-writer let out an hysterical shriek and threw himself face down on the ground, where he lay crying quietly and plaintively like a sick child.

"Nikolai," said Foma, taking him by the shoulder, "stop it. What's the matter? Aren't you ashamed?"

But he was not ashamed; he flung himself about on the ground like a fish on dry land, and when Foma lifted him to his feet he threw his skinny arms about him and went on sobbing.

"Come, come," said Foma through clenched teeth. "Calm yourself, dear fellow."

Indignant that life should cause a man such suffering, full of resentment on his friend's behalf, Foma turned to where the lights of the city glimmered in the darkness and, in an upsurge of bitterness, thundered hoarsely:

"Curses on you, you fiends!"

XI

"LYUBA," said Mayakin one day on returning from the
exchange, "prepare yourself to receive a suitor this evening.
Lay a fine table. Bring out all our old silver, and the fruit vases
too. Let the table impress him. Let him see all the precious things
we own."

Lyuba was sitting at the window darning her father's socks,
her head bent low over her work.

"Why all that show, Father?" she said, vexed and disapproving.

"As a sauce—for the flavour. And because that's as it should
be. A girl's not a horse; no one will buy her without trappings."

Lyuba gave a little toss of her head, threw down her work,
glanced at her father with a blush of indignation, and then
picked up the sock again, bending her head still lower. The old
man walked to and fro, staring into space and tugging anxiously
at his beard, as if pondering some deep and difficult problem.
His daughter knew he would not listen to her if she spoke and
would be indifferent to the humiliation his words had caused
her. Her romantic dreams of a husband who would be a friend as
well, a cultivated husband who would read fine books with her
and help her to understand her vague longings—these dreams
were wiped out by her father's inflexible decision to marry her to
Smolin. It left a bitter sediment in her soul. She had come to
look upon herself as superior to the ordinary run of girls of the
merchant class, who thought of nothing but clothes and who
married the men their parents decided were a good match,
rarely taking into consideration the young people's feelings.
And now she, too, was about to marry simply because it was
high time, and because her father needed a son-in-law who would
take over his business. Evidently her father thought her incapable
of attracting a husband, and therefore adorned her with silver.
She pricked her finger and broke her needle in her agitation,

but said nothing, knowing only too well that her words would not reach her father's heart.

The old man kept on pacing the room, now chanting a psalm under his breath, now instructing his daughter how to behave in the presence of the suitor. Suddenly he made some calculation on his fingers—frowned—then smiled.

"H'm . . . may the Lord be my judge, and may He deliver me from the fawning and the ungodly . . . H'm . . . Put on your mother's emeralds, Lyuba."

"Oh, enough of this, Father!" she burst out unhappily. "Do leave me alone!"

"None of your tricks, now! Do what you're told!"

And he went back to his calculations, narrowing his green eyes as he counted on his fingers.

"Thirty-five per cent, the swindler! . . . Shed Thy light upon us. . . ."

"Father!" exclaimed Lyuba in a frightened voice.

"Ay?"

"Does he . . . do you like him?"

"Who?"

"Smolin."

"Smolin? He's a sharp one. Got a good head on his shoulders. Well, I must be going. Put on your fine clothes, Lyuba."

When he was gone Lyuba flung down her work and leaned back in her chair, closing her eyes. The knuckles of her hands were white, so tightly were her fingers clenched. Overwhelmed by the bitterness of her humiliation and fearful of the future, she sat there praying soundlessly:

"Dear God, Blessed Lord and Saviour . . . if only he turns out to be kind! . . . Make him kind, dear Lord . . . and gentle. Some unknown man comes and gapes at you . . . then makes you his for years and years. How fearful! How shameful! Oh God, dear God! If only there were someone I could talk to! But I'm still alone. If Taras were here. . . ."

At the thought of her brother she felt still more wronged, still more sorry for herself. She had written Taras a long and exuberant letter in which she had told him that she loved him dearly and placed all her hopes in him; she implored him to come and see their father as soon as possible, painting a bright picture of the life they would live together, assuring him that their father was a clever man who would understand everything, that he was old and lonely, but had an amazing zest for life. And she complained of the way the old man treated her.

For two weeks she had waited anxiously for the answer, and on receiving it had wept hysterically with joy and disappointment. The answer was dry and terse. Taras informed her that in a month's time he would be on the Volga on business and would pay his father a visit if the old man had no objections. It was a cold letter. She wept over it, she folded and crumpled it, but the moistening of the paper did not soften its message. From the surface of the stiff writing-paper covered with letters in a large, bold hand, a face seemed to frown at her distrustfully—a face as thin and sharp and winkled as her father's.

His son's letter produced quite a different effect on Mayakin. On learning that Taras had written, he became greatly excited and hastened to his daughter with a peculiar smile twisting his lips.

"Come, let's have it," he said. "Show it to me. He-he-he! Let's see how the wise men write. Where are my spectacles? 'Dear sister'. H'm."

The old man read his son's message in silence. When he had finished he laid it on the table and took a turn up and down the room, his eyebrows raised in astonishment. Then he read it a second time, after which he stood drumming the table lost in thought.

"Not bad," he uttered at last. "A good solid letter. No unnecessary words. Perhaps the cold has hardened him. The cold is fierce there. Let him come. We'll have a look at him. Curious. H'm. As is said in the Psalm of David: 'When mine enemies are turned back'—I've forgotten how it goes after that, something like: "My enemy's weapons have weakened in the end, and his memorial hath perished amid noise'. Well, he and I will have things out without any noise."

The old man tried to speak calmly, with a supercilious smile, but the smile was a failure; his wrinkles quivered with excitement and his eyes glittered strangely.

"Write to him again, Lyuba. Tell him to come without any fear."

Lyuba wrote him a second letter that was shorter and more restrained than the first. And now she was waiting for the answer and trying to imagine what this mysterious brother of hers would be like. Formerly she had thought of him with the reverence in

which believers hold saints and pilgrims. Now she was intimidated by the thought of him, for at the price of great suffering,
at the price of a youth spent in exile, he had bought the right to
judge of men and their actions, and he would be sure to say to her:

"Is it of your own free will, for love, that you are marrying this
man?"

One after another dark thoughts rose in her mind to confuse
and torment her. In a nervous state verging on despair, scarcely
holding back her tears, she carried out exactly, if half-uncon-
sciously, her father's orders: laid the table with old silver, put on
a grey silk dress, and seated herself in front of the mirror to screw
into her ears the enormous emeralds that had once been part
of the family jewels of Prince Gruzinsky and had fallen into
Mayakin's hands, along with many other valuables, as unre-
deemed security for a loan.

As she gazed in the mirror at her agitated face, whose round,
ripe lips seemed even redder by contrast with the pallor of her
cheeks, at her full breasts firmly encased in silk, she saw that she
was pretty and worthy of the attention of any man. The green
stones sparkling in her ears were a superfluous touch that
offended her taste and, besides, they seemed to cast a pale yellow
shadow on her cheeks. She took out the emeralds and put in tiny
rubies instead, wondering the while what Smolin would be like.

Displeased with the dark circles under her eyes, she began to
powder them away, still thinking of Smolin and the misfortune
of being a woman, and reproaching herself for lack of character.
When the dark circles were gone she found that the powder had
robbed her eyes of their lustre, and so she rubbed it off. One
last glance into the mirror convinced her that she was strikingly
beautiful, with the sturdy, sound beauty of a young pine tree.
This flattering conviction somewhat quieted her fears, and she
entered the dining-room with the firm step of a rich and marriage-
able young woman who knows her own worth.

Her father and Smolin were waiting for her.

Lyuba lingered a moment in the doorway, screwing up her
eyes in a pretty way and compressing her lips proudly. Smolin
got up, took a step towards her, and bowed. She liked the bow,
and she liked the coat that sat so well on his lithe body. He had
changed very little; his hair was still red and close-cropped and
his face was covered with freckles, but he wore a handsome
moustache and his eyes seemed to have grown larger.

"A fine specimen, eh?" Mayakin cried to his daughter, pointing at Smolin.

The young man squeezed her hand and smiled.

"May I hope you have not forgotten your old school-friend?" he murmured in a rich baritone.

"You two can talk later," said the old man, examining his daughter with his eyes. "You make arrangements here, Lyuba, and he and I will finish our little talk. And so, Afrikan Dmitriyevich, as you were saying. . . ."

"I must ask you to excuse me, Lyubov Yakovlevna," said Smolin in winning tones.

"Oh, think nothing of it," said Lyuba.

He's very polite, she thought, and as she moved between table and sideboard she listened carefully to what he said. His voice was soft and full of self-confidence.

"As I was saying, for four years I have made a careful study of Russian leather in foreign markets. Thirty years ago our leather was considered the best, but now the demand for it is falling off and so is the price. And that is perfectly natural. Lacking the capital and the knowledge all these small leather producers are unable to raise their product to the proper standard and, at the same time, reduce the price. Their goods are extremely bad and dear. And they are to blame for having spoilt Russia's reputation for the manufacture of the best leather. On the whole your small producers, without the capital and technical knowledge, are incapable of keeping up with the latest developments in industry, and therefore they are a curse to the country, are parasites on her trade."

In the studied simplicity of Smolin's words Lyuba sensed a condescending attitude towards her father which she resented.

"H'm," murmured the old man, one eye on his guest, the other on his daughter. "In other words, you are thinking of building a huge factory that will gobble up all the small fry?"

"Oh, no," said Smolin, dismissing the old man's accusation with a mild gesture. "My purpose is to restore the reputation and the price of Russian leather in foreign markets; and so, armed with a knowledge of modern methods of production, I intend to build a model factory and market model goods. The honour of the country. . . ."

"And how much money did you say was needed for this?" asked Mayakin thoughtfully.

"About three hundred thousand."

Father won't give that much for me, thought Lyuba.

"My factory will turn out leather goods, such as trunks, foot-wear, harness, straps and so on."

"And what is the interest you dream of getting?" put in the old man.

"I don't dream, I calculate with all the exactness possible under conditions in Russia," said Smolin with emphasis. "The manufacturer must be as coldly practical as a mechanic invent-ing a machine. If he wishes to do a big job in a big way, he must calculate the friction of even the tiniest wheel in the mech-anism. I should like you to read the notes I have made, based on a thorough study of cattle-breeding and the meat market in Russia."

"Just fancy that now!" said Mayakin with a little laugh. "Bring me the notes. Very interesting. Anyone can see you didn't waste your time in Europe. And now let's have a bite to eat, in the good old Russian fashion."

"And how are you getting on, Lyuba Yakovlevna?" asked Smolin as he picked up his knife and fork.

"Getting on poorly," answered Mayakin for his daughter. "She's the housekeeper here—runs the whole household, and that leaves her no time to enjoy herself."

"No time and no inclination," added Lyuba. "I can't endure the balls and parties the merchants give."

"And the theatre?" asked Smolin.

"I don't go to the theatre often. I have no one to go with."

"Theatre!" snorted Mayakin. "Perhaps you'll be so kind as to explain to me the new fashion of representing the merchants as a pack of fools. Very amusing of course, but not true at all. It's the merchant who's the master in the Town Council, the master in commerce, the owner of those very theatres, and they dare to call him a fool. That play-merchant of theirs is not true to life. Oh, I understand if you're putting on something historical, say 'Life of the Tsar' with songs and dances, or 'Hamlet', or 'The Sorceress', or 'Vasilisa'—truthful representation isn't needed because they deal with the past and don't concern us; true or untrue, it doesn't matter so long as they're well done. But if you're dealing with *our* day, then don't lie, but show a man in his true light."

217

Smolin smiled politely as he listened to the old man, and he threw Lyuba a glance that seemed to challenge her to answer her father.

"After all, Father," she said with some embarrassment, "you must admit that most of the merchants and their families *are* coarse and uneducated."

"Yes," said Smolin with a nod of agreement, "unfortunately that is the truth. But aren't you a member of some society? There are all sorts of societies in this town."

"I know," sighed Lyuba, "but somehow I seem to be out of everything."

"The housekeeping," put in her father. "Just see all the knick-knacks we've collected. They've all got to be accounted for, and kept clean and in order."

With a self-satisfied air he nodded at the table, piled high with silver, and at the china-closet that was groaning under the weight of expensive ware, reminding one of a display in a shop window. As Smolin noted all this an ironical smile touched his lips. He turned to Lyuba, and his glance told her that he felt friendly towards her and sympathized with her. Thank God! she said to herself, a feeling of happiness tugging timidly at her heart.

The cut-glass glittered more brilliantly in the light of the heavy bronze chandelier, and the room seemed to grow brighter.

"I'm very fond of our dear old town," said Smolin, smiling gently at her. "It's so lively and picturesque. There's something stimulating about it, something that makes one want to work. Its very picturesqueness inspires one somehow, makes one want to live a full life, to work hard and seriously. And it's an intellectual town. Just see what a serious newspaper it puts out. By the way, we are thinking of buying it."

"Who's 'we'?" asked Mayakin.

"Urvantsov and Shchukin and myself."

"Excellent!" said the old man, bringing his hand down on the table with a bang. "It's high time we shut their mouths for them —was high time long ago. Especially that Yezhov. Sharp teeth he's got. File them down for him, and see that you make a good job of it."

Once more Smolin threw Lyuba a smiling glance, and once more joy stirred in her heart.

"If I'm not mistaken, it isn't to 'shut their mouths for them' as you put it, that Afrikan Dmitriyevich wants to buy the paper," she said with a blush, outwardly addressing her father, inwardly her suitor.

"Why else should he buy it?" said the old man with a shrug of his shoulders. "Nothing but sound and fury comes out of that paper. Oh, of course, if it was the business men who wrote for it, the merchants themselves, we—"

"The publishing of a paper," interrupted Smolin sententiously, "can be a very profitable undertaking even if considered only from a commercial point of view. But besides this, a paper has another and more important purpose, namely, to defend the rights of private property and the interests of trade and industry."

"Just what I was saying—if the merchant takes it over, the paper can be put to good use."

"But, Father—" began Lyuba.

She felt an urge to express herself in the presence of Smolin. She wanted to show that she understood him, that she was not the ordinary merchant's daughter, interested only in clothes and dancing. She liked Smolin. Never before had she met a merchant who had lived abroad for a long time, who talked so impressively, had such good manners, wore such good clothes and spoke to her father, the cleverest man in the town, with the condescending air of an adult to a child.

After the wedding I'll get him to take me abroad, she thought, and the embarrassment of this thought made her forget what she had intended to say to her father. She blushed furiously and could not utter a word, and this, she feared, would discredit her in Smolin's eyes.

"You've been talking so much you've forgotten to offer our guest some wine," she managed to stutter at last.

"That's for you to do; you're the hostess," said her father.

"Oh, don't trouble yourself," Smolin hastened to say. "I hardly drink at all."

"Now, now," said Mayakin.

"Truly. On rare occasions I may drink a glass or two—if I'm very tired or not feeling well. I can't understand drinking wine for pleasure. There are so many other pleasures more worthy of a man of education."

"Women, for instance?" said Mayakin with a wink.

"Books, theatres, music," said Smolin dryly, glancing at Lyuba.

219

Lyuba rejoiced on hearing these words.

But Mayakin glowered at the worthy young man and gave a caustic little grunt.

"Life is changing!" he burst out suddenly. "Once big dogs lived on crusts; nowadays puppies turn down cream. Forgive me the sharp remark, my dear sir, but it's to the point. Not that I refer to you, of course."

Lyuba turned pale and glanced at Smolin in fright. He was calmly examining a *cloisonné* salt cellar of old workmanship and twirling his moustache as if he had not heard the old man's words. But his eyes were darker than usual and his lips formed a tight line that emphasized the prominence of his chin.

"And so, my future Factory Owner, three hundred thousand roubles and your sails are hoisted, is that it?" said Mayakin as if the even tenor of their conversation had not been interrupted.

"In a year and a half my first goods will be ready for market and they will be fairly torn out of my hands," said Smolin with unwavering conviction, fixing the old man with a hard cold eye.

"And the firm will consist of Smolin and Mayakin and nobody else? Very well. Rather late for me to be launching on a new venture, don't you think? A coffin's been waiting for me for some time now. How do you look at that?"

To evade replying, Smolin laughed loudly, though with cold indifference.

"Come, now, you're joking," he said at last.

A little shudder passed over the old man at the sound of his laughter, and he recoiled almost imperceptibly. All three of them were silent for a moment.

"Ye-es," said Mayakin, without lifting his head. "We've got to think of that. *I've* got to think of it," Lifting his head, he stared intently at his daughter and Smolin, got up, and said roughly: "I'll leave you two alone for a minute—I've something to attend to in my study."

And he went out with drooping head and shoulders, dragging his feet.

When he was gone the young people tried to make conversation, but since this only increased the strain, abandoned the attempt and maintained an awkward, expectant silence. Lyuba took an orange and concentrated all her attention on peeling it. Smokin looked down his nose at his moustache, smoothed it carefully with his left hand, picked up and toyed with a knife and said at last in lowered tones:

"Forgive me my indiscretion, but you must find it hard to live with your father, Lyubov Yakovlevna. He's of the old school, I see; and, if you don't mind my saying so, he's rather—er—callous."

Lyuba started and looked gratefully at this red-haired young man.

"It *is* hard," she admitted, "but I'm used to it. And he has his good qualities."

"Oh, there can be no doubt of that! But you—so young, so attractive, so cultivated; you, with your views on life. . . ."

There was tender sympathy in his smile and his voice was indescribably soft. She felt her heart fill with warmth, and the timid hope of finding happiness grew brighter and brighter.

XII

FOMA was sitting in Yezhov's room listening to him recount the town gossip.

"The election campaign has begun," said Yezhov, who was sitting on a table piled high with newspapers, swinging his legs vigorously. "The merchants have nominated your godfather, the old weevil. He's deathless—must be a hundred and fifty years old. He's marrying his daughter to Smolin—remember him? The red-haired one. They say he's a decent fellow, but then they call anyone decent who has brains, even if he's a scoundrel, because there aren't any really decent people to be found these days. Afrikan makes himself out to be one of your enlightened men—he's already wormed his way into intellectual circles and is attracting attention. Judging from his looks, he's a swindler of the first water, but he's sure to make his mark in the world because he knows just how far he can go. Yes, friend, Afrikan Smolin is a liberal, and a liberal merchant is a cross between a wolf and a pig."

"The devil take him!" said Foma with a wave of his hand. "What do I care about him? Are you drinking as hard as ever?"

"Why shouldn't I?"

The tousled, half-naked Yezhov looked like a plucked cock that has not yet cooled off after a fight.

"I drink because from time to time I must quench the fires burning in my soul. As for you, you wet log, are you still smouldering?"

"I ought to go and see the old man," said Foma, making a face.

"Take the bull by the horns."

"I don't feel like it."

"Then don't go."

"But I must."

"Then go."

"Oh, for God's sake, stop playing the clown," said Foma testily. "As if you really got any pleasure out of it."

222

"But I do!" exclaimed Yezhov, jumping off the table. "The mincemeat I made of one of our leading citizens in yesterday's paper! And, besides, I had the pleasure of hearing a very profound joke: a group of people are sitting on the seashore philosophizing about life, and suddenly a Jew breaks in and says: Gentlemen, why waste words? I can put it all for you in one word: life is not worth a kopek, no more than that sea. . . ."

"Oh, stop it," interrupted Foma. "Goodbye."

"Get along with you. I'm in an elevated mood today and have no mind to listen to your groaning, particularly since you don't groan, but grunt like a pig."

Foma went out, leaving Yezhov singing at the top of his voice:

Take up your drum without fear. . . .

You're a drum yourself, thought Foma irritably.

At Mayakin's he was met by Lyuba, who appeared before him suddenly and in a state of great excitement.

"You?" she said. "Good heavens! How pale you are! And how thin! You seem to be taking good care of yourself." Then a look of alarm came over her face and she said almost in a whisper: "Oh, Foma! Haven't you heard? Today—there! hear that? It's the bell—perhaps it's he."

And she rushed out of the room leaving a rustle of silk and an astonished Foma behind her. He had not even had a chance to ask where her father was. Yakov was at home. Attired in a long frock coat, with all his medals on his chest, he was standing in the doorway with his arms spread wide, holding on to the doorposts and exploring Foma with his little green eyes. Conscious of the old man's gaze, Foma lifted his head.

"How do you do, my fine gentleman?" said the old man with a reproving shake of his head. "And where might you have come from? And who has been sucking the juice out of you? Or is it, as the saying goes: pigs will swill?"

"Is that all you have to say to me?" asked Foma sullenly, looking hard at his godfather.

Suddenly he saw the old man start; his legs began to tremble, his eyes to blink, and he tightened his grip on the doorposts. Foma took a step towards him, fearing that the old man was ill, but Mayakin stopped him with an impatient: "Get away. Stand aside."

Foma stepped back and found himself next to a rather round, small man who was bowing to Mayakin.

"How do you do, Father," he said.

"How do you do, Taras Yakovlevich, how do you do," said the old man, nodding and smiling crookedly. His legs were shaking so that he dared not let go of the doorposts.

Foma moved away and sat down, filled with curiosity.

Mayakin's frail body swayed in the doorway and he cocked his head as he stared at his son without speaking. His son was standing in front of him with his head held high and his brows drawn over his large dark eyes. He had a lean face and a fleshy nose like his father's, and he wore a pointed beard and little black moustache that was twitching now. Over his shoulder Foma caught a glimpse of Lyuba's pale, startled, but happy face; she was gazing imploringly at her father, and it seemed as if she was about to cry out. All of them were too absorbed in their emotions to say a word or make a movement. The silence was broken by the quiet, strangely hushed voice of Mayakin:

"You've grown old, Taras," he said.

His son gave a little laugh and swept his father from head to foot with a swift glance.

Letting go of the doorposts, Mayakin moved towards his son, but suddenly he stopped and frowned. Seeing this, Taras Mayakin stepped forward and held out his hand.

"Very well . . . let's kiss," said Mayakin softly.

They embraced each other impulsively, exchanged warm kisses, and separated. The old man's wrinkles were working, but his son's lean face was composed and almost stern. Lyuba was whimpering happily. Foma shifted in his chair, finding it hard to breathe.

"Children—they're not the joy of our hearts, but a cancer eating into them," wheezed Mayakin plaintively, and he must have unburdened his soul in these words, for when they were spoken his face beamed, he was infused with new energy, and he said to his daughter in a lively tone: "You've gone soft from all this treacle. Come, now—lay the table and we'll entertain the prodigal son. You've probably forgotten what your father's like, haven't you, old man?"

Taras Mayakin, dressed all in black that set off the grey in his hair and beard, smiled at his father without comment.

"Well, sit down. Tell us what your life's been like—what you've been doing. What are you looking at? That's my godson, Ignat Gordeyev's son, remember Ignat?"

"I remember everything," said Taras.

"That's good—if you're not bragging. Are you **married**?"

"A widower."

"Children?"

"They died. I had two."

"A pity. I'd like to have grandchildren."

"May I smoke?"

"Go ahead. H'm—a cigar."

"Do you object?"

"It's all the same to me. What I meant was, it seems sort of— sort of aristocratic to smoke cigars. I just said it because—well, it seems funny. Such a sedate old fellow with whiskers of a foreign cut and a cigar between his teeth. And who might he be? Mayakin's son. He-he-he!" The old man slapped Taras on the shoulder, but instantly recoiled as if in fright: was he not rejoicing too soon? Was this the way he should receive this man with the irongrey hair? He peered suspiciously into the large dark eyes with the yellow pouches under them.

Taras gave his father a warm smile.

"That's how I remember you—gay and lively," he mused. "The years have not changed you in the least."

The old man squared his shoulders proudly and beat his chest with his fist.

"And they'll never change me," he said, "because life has no power over a man who knows his own worth."

"Oho! What a proud one you are!"

"I must take after my son," said the old man with a cunning grin. "My son was silent for seventeen years out of pride."

"That was because his father didn't want to hear from him," rejoined Taras.

"Enough of that; God alone knows who's to blame, and He, in his wisdom, will make it clear to you some day. This is no time to talk about such things. Tell me now—what have you been doing all these years? How did you come to be at the soda factory? How have you made your way in the world?"

"It's a long story," said Taras with a sigh, and when he had blown out a great cloud of smoke, he began unhurriedly: "When I got my freedom, I went to work in the goldfields—in the offices of the Remezovs—"

"I know them. Three brothers. I know all three. One's a cripple, another's a fool, the third's a skinflint."

"He's the one I worked for for two years, at the end of which I married his daughter," went on Taras in a husky voice.

"Clever of you."

Taras became lost in thought. His father studied his sad face.

"I can see you loved her," he said. "It can't be helped—the dead go to heaven, the living keep the ball rolling. You're not so old. Have you been a widower long?"

"Over two years."

"How did you come into the soda factory?"

"The works belong to my father-in-law."

"Oh. How much does he pay you?"

"About five thousand."

"A juicy morsel. H'm. So that's your convict for you!"

Taras threw his father a cold glance.

"By the way," he said dryly, "where did you get the idea that I was a convict?"

The old man showed a surprise that was soon supplanted by joy.

"Why, weren't you? Damn it all! But then . . . how's that? Don't be offended. How was I to know? They said you were sent to Siberia, and that's where convicts are sent."

"To put an end to this once and for all," said Taras impressively, patting one knee with his hand, "I'll tell you exactly how it was: I was exiled to Siberia for six years, and all that time I lived in the Lena goldfields. And I was in jail in Moscow for nine months. And that's the whole story."

"I see. But then, why—?" murmured Mayakin, relieved, but puzzled.

"All those idiotic rumours that were circulated here!" snorted Taras.

"I see now they really were idiotic," said Mayakin indignantly.

"And they once did me a lot of harm."

"Really?"

"Yes. I had just gone into business—"

Foma sat in his corner blinking incredulously as he listened to the talk of the two Mayakins and studied the younger man. Lyuba's attitude towards her brother, based principally on rumours of his activities, had led Foma to think of him as an exceptional person, in no way resembling ordinary people. He had imagined he would speak in a special way and dress in a special way and be, on the whole, a man unlike all others. But here in front of him was sitting another one of your prosperous-looking citizens, carefully dressed, looking exactly like his father except for the cigar in his mouth. He spoke commonplaces in a terse, matter-of-fact way. What was there exceptional about him? Now he was telling his father how profitable the soda trade was. And he had never been a convict—Lyuba had invented that.

She kept coming and going. Her face was shining with joy and she could not tear her eyes from Taras, who was wearing a frock-coat of particularly heavy black cloth with pockets on the sides and big buttons. She walked on tiptoe and kept craning her neck in his direction. Foma looked at her inquiringly, but she did not even notice him as she hurried through the door with plates and bottles in her hands.

It so happened that she entered the room at the very moment when her brother was telling his father about his exile. She stood stock-still, holding her tray in outstretched hands and drinking in every word he said about the punishment he had suffered. And when he finished she turned and went away slowly, without noticing Foma's mocking glance. Foma became so lost in thoughts of Taras and of the neglect he himself was being shown, that he ceased for a while to follow the conversation and when someone suddenly seized him by the shoulder he started and jumped up, almost upsetting his godfather.

"There's a Mayakin for you! Look! He's been boiled in seven pots and come out alive and rich. Does that mean anything to you? And without any help—made his way in the world alone. That's what it means to be a Mayakin! A Mayakin holds his fate in his own hands. Understand that? Take a lesson from him. If you don't find his like in a hundred, seek it in a thousand. A Mayakin will be a man no matter what happens. No force in the world can change him into a saint or a devil, bear that in mind!"

Foma was so taken aback by this unexpected bombast that he did not know what to say in reply. He saw a smile quivering at the corner of Taras's mouth as he calmly smoked his cigar and watched his father. There was an expression of arrogant satisfaction on his face, an air of pride and superiority in his whole figure. He seemed amused by the old man's delight.

"I don't know my own son—he hasn't opened his heart to me," went on Mayakin, tapping Foma on the chest. "Perhaps

227

there's a gulf between us that an eagle couldn't fly or a devil leap over. Perhaps his blood has been boiled so long there's not a smell of his father left in it. And even so, he's a Mayakin! I saw that at once. I saw it, and said to myself: now may Thy humble servant commit himself into Thy hands, oh Lord!"

So violently was the old man trembling that he cut a sort of caper in front of Foma.

"Come, calm yourself, Father," said Taras, getting up unhurriedly and coming over to him. "Let's sit down."

He smiled at Foma casually and led his father over to the table.

"I believe in blood," said Mayakin. "All a man's strength is in his blood. My father used to say to me: you've got my blood in your veins, Yasha. The Mayakin blood is too thick to be thinned down by any woman. So let's have a bottle of champagne on it, shall we? And you'll tell me everything—all about yourself —how are things in Siberia?"

And again, as if struck by some frightening and sobering thought, Mayakin stared fixedly at his son. But in a few moments the latter's reassuring answers threw the old man into a new fit of ecstasy. Foma watched and listened as he sat in the corner.

"It goes without saying that gold mining is a very good business," said Taras, very calm and important, "but it is full of risk and requires large capital. Trade with the natives is very profitable; it brings in a lot of money even if it's badly organized. It is always a paying proposition, but it's tedious. It doesn't require much intelligence, and doesn't give a man of big ideas a chance to express them."

At this moment Lyuba came in and invited them to the table. When father and son had gone out of the room, Foma caught Lyuba by the sleeve and held her back.

"What do you want?" she asked quickly.

"Nothing," said Foma with a smile. "I just wanted to ask if you were glad."

"Terribly!" she exclaimed.

"Why?"

"How funny you are!" she said, looking at him in surprise. "Can't you see for yourself?"

"Bah!" said Foma contemptuously. "As if anything good could come of your father, or of the merchant class! And you lied to me. You said Taras was this, Taras was that, and he's just an ordinary merchant—with a merchant's paunch." He was pleased to see her turn red, then white, and bite her lip in indignation.

"You—you—" she gasped, then, stamping her foot: "Don't dare speak to me!"

When she reached the door she turned a wrathful face to him and said under her breath:

"You misanthrope!"

Foma laughed. He did not want to sit at table with those three happy people. He heard their gay voices, their contented laughter and the clatter of dishes, and knew there was no place among them for him with his heavy heart. There was no place for him anywhere. As he stood by himself in the middle of the room, he decided to leave this house where people were rejoicing. When he got outside, he was filled with resentment against them for the way they had treated him. After all, they were the only people who were close to him. In his mind's eye he saw the face of his godfather with its quivering wrinkles and the green eyes flashing joyfully.

A rotten log glows in the dark, he thought bitterly. Then he recalled the calm, serious face of Taras and the figure of Lyuba straining towards him. This made him sad and jealous.

Who will ever look at me in that way? he thought. He was brought to himself by the bustle on the wharves by the river. All round him people were loading and unloading cargoes; their movements were anxious and hurried, they urged on their horses and shouted at each other irritably, filling the street with the vain confusion and deafening noise of work. They were rushing up and down a narrow cobbled street with high buildings on one side and a steep drop to the river on the other. Foma got the impression that they were all planning to run away from their work in that crowded, dirty street, and were hurrying to finish the tasks that held them there so that they could escape as soon as possible. Enormous steamers with smoke billowing from their funnels were waiting for them near the shore. The turbid water of the river, cluttered with ships and craft of all sorts, beat plaintively against the shore, as if begging a moment's peace and quiet.

For some time the strains of the workmen's cheerful song *Dubinushka* had been coming from one of the wharves. The stevedores were doing an urgent job, and they adapted the rhythm of their song to the rhythm of their movements:

In the tavern merchants fine,
Guzzle vodka, guzzle wine. . . .

sang the soloist, and the other men joined in lustily:

Oh! dubinushka, heave-ho!

Bass voices tossed solid notes up into the air:

Here she comes! Here she comes!

And tenor voices echoed them:

Here she comes! Here she comes!

Foma listened to the song for a while, then followed it to the
wharf. He found the stevedores drawn up in two lines pulling
enormous barrels out of the hold of a ship. Dirty, in red shirts
open at the throat, with mittens on their hands, their arms bare
to the elbow, they were standing over the hold pulling on the
ropes in a gay, joking, companionable way, in time to their
song. Out of the hold came the laughing voice of the invisible
soloist:

But we the chaps who work in boats,
Can't so much as wet our throats.

And the others joined in loudly in unison as from one pair of
lungs:

Oh! dubinushka, heave-ho!

Foma found their work as harmonious as music, and it pleased
him to watch them. The grimy faces of the stevedores were lit
with smiles, the work was easy and went smoothly, the soloist was
touched by inspiration. Foma thought how pleasant it would be
to work with such good companions to the accompaniment of that
jolly song, and when worn out with work, to drink a glass of
vodka with them and eat a dish of rich cabbage soup made by
the buxom wench who cooked for the stevedores.

"Lively, men, lively!" said someone beside him in a rasping
voice. Foma turned round. A fat man with a bloated belly was
tapping the boards of the wharf with his walking-stick and
watching the stevedores with small eyes. His face and neck were
bathed in sweat which he kept mopping with his left hand. He
breathed as hard as if he had just climbed a mountain.

Foma gave him a hostile look and thought to himself: other people do the work and he does the sweating. But I'm even worse.

Every new impression gave rise to painful thoughts of his own worthlessness. Everything held a rebuke for him, and each rebuke was a brick laid upon his chest.

That evening he went to the Mayakins again. The old man was not at home, but Lyuba and her brother were having tea in the dining-room. As he came near the door, Foma heard Taras's husky voice saying:

"Why does father bother about him?"

The moment Foma appeared he fell silent and sat staring hard at him. Lyuba looked confused.

"Oh, it's you," she said, as if apologizing.

They were talking about me, thought Foma as he sat down. Taras looked away and settled himself more comfortably in his chair. There was a minute of strained silence that Foma enjoyed.

"Are you going to the banquet?" asked Lyuba at last.

"What banquet?"

"Didn't you know? Kononov is launching a new ship. There's to be a dedication service, and then a trip up the Volga."

"I haven't been invited," said Foma.

"Nobody has. He just announced on the exchange that anybody who cared to do him the honour was welcome."

"Well, I don't care to."

"Don't you? Don't speak too soon: the wine will flow in rivers," said Lyuba, throwing him a sidelong glance.

"I can get drunk at my own expense if I want to."

"I know!" said Lyuba with an expressive shake of her head.

Taras was playing with a teaspoon and watching them from under his brows.

"Where's godfather?" asked Foma.

"He went to the bank. There's a meeting of the board of directors today. Elections are to be held."

"Will he be elected again?"

"Naturally."

There was another pause. Taras drank his tea in big, slow sips, then smiled at his sister and pushed his glass towards her without speaking. She smiled back at him happily, took up the glass and rinsed. it. As she handed it back a grave look came over

231

her face and she strained forward to say in an undertone, almost reverently:

"Can we go on with what we were talking about?"

"Let's," said Taras briefly.

"You were saying ... I didn't quite understand ... I said that if you found all that Utopian ... that is, if it is impossible to—to dream, then what is a person to do who is not content with life?"

She looked into her brother's calm face with tense expectation. He glanced at her, shifted in his chair, dropped his head, and began to speak very calmly and emphatically.

"We must consider the reason for one's dissatisfaction with life. Perhaps it comes from an inability to work, from lack of respect for work. Or from a wrong idea of one's own powers. The mistake of most people is that they imagine themselves more capable than they actually are. As a matter of fact, very little is demanded of a person; he is only expected to choose a task he can accomplish and do it to the best of his ability. If a person loves what he does, even the roughest work becomes creative. A chair into which the maker has poured his whole heart is bound to be a good, strong, beautiful chair. And this applies to everything. Read Smiles—haven't you read him? A very good book. A beneficial book. And then read Lubbock. Bear in mind that there are no people as hard working as the British, and this explains their extraordinary success in trade and industry. Labour for them is almost a cult. The cultural level of a nation is always in direct proportion to their love of work. The more cultured a people and the more completely their demands are satisfied, the fewer the barriers to the further satisfying of their demands. Happiness lies in the fullest satisfaction of a man's demands. And so, you see, a man's happiness depends upon his attitude to work."

Taras Mayakin spoke so slowly that one might have thought he found talking tedious. But Lyuba leaned towards him with an eager face and eyes, ready to accept anything he said as a pearl of wisdom to be stored away in her soul.

"And what if a man finds everything repulsive?" asked Foma.

"What, in particular?" asked Taras calmly, without looking at him.

"Everything—business, work, people. If, for instance, he sees that everything is a sham. That business is not real business, but just a stopper. A stopper for the empty soul. Some people work; others just sweat and order them about, but get all the profit. How do you explain that?"

"I don't understand what you mean," said Taras when Foma, conscious of Lyuba's withering look, stopped talking.

"You don't?" said Foma with a mocking glance. "Well, let's put it this way: a man goes out into the middle of the river in a boat; it's a good boat, but the water is very deep underneath it, and no matter how sound the boat, once the man begins to fear the deepness and the blackness of the water, it won't save him."

Taras gazed at Foma with calm indifference. He gazed at him without speaking, softly tapping the edge of the table with his fingers. Lyuba shifted uneasily in her chair. The pendulum of the clock told the passage of time with little hushed sounds that were like sighs. And Foma's heart beat slowly and heavily, for he knew that no one in this house would offer him a kind word in this, his hour of painful perplexity.

"Work is not everything a man needs," he said, more to himself than to them. "It's not true that work justifies everything. Some people don't do a stroke of work all their lives, yet they live better than those who do. How do you explain that? As for your working men—they're just miserable dray-horses. Others drive them along and they suffer it, that's all. But they are justified in the eyes of God. If they're asked: what was your purpose in life? they'll answer: we never had time to think about it—we worked all our lives. But what is *my* justification for living? And what is the justification of all those who don't do anything but order others about? What is their purpose in life? It seems to me everyone ought to know very definitely what he is living for." He paused, threw back his head, and cried in stifled tones: "Can it be that a man is born just to work, to make money, build a house, breed children, and die? I don't believe it; there must be *some* meaning to life. A man's born, lives, and dies. What for? We've got to find out what we live for. There's no sense in the lives we live. And there's no equality—anyone can see that. Some are rich, have enough money for a thousand people, and live in idleness, while others sweat all their lives and haven't a kopek to show for it. And yet there isn't a very big difference between people. Some men without a shirt to their backs understand things better than those who wear silk."

233

Foma was so carried away by his thoughts that he would have gone on talking all day had not Taras interrupted by pushing his chair away from the table and getting up.

"No thank you; I've had enough," he said with a sharp intake of breath.

Foma shrugged his shoulders and glanced at Lyuba with a sardonic smile.

"Where did you pick up such philosophy?" she said dryly.

"That's not philosophy, it's torture," said Foma in an undertone. "Open your eyes and look about you, and such thoughts will come into your head of their own accord."

"By the way, Lyuba, have you ever noticed that pessimism is quite alien to the Anglo-Saxon race?" said Taras from where he stood with his back to the table, examining the clock on the wall. "What is called the pessimism of Byron and Swift is nothing but a clamorous protest against the imperfections of life and mankind. But a cold, detached, passive pessimism is not to be found among the English." Then, as if suddenly remembering Foma, he turned to him and said, clasping his hands behind his back and jerking his calf muscle: "You raise very important questions. Some people would call them childish. But if they seriously trouble you, you must read books. In books you will find many valuable observations on the meaning of life. Do you read?"

"No," said Foma shortly. "I can't bear it."

"But books would be of help to you," said Taras, a faint smile touching his lips.

"If people can't help me think, books certainly won't," said Foma morosely.

He was tired of talking to this impervious man. He felt like going away, but at the same time he wanted to say something insulting to Lyuba about her brother, and so he waited in the hope that Taras would leave the room. Lyuba was washing the tea-cups. Her face was thoughtful, her hands moved listlessly. Taras was wandering about the room, stopping in front of the china-closet filled with silver, whistling softly, tapping the glass with a finger-nail and screwing up his eyes as he examined the objects. Once or twice Lyuba threw Foma a questioning and disapproving glance plainly indicating that she would be glad if he left.

"I shall spend the night here," he said with a smile. "I want to speak to godfather. And, besides, it's lonely in that house of mine."

"Then go and tell Marfusha to make up your bed in the corner room," said Lyuba hurriedly.

"Very well."

He got up and went out of the room and as soon as he was outside he heard Taras ask his sister something in a hushed voice.

About me, thought Foma. Suddenly an evil inspiration came to him: why shouldn't he listen to what these clever people thought of him?

He went noiselessly into the room adjoining the dining-room. It was in darkness, the only light being a strip that came through the crack of the door leading to the dining-room. Softly, with bated breath, Foma went over to the door and stood listening.

"A difficult character," said Taras.

"He's been living a wild life," said Lyuba in a quick, low voice. "Behaving preposterously. It began all of a sudden. First he thrashed the vice-governor's son-in-law. Father moved heaven and earth to avoid a scandal. Fortunately the man had a bad reputation. But it cost Father over two thousand roubles all the same. And while Father was doing his best to hush this up, Foma nearly drowned a whole party in the Volga."

"A queer customer. And gives himself up to meditations on the meaning of life!"

"On another occasion he was in a boat with a group of people like himself. When they were all drunk, he said: 'Say your prayers because I'm going to throw you all into the river'. He's horribly strong. They began shouting and pleading, and he said: 'I want to do my country a service by ridding it of such riff-raff'."

"Very witty!"

"He's dreadful. If you only knew all the appalling things he's done these last few years, and all the money he's squandered!"

"Tell me this: what are the conditions under which Father manages his business for him? Do you know?"

"No, I don't. But Father holds it in trust. Why do you ask?"

"Oh, I just wondered. It's a good business. Of course it is organized abominably, in the good old Russian way, but it's an excellent business none the less. If one were to pay it serious attention. . . ."

"Foma does nothing at all. Everything falls on Father."

235

"Does it?"

"Sometimes it seems to me that Foma's moods of thoughtfulness and those speeches he makes are quite sincere, and that he could be very decent. But I can't reconcile the wild life he leads with the things he says."

"And it isn't worth trying. He's lazy and underdeveloped and tries to find an excuse for his laziness."

"But sometimes he's—he's like a child."

"Just what I said—underdeveloped. It's a waste of time to worry about a savage ignoramus who *wants* to be a savage ignoramus. You heard him; he judges things as the bear in the fable bent the yokes."

"You're very hard."

"I am. And that's what people need. All we Russians are much too easygoing. Fortunately life has taken a turn that makes us stiffen up whether we want to or not. It's for youths and girls to indulge in dreams, but for serious people there is serious work."

"Sometimes I feel very sorry for Foma. What will become of him?"

"Nothing in particular—neither good nor bad. He'll go through all his money and become a pauper. But enough of him! People of his sort are rare these days. The merchant has come to appreciate the value of education. And he—that Foma of yours—will come to ruin."

"Quite right, my good man," said Foma, appearing in the doorway. He was white and frowning, his mouth was twisted, and he kept his eyes glued on Taras as he spoke. "Quite right. I'll come to ruin, amen. And the sooner the better."

Lyuba jumped up in fright and ran over to Taras, who was standing calmly in the middle of the room with his hands in his pockets.

"Foma!" she cried in distress. "Oh, Foma! How shameful! Eavesdropping!"

"Shut up, you sheep!"

"True, eavesdropping is not . . . er . . . nice," said Taras, looking at Foma contemptuously.

"What do I care?" said Foma with a wave of his hand. "Is it my fault if the only way a person can hear the truth is by eavesdropping?"

"Go away, Foma, please do," said Lyuba, drawing closer to her brother.

"Perhaps there is something you wanted to say to me?" asked Taras calmly.

"Me?" exclaimed Foma. "What can I say? Nothing. You're the one—you're good at saying things."

"And so you have nothing to say to me?" Taras asked again.

"Nothing."

"I am very glad." Turning away from Foma, he said to Lyuba: "Are you expecting Father home soon?"

Foma looked at him for a moment with a feeling akin to respect, then he went out quietly. He did not want to go home to that enormous empty house that echoed with every step he took, and so he strolled along the street, now wrapped in the sad twilight of late autumn. His mind was filled with thoughts of Taras Mayakin.

"A hard man. Like his father, but not so fidgety. And probably the same kind of swindler. And Lyuba thinking he was a saint, the little fool! The things he said about me! A worthy judge. She feels more kindly towards me."

These thoughts did not make him resent Taras or like Lyuba the more.

His godfather's horse went trotting past. Foma caught a glimpse of the wizened form of Yakov Mayakin, but this aroused no feeling in him either. A lamp-lighter ran past him, put his ladder against the lamp-post and climbed up; suddenly the ladder slipped, the lighter hung on to the post with both hands and let out a loud oath. A young girl jostled Foma in passing.

"Oh, I beg your pardon," she said.

He glanced at her without speaking. A nasty drizzle began to fall. Fine drops of moisture covered the lamps and the shop windows with a dust-like spray that got into the throat and made breathing difficult.

Shall I go to Yezhov's? thought Foma. We'll drink and I'll spend the night there.

And he went to Yezhov's, though he did not have the least desire either to drink or to see his friend.

A shaggy man wearing a blouse and grey trousers was sitting on the couch in Yezhov's room. His face was as dark as a smoked herring, his eyes had an angry look in them, and he wore a bristly moustache over his thick lips. He was sitting with his feet drawn up on the couch, clasping his legs with massive arms and resting his chin on his knees. Yezhov was sitting sideways in an easy chair with his legs thrown over the arm. A bottle of vodka was standing among the books and papers on the table, and there was a smell of salt fish in the room.

"What's the matter with you?" Yezhov asked Foma, then, with a nod in his direction, he said to the man on the couch: "Gordeyev."

"Krasnoshchekov," responded the man in a shrill voice.

Foma sat on the other end of the couch.

"I've come to spend the night," he said to Yezhov.

"Quite right. Go on with what you were saying, Vasili."

The man glanced at Foma out of the corner of his eye before he went on in his shrill voice.

"As I see it," he said, "there's no sense in your attacking stupid people as you do. Masaniello was a fool, but he did what he had to do in the best possible way. And your Winkelried was probably a fool, too, but if he hadn't run the imperial bayonet into himself he'd have beaten the Swiss. There are lots of fools like that, but the fact is that they're the heroes, and the clever people are the cowards. When the time comes to strike with all their strength, they stop to think: What will be the result? What if my efforts are in vain? And there they stand, like posts, until it's too late. But a fool is brave. He drives his head slam into the wall. What if he breaks it? Calves' heads are cheap. And if he makes a little crack in the wall, the clever ones come along, widen it, pass through, and take all the credit. No, you're quite wrong, Nikolai Matveyevich; bravery's a good thing, even without brains."

"You're talking nonsense, Vasili," said Yezhov, holding out his hand to him.

"I daresay," agreed Vasili. "How can you make a silk purse out of a sow's ear? But still, I'm not blind. I see there are lots of brainy fellows, but little good comes of them."

"Don't go yet," said Yezhov.

"I've got to. I'm on duty tonight—I'm late as it is. I'll drop in tomorrow, shall I?"

"Do. And I'll make mincemeat of you."

"That's what you're for."

Vasili stretched himself slowly, got up from the coach, and took Yezhov's skinny yellow hand in his big brown one.

"Goodbye."

He nodded to Foma and went with a lopsided gait to the door.

"How did you like him?" asked Yezhov, pointing in the direction to where heavy footsteps could be heard receding.

"Who is he?"

"Vasili Krasnoshchekov, mechanic's assistant. Let him be an example to you—he was fifteen years old when he learned to read and write and now, at twenty-eight, he's read I don't know how many books and learned two languages. He's going abroad."

"What for?" asked Foma.

"To study, and to see how other people live. And you go about with a long face!"

"What he said about fools was quite right," said Foma.

"I don't know, not being a fool myself."

"Blockheads have got to act on the spur of the moment—rush at things—overturn them!"

"Off again! Let's change the subject. Tell me, is it true Mayakin's son has come back?"

"Yes. What of it?"

"Nothing in particular."

"I can see by your face there is something."

"I know that son of his. I've heard all about him. Is he like his father?"

"Fatter. And more serious. But just as cold."

"Watch yourself, friend, or they'll swallow you up before you know it. That Taras made quick work of his father-in-law in Yekaterinburg."

"Let them if they want to. I'll only thank them for it."

"The same old tune. So you want your freedom, do you? What for? What will you do with it? You're not fit for anything—you can hardly read or write. If it were *me* now—" Yezhov leaped to his feet and took up a position in front of Foma, declaiming in a high voice: "If only I could free myself of the necessity of drinking vodka and eating bread, I'd gather up the remains of my tormented soul and spit it, along with my heart's blood, straight in the face of our respected intelligentsia, may they be damned forever! And I'd say to them: 'For shame, you who are the sap of our country, you whose very existence has been bought with the blood and tears of tens of generations of Russians—shame on you! Lice, that's what you are! How dearly you have cost your country! And what are you doing for her? Are you turning the tears of the past into pearls? What have you ever done to make life better? What have you ever done that was worth doing?

239

Allowed yourselves to be defeated! And what are you doing now? Allowing yourselves to be made a laughing stock'." He stamped his foot in rage, clenched his teeth, and looked at Foma with the blazing eyes of an infuriated beast. "I would say to them: 'You waste endless time talking, but you have little intelligence and no power, and you are all cowards. Your hearts are like feather-beds stuffed full of morality and noble intentions—snug feather-beds in which the creative spirit sleeps soundly on. And instead of beating, your hearts rock like cradles'. I would dip my finger in my heart's blood and write my denunciation on their brows, and they would suffer, these intellectuals with their impoverished spirits and contemptible self-righteousness—oh, how they would suffer! My lash is heavy and my hand is firm. And my love is too deep to spare them. At present they don't suffer, for they talk too much and too loudly of their sufferings. They lie. Genuine suffering is silent; genuine passion knows no bounds. Passion! Will the human heart ever again know what passion is? It is the misfortune of all of us that we are dispassionate."

His breath gave out and he began to cough. He coughed for a long time, flinging about the room and waving his arms like a madman. When he came to a halt in front of Foma his face was white, his eyes bloodshot, he was breathing hard and his lips trembled, revealing little pointed teeth. With his damp, short hair sticking out on all sides, he looked like a perch thrown out of the water. Foma had often seen him in such a state and this time, as always, he caught his mood. He listened in silence to the little man's tirade, not trying to grasp its meaning or understand against whom it was directed—merely absorbing its strength. The words poured over him like a hot spring warming his soul.

"I know my own powers," went on Yezhov. "They shout at me to hold my tongue; they shoo me away, and they do it very calmly, very wisely, looking down on me from a great height. I know I'm only a small bird—oh, I'm no nightingale! I'm a dunce compared with them. I'm just a feature-writer, whose sole purpose in life is to amuse the public. But let them shout at me and shoo me away! I'll accept their slaps, but my heart will go on throbbing. And I'll say to them: 'Yes, I'm a dunce, but the one great advantage I have over you is that I don't hold a single truth printed in books to be dearer than man. Man is the universe, and may his name be praised forever, for in him lies the whole world. But you? For the sake of words whose meaning you don't even understand—for the sake of mere words, you wound and injure one another, for the sake of mere words you vent your spleen on one another and do violence to your souls. You will yet pay dearly for this, believe me! The storm will break and wash you off the face of the earth as rain washes dust off a bough. There is only one word in human speech that is clear and dear to everyone, and that word is Freedom'."

"That's right, go for them!" cried Foma, jumping up from the couch and seizing Yezhov by the shoulders. He peered into Yezhov's face with burning eyes, and there was pain and bitterness in his voice as he said: "Poor Nikolai, I'm deeply sorry for you! I can't say how sorry I am!"

"What's that? Oh, no!" cried Yezhov, pushing him away, shocked and hurt by Foma's strange words and unexpected show of feeling.

"Ah, brother," said Foma, dropping to a lower key that made his voice sound richer and more sincere, "You're a flaming spirit. What a pity your efforts should all be in vain!"

"What? In vain? That's a lie!"

"Dear old chap! You'll never speak your mind to anyone. There's no one to speak it to. Who would listen? Nobody but me."

"Go to the devil!" cried Yezhov viciously, leaping away as if stung.

But Foma said to him urgently and with pain in his voice:

"Speak to me. I'll carry your message where it is needed. I understand it. And oh! I'll sear men's souls with it! Just wait! My time will come!"

"Go away!" screamed Yezhov hysterically, backing to the wall where he stood crumpled, crushed, infuriated, waving off Foma's outstretched arms. At that moment the door opened and a woman in black appeared. She looked irate and indignant, and her face was tied up in a handkerchief.

"Nikolai Matveyevich," she said with a wheeze and a whistle, throwing back her head and stretching out a hand towards Yezhov. "Excuse me, but I've had just about enough of this. Shouting, squabbling. Visitors every day. You're attracting the attention of the police. I've come to the end of my tether. I'm nervous. You'll have to get out tomorrow. You're not living in a desert, you know. There are people all round. They want to live in peace and quiet. And I've got toothache. Tomorrow, if you please."

She spoke quickly and many of her words were lost in the wheeze and the whistle—only the ones she shrieked could be heard distinctly. The ends of the handkerchief stuck out on the top of her head like little horns that shook as she spoke. Altogether she looked so comical in her agitation that Foma dropped on to the couch again. Yezhov remained standing where he was, mopping his brow and straining to catch what she was saying.

"And now you know!" she screamed; then, once more, from behind the closed door: "Tomorrow, don't forget. A disgrace!"

"Damn it all!" muttered Yezhov, staring dully at the door.

"She's a strict one," said Foma in some surprise.

Yezhov hunched his shoulders and went over to the table where he poured himself out half a glass of vodka. When he had gulped it down, he sank in a heap on a chair. Neither of the men said anything for a minute or two.

At last Foma ventured timidly: "It all happened so suddenly. Such an outburst before we had a chance to catch our breath!"

"As for you," said Yezhov under his breath, throwing Foma a savage look, "you shut up! Lie down and go to sleep, damn you. You monster. You scarecrow."

He shook his fist at Foma. Then he poured out some more vodka and drank it.

A few minutes later Foma was lying undressed on the couch watching Yezhov through half-closed eyes. He was sitting hunched up at the table, staring hard at the floor and moving his lips. Foma could not understand why he should have turned on him so. Was it because his landlady had put him out? But Yezhov himself was the one who had done the shouting.

"The devil!" muttered the feature-writer, grinding his teeth.

Foma lifted his head from the pillow. With a loud intake of breath, Yezhov reached for the bottle again.

"Let's go to an hotel," suggested Foma softly. "It isn't very late yet."

Yezhov glanced at him and gave a queer laugh. Then he rubbed his head vigorously and got up.

"Put on your clothes," he snapped, adding, as he watched Foma's slow progress: "Hurry up, can't you, you block?"

"None of your abuse, now," said Foma with a placating smile. "Is it worth quarrelling just because a woman squawked?"

Yezhov looked at him, spat, and burst out laughing.

XIII

"IS everyone present?" asked Ilya Yefimovich Kononov from where he stood in the bow of his new steamer and surveyed the guests gathered round him with shining eyes. "It looks as if everyone was." Then he lifted his beaming red face and called to the captain up on the bridge;

"Cast off, Petruha!"

"Ay, ay!"

The captain bared his bald head and crossed himself, after which he glanced up at the sky and ran a hand over his broad black beard.

"Engines in reverse! Slow!" he commanded.

Following the captain's example, the guests, too, began to cross themselves, taking off their caps and silk hats, which flashed in the air like a flock of blackbirds.

"Thy blessing, Lord!" cried Kononov reverently.

"Let go astern! Full steam ahead!" ordered the captain.

With a shudder that shook its whole great bulk, the *Ilya Muromets* poured a cloud of white steam over the pier and moved upstream as gracefully as a swan.

"Off she goes," exclaimed Commercial Counsellor Reznikov, a tall, thin, handsome man. "Smooth as cream. Like a maid gliding into the dance."

"A leviathan," breathed the pockmarked, stooping Trofim Zubov, an elder of the cathedral and the town's principal money-lender.

It was a grey day. The sky was veiled in autumnal clouds whose reflection gave a cold, leaden hue to the river. Against this dull background the freshly-painted steamer was a bright splash of colour trailing the heavy black cloud of its breath. The boat was white with pink paddle-boxes and bright-red blades, and as it cut easily through the cold waves, sending them scuttling to the river-banks, its round port-holes flashed as with happy, self-satisfied smiles.

"Worthy friends," said Kononov, taking off his hat and making a low bow to his guests. "Now that we have, so to speak, rendered to God what is God's, let us, with the help of the band, render to Caesar what is Caesar's."

And without waiting for any response from his guests he put his hand to his mouth and called out "Bandmaster! The hymn to the Tsar!"

The military band began to play.

Makar Bobrov, director of the Merchants' Bank, sang in a pleasant bass voice, while his fingers beat out the time on his enormous paunch.

"Glory to the Tsar, our Russian Tsar . . . tra-la-la! Boom, boom!"

"And now to the table, friends! Be so kind as to partake of our modest fare. Be so kind," Kononov kept saying as he made his way through the group of guests.

There were about thirty of them, all prominent citizens, the cream of the local merchants. The older representatives (those who were bald and grey) were wearing old-fashioned frock-coats, caps, and high boots. But there were not many of these older representatives. They were outnumbered by men in silk hats, patent-leather boots and fashionable cut-aways. All of them were standing in the bow of the boat, but at Kononov's request they gradually retired to the stern, where tables were laid under awnings. Lupe Reznikov took Yakov Mayakin's arm and whispered in his ear as he led him away, and what he said brought a faint smile to Mayakin's lips. Foma, whom his godfather had at last persuaded to come to the celebration, did not find a companion among these people he detested. Pale and sullen, he kept himself aloof. Two days of heavy drinking with Yezhov had left him with a splitting headache. He felt uncomfortable in such highly respectable company, and his nerves were set on edge by the noise of the band, the crowd and the engines.

He had an irresistible desire to get drunk. He could not imagine why his godfather had been so amiable today, nor why he had brought him here, among the town's leading citizens. Why had he urged him, even begged him to attend Kononov's dedication and banquet?

Foma had arrived in the middle of the dedication and taken a stand on the side where he could watch the merchants.

They stood in reverent silence, a devout expression on their faces. They prayed with great fervour, sighing heavily, bowing low, and rolling their eyes up to heaven. As Foma watched first one, then another, he went over in his mind what he knew about each of them.

Here, for instance, was Lupe Reznikov. He had begun his career by keeping a brothel which made him rich overnight. It was said he had murdered one of his clients, a rich Siberian. Zubov in his early days had bought up peasant yarn wholesale. Twice he had gone bankrupt. Kononov had been arrested twenty years before for setting fire to insured property, and recently a charge of seducing juveniles had been brought against him and was now being investigated. Zahar Kirillov Robustov, a short fat man with a round face and merry blue eyes, was charged with the same crime for the second time in his life. There was scarcely a man among them about whom Foma did not know something incriminating.

He knew that all of them were envious of Kononov, who added a new boat to the number he owned every year. Many of them were at daggers' drawn with one another, they fought ruthlessly on the battleground of business, and they knew all about each other's shady dealings. Yet now, as they gathered about the happy, triumphant Kononov, they merged in a solid dark mass that lived and breathed as a single being, utterly silent, and surrounded by a hard, invisible something that repelled Foma and made him feel shy in their presence.

"Frauds," he said to himself by way of encouragement. They were coughing and sighing in a genteel manner, bowing and crossing themselves where they stood in a solid, impenetrable black wall round the clerics.

"All sham!" exclaimed Foma to himself at the very moment that hunchbacked, one-eyed Pavlin Gushchin (who had recently turned the children of his imbecile brother into the street to beg) whispered soulfully, his one eye raised to the dull sky: "Dear Lord, let not Thy wrath descend upon me, nor yet Thy righteous anger. . . ."

Foma could see that this man was appealing to God with a deep and unshakable faith in His mercy.

"Oh Lord, God of our fathers, who commanded Noah, Thy servant, to build an ark for the preservation of mankind . . ." chanted the priest in a deep bass voice, raising his arms and casting his eyes up to heaven, "protect likewise this vessel and send a guardian angel to watch over it . . . spare those who sail in it. . . ."

All the merchants flung out their arms simultaneously to make the sign of the cross, and all their faces wore the same expression: an expression of faith in the power of prayer.

All this impressed Foma deeply and made him wonder how people with such firm faith in the mercy of God could be so cruel to human beings.

He was infuriated by their adamantine respectability, their self-confidence, their triumphant faces, their loud voices and laughter. By this time they had seated themselves at the tables and were greedily admiring the monster sturgeon decorated with vegetables and large crabs. Trofim Zubov's eyes filmed at the sight as he tied his napkin round his neck.

"Just look at that, Ion Nikiforovich," he gurgled to the miller who was sitting on his right. "A whale, upon my word! Quite large enough to pack you into it. You'd fit inside like a foot in a boot, eh? Ha-ha-ha!"

Little pot-bellied Ion stretched out a short arm to lift a silver bowl of fresh caviar, smacking his lips and keeping a wary eye on the bottles in front of him for fear of knocking them over.

Next to Kononov stood a wooden trestle holding a barrel of seasoned vodka he had brought from Poland. Oysters lay in an enormous shell lined with silver, but the *pièce de résistance* was a colourful pastry in the form of a tower.

"Help yourselves, gentlemen, help yourselves," cried Kononov. "Everything stands before you—help yourselves to whatever you fancy. Our good old Russian dishes, and foreign ones as well—all at the same time. That's the best way, as I see it. What will you have? Snails? Crabs? Straight from India, they say."

"The prayer the priest read is hardly fitting for the launching of tow-boats or river craft," Zubov was saying to his neighbour Mayakin. "That is, not that it isn't suitable, but it's insufficient. A river-boat in which the crew lives day in day out, is the same as a house. Accordingly, a prayer for the dedication of a house should have been added to the one that was read. What will you have to drink?"

"I'm not a wine-drinker. Pour me out a glass of vodka," said Mayakin.

Foma, who was sitting at the end of the table among the more humble guests, felt his godfather's eye on him.

He's afraid I'll make a scene, he thought.

"Brothers!" roared a pot-bellied shipowner named Yashchurov. "I can't live without herring! I've just got to begin with herring! That's my nature!"

"Music! Let's have the *Persian March*."

"Wait. Make it *Glory to the Tsar*."

"Very well! *Glory to the Tsar*."

The wheeze of the engines and the noise of the paddle-wheels mingling with the music of the band filled the air with something that sounded like the wild song of a snowstorm. The flutes whistled, the clarinets warbled, the French horns blared, the little drum went rat-a-tat, the big one boom-boom, and all these sounds went crashing into the steady beat of the paddle-wheels, stampeding through the air and rushing past the boat like a tornado, so that people had to shout at the tops of their voices to be heard. Every now and again the engines would give an angry hiss, and there was annoyance and contempt in this sound, which kept intruding itself into the chaos of screeching, roaring and shouting.

"I'll never forgive you for refusing to take my promissory note," shouted someone furiously.

"That's enough! Is this the time to bring up such things?" came Bobrov's deep voice.

"Time for speeches, gentlemen!"

"Bandmaster! Silence!"

"Drop in to see me at the bank and I'll explain to you why I didn't endorse it."

"A speech! Silence!"

"Stop the music!"

"*The Merry Widow*."

"*Madame Angot*."

"No, don't. Make a speech, Yakov Tarasovich!"

"It's called 'Strassburg pudding'."

"A speech! A speech!"

"Pudding? Doesn't look like it. But I'll try it."

"Mayakin! A speech!"

"Very jolly, I must say!"

247

"And in *La Belle Hélène* she comes out on the stage almost naked," came the reedy voice of Robustov through the noise.

"So Jacob cheated Esau, did he? Aha!"

"Come Mayakin, don't put us off."

"Silence, gentlemen! Yakov Mayakin has the floor."

In the sudden silence that followed, someone was heard to whisper indignantly:

"How she pinched me, the little bitch!"

"Where?" roared Bobrov.

There was a burst of laughter that instantly subsided as Mayakin rose, cleared his throat, ran a hand over his bald crown, and glanced gravely about him in expectation of silence.

"Prick up your ears, friends," called out Kononov.

"Fellow merchants!" began Mayakin with a little laugh, "there's a foreign word you'll often hear learned and educated people using, and the word is 'culture'. So now, as a simple man, I'm going to talk to you about that word."

"Hear, hear!"

"Worthy gentlemen," went on Mayakin, raising his voice, "the papers keep saying that we merchants have no culture, that we don't know what it is and don't want to know. They call us savages. Now, then, just what is this 'culture'? It's not easy for an old man like me to hear such hard things said, and so one day I took it upon myself to find out what the word means."

Mayakin stopped and ran his eyes over his audience before he resumed, with a little chuckle of triumph:

"It turns out this word means love—love of order, a fierce love of improvement. So that's what it means! I think to myself: in other words, a cultured person is one who loves order and improvement, who loves to arrange things, who loves life and knows its worth, and knows his own worth, too. Very well." A shudder seemed to pass through the old man. The wrinkles of his face spread out in rays from his smiling eyes down to his lips, and his whole bald head twinkled like a dark star.

The merchants hung on his every word, their faces filled with attention, their bodies frozen in the attitudes in which Mayakin's opening words had caught them.

"But if that's how it is—and tha* *is* the precise interpretation of the word—if that's how it is, I say, then those who call us

248

uncultured savages are slandering us, for they are in love with the word, but not its meaning, while we love the very roots of the word, the very core and essence of it. We love to work. We have a real cult of life—that is, we worship life—but they don't. They love talk, we love action. And behold, fellow merchants, the proof of our culture, of our love of development: the Volga! Our beloved Mother Volga! Every drop of her water speaks in our defence and refutes their slander. Only a hundred years have gone by since the day when Peter the Great launched his flat-bottomed boats on her waters, and today, gentlemen, thousands of steamers are plying between her ports. Who built them? The Russian peasant, a totally unlettered man. Who owns all these huge steamers and barges? We do. Who invented them? We did. Everything here is ours. Everything was born of our minds, of our daring, of our love of action. No one has ever helped us. We ourselves got rid of the robber bands that preyed on the Volga; at our own expense we hired troops to wipe them out, and then we launched thousands of river-craft along the thousands of versts of the Volga. Which are the best towns on the Volga? The ones that have the most merchants. Whose are the best houses in the towns? The merchants' houses. Who gives most help to the poor? The merchants. We donate hundreds of thousands of roubles to charity, collecting it kopek by kopek. Who builds the churches? We do. Who contributes most to the State? We do. Gentlemen, we alone do things for the love of the work, for the love of making life better. We alone love life and order. And what they say against us is—is. . . ." he pronounced a foul word with gusto. "That's what it is. Let them talk! The wind blows, the willow rustles; the wind drops, the willow is silent. And you can't make either shaft or broom out of the willow. It's a useless tree. From its uselessness comes all the rustling. And what have those men who set themselves up as our judges ever done that was worth doing? How have they ever improved life? We do not know. But *our* work is plainly to be seen. Fellow merchants! You are the salt of the earth; no others are as hard-working and energetic as you are; all that has been done has been done by you, and there is no limit to what you can still do, and therefore I drink this toast to you: I love and respect you deeply, and with all my heart I say: Long live the gallant, hard-working merchants of Russia! May they prosper to the glory of our motherland! Hurrah!"

249

Mayakin's shrill cry called forth a thunderous roar of applause. All these massive, fleshy bodies suddenly began to move, and so mighty was the roar that came from their throats that everything about seemed to tremble and quake.

"Yakov! Trumpet of the Lord!" shouted Zubov, holding up his glass to Mayakin.

Chairs were overturned, tables jarred, bottles fell and dishes clattered as the happy, excited merchants streamed towards Mayakin with raised wine-glasses in their hands and tears in their eyes.

"How do you like that?" asked Kononov, seizing Robustov by the shoulder and shaking him. "Do you realize what has happened? We've just listened to a great speech!"

"Let me kiss you, Yakov!"

"Toss him into the air! Hurrah!"

"Music!"

"Music! The *Persian March!*"

"To hell with your music!"

"Wasn't his speech music enough?"

"Small in stature but great in mind!"

"That's a lie, Trofim!"

"What a shame you're so on in years, Mayakin. What will we do when you're gone?"

"Oh, what a funeral we'll give him!"

"Gentlemen, let's start a Mayakin fund. I'll give the first thousand."

"Hold your tongue! What's your hurry?"

"Gentlemen!" began Mayakin again, quivering. "One of the main reasons why we are the salt of the earth and the true rulers of our country is that the blood of the peasant runs in our veins."

"True, how true!"

"God, what a man!"

"Don't interrupt!"

"We are pure-blooded Russians, and everything that comes from us is pure-blooded Russian. And so it is the most genuine, the most important and essential."

"As true as two and two make four!"

"And so simple!"

"The old man's as wise as a serpent."

"And as meek as . . ."

"As a hawk! Ha-ha!"

The merchants crowded about their orator and gazed upon him with unctuous eyes, unable to listen to him calmly for their excitement. The babble of their voices, the throbbing of the engines and the pounding of the paddle-wheels formed a rush of sound in which the old man's voice was lost.

"A Russian dance! A Kamarinsky dance!"

"Behold the work of our hands!" shouted Mayakin, pointing to the river. "Ours, and ours alone! We're the ones who have made life what it is!"

Suddenly a voice was heard that drowned all others.

"So you're the ones, are you?" it cried. "You—" and there followed a string of foul epithets. Everyone heard them, and for an instant there was a dead silence while all eyes sought out the speaker. In that instant the only thing to be heard was the sighing of the engines and the screech of the rudder chains.

"Who said that?" asked Kononov with a frown.

"Ugh, we just can't do without a scene," sighed Reznikov.

The faces of the merchants expressed alarm, wonder, curiosity and reproach, and all the men gave vent to some sort of protest. Yakov Mayakin alone preserved his composure and even seemed to derive satisfaction from what had happened. He stood on his toes and craned his neck to catch sight of something at the other end of the table, and there was a glitter in his eye, as if he were highly pleased with what he saw.

"Foma Gordeyev," whispered Ion Yushkov.

All heads turned in the direction in which Mayakin was looking.

There, with his hands resting on the table, stood Foma. His face set with rage he was staring at the merchants with burning, wide-open eyes. His lower jaw trembled, his shoulders twitched and the fingers grasping the edge of the table kept scratching at the cloth convulsively. His wrathful pose and the wild look in his eye silenced the merchants.

"What are you staring at?" asked Foma, unburdening himself of another string of profanities.

"Drunk," said Bobrov with a shake of his head.

"Why did they invite him?" whispered Reznikov.

"Foma Ignatiyevich, do try to behave," said Kononov in dignified tones. "If you . . . er . . . have had a drop too much . . . er . . . just go quietly into one of the cabins and lie down. Lie down, my boy, and—"

"Silence, you!" roared Foma, turning his eyes upon him. "Don't dare talk to me! I'm not drunk! I'm more sober than any of you, do you understand?"

"Just a minute, my good man—who invited you here?" said Kononov, reddening at the insult.

"I did," said Mayakin.

"Oh. In that case I beg your pardon, Foma Ignatiyevich. But since it was you who brought him, Yakov, it's you who will have to take him in hand. This is . . . er . . . rather unpleasant."

Foma smiled and said nothing. And the merchants said nothing as they watched him.

"Ah, Foma, Foma!" said Mayakin. "Disgracing me in my old age again!"

"My dear godfather," returned Foma, still grinning, "I haven't done anything yet, so it's too soon to scold me. I'm not drunk. I have drunk nothing, but I have heard everything. Gentlemen, allow *me* to make a speech now. You have just heard my godfather speak, now listen to his godson."

"Speeches?" said Reznikov. "Must we listen to speeches? We came here to enjoy ourselves."

"Enough of that, Foma Ignatiyevich."

"Have something to drink instead."

"Yes, let's have a drink. Ah, Foma, what a fine man your father was!"

Foma let go of the table, straightened up and, still smiling, stood listening to their efforts to placate him. He was younger and better-looking than any of these eminent townsmen. His handsome figure in its well-fitting frock-coat stood out in striking contrast to their shapeless bodies and bloated bellies. His brown face with its large eyes had a freshness and regularity of feature that their puffy red faces lacked. He threw out his chest, clenched his teeth, threw open his coat, and thrust his hands into the pockets of his trousers.

"You can't stop my mouth with fine phrases," he said in a hard, threatening voice. "I intend to have my say whether you listen or not. You can't put me off the boat." He threw back his head and squared his shoulders. "And I'll kill anyone who lays a finger on me. I swear to God I will."

The group of people standing in front of him swayed like bushes in the wind. Frightened whisperings were heard. Foma's face darkened and his eyes grew larger still.

"It was said that you are the ones who have made life what it is, that all that is good and sound is the work of your hands." He sucked in his breath and gazed with inexpressible hatred into these faces that seemed swollen with indignation. The merchants pressed closer together and said not a word.

"What's it all about, eh? From a paper, or is it his own?" muttered someone in the back row.

"You scoundrels!" exclaimed Foma, shaking his head. "What have you done? Instead of improving the world, you've turned it into a jail; instead of bringing order into it, you've put people in chains. No person with a spark of life in him can breathe in this suffocating world of yours. Murderers, that's what you are! And it's only because people are so long-suffering that you're still alive, bear that in mind!"

"I never heard anything like it!" exclaimed Reznikov, wringing his hands in futile protest. "I won't listen to another word!"

"Careful, Gordeyev," called out Bobrov. "You're saying things you may be sorry for."

"Do you know what you can get for saying such things?" warned Zubov.

"Bah!" fumed Foma, with bloodshot eyes. "Rave as much as you like, you swine!"

"Gentlemen," said Mayakin, his voice menacingly calm and as rasping as a file on metal, "I beg you not to interrupt. Let him speak if it gives him any pleasure. It won't hurt you."

"Oh, won't it?" cried Yushkov.

Smolin, who was standing next to Foma, whispered into his ear: "Stop it; have you gone mad?"

"Get away!" said Foma sharply, looking at him with blazing eyes. "Go and lick Mayakin's hands, perhaps he'll throw you a crust."

Smolin gave a low whistle and moved away. And one by one the other merchants dispersed. This enraged Foma the more: he wanted to hold them with his words, but he could not find words powerful enough to do so.

"So you are the ones who have made life what it is, are you?" he cried. "And who are you? Robbers! Swindlers!"

A few of the men turned back as if he had called them by name.

"Kononov! When are you to be tried for what you did to that little girl? You'll get hard labout for it. It'll be farewell, Kononov!

You've built your fine steamer in vain. They'll transport you to Siberia for certain."

Kononov sank into a chair. The blood rushed to his face and he shook his fist in the air.

"Just wait . . . you'll see . . . I won't forget this in a hurry!"

His face was so distorted and his lips were trembling so violently that Foma understood with what weapons he could deal these men the most effective blows.

"Improvers of life, you say? Well, then, Gushchin, do you give alms to your nephews? You might give them at least a kopek a day—you've stolen enough from them to afford it. Or Bobrov, here—why did you have your mistress thrown in jail by telling that lie about her stealing your money? If you were tired of her, you could have passed her on to your son—he's taken up with your latest woman anyway. Didn't you know it? Ugh, you fat pig! As for you, Lupe, why don't you open a brothel again so that you can fleece your gentlemen clients before you break them. I can just see you doing it, ha-ha! It must be easy for a man with a pious face like yours to get away with murder. Who was that fellow you murdered, Lupe?"

Foma laughed as he spoke, and he could see the telling effect his words had on his listeners. At first, when he had addressed them as a whole, they had turned away from him—had stepped aside and stood in little groups watching him from a distance with contemptuous smiles on their faces. He saw their smiles and read scorn in their every movement, and while his words angered, they did not strike deeply. This chilled his spirits, and he faced the bitter recognition that his attack was a failure. But the minute he began to speak to each of the merchants separately, his audience underwent a sudden shange.

When Kononov collapsed on the chair as if felled by Foma's ridicule, Foma noticed gloating smiles playing over the lips of some of the merchants. And he heard somebody whisper in wonder and approval:

"That's well aimed!"

This infused Foma with new strength, and he began to hurl his jibes and rebukes at whomever his eyes fell on. He growled with joy on realizing the power of his words. His audience listened in breathless silence, some of them even drawing nearer.

A few cries of protest were made, but not loudly or emphatically and each time Foma shouted someone's name the merchants pricked up their ears and cast sidelong glances full of malicious pleasure at the man who was the new target.

Bobrov gave a discomfited little laugh and his sharp little eyes bored Foma through and through. Lupe Reznikov waved his arms in the air and hopped about, gasping: "You're my witnesses— I'll never forgive this! I'll take him to court! How dare he?" Then, suddenly, stretching out his arms towards Foma he shrieked:

"Tie him up!"

Foma laughed.

"There's no tying up the truth!" he said.

"We'll see about that," said Kononov hoarsely.

"Gentlemen," came Mayakin's shrill voice, "I beg you to take a good look at him. See for yourselves what he's like."

One by one the merchants drew closer to Foma and he saw expressions of fear, fury, curiosity and gloating satisfaction on their faces. One of the more humble guests whispered to him:

"Go on, give it to them. It'll all be counted to your credit!"

"What are you laughing at, Robustov?" cried Foma. "What are you so happy about? Do you think *you* won't be sent to Siberia?"

"Put him ashore!" shouted Robustov, leaping to his feet.

"Turn back! Back to town! To the mayor!" called Kononov to the captain of the boat.

"It's a put-up job. Done on purpose. They put him up to it— made him drunk first."

"This is open rebellion!"

"Tie him up! Simply tie him up!"

Foma picked up an empty champagne bottle and waved it in the air.

"Hands off! You've got to listen to me whether you like it or not!"

And in a wave of fury, in the frenzy of his joy at seeing these men writhe under his blows, he began to call out other names and to swear at his victims in the foulest language. And again the mutter of protest died down. Those who did not know Foma looked at him in wonder and curiosity, some even with approval. One of them, a little grey-haired old man with pink cheeks and mouse-like eyes, turned to the insulted merchants and said in wheedling tones:

"It's his conscience prompts him to say these things. Don't mind them. They've got to be suffered. The judgment of a prophet. We *are* sinners. And we ought to speak the truth because we're so—"

They hissed him into silence and Zubov gave him a little push that made him slink out of sight.

"Zubov!" called out Foma, "How many people have you turned out without a kopek? Aren't your dreams haunted by Ivan Petrovich Mayakinnikov, who hanged himself on your account? And is it true that you steal ten roubles out of the collection plate every Sunday?"

This attack caught Zubov unawares and he remained standing with one arm in mid-air. When he recovered, he jumped up and down, screeching:

"So you're after me too, are you? Me too?" He blew out his cheeks, shook his fist at Foma, and went on screeching: "I'll report you to the bishop! Heretic! You're the one who'll be sentenced to hard labour!"

The turmoil on the steamer increased and the sight of these flustered, infuriated people made Foma feel like a legendary hero slaying dragons. They walked about shouting and gesticulating, some of them red in the face, others white, powerless to stop the stream of his invective.

"Call the boat-hands!" shouted Reznikov as he seized Kononov by the shoulder. "What do you mean by this, Ilya? Did you invite us here to be ridiculed?"

"The puppy!" squealed Zubov.

A group of merchants had gathered round Yakov Mayakin. He was speaking to them quietly and they listened with fierce faces, nodding their heads from time to time.

"Go on and do it, Yakov," said Robustov in a loud voice. "We are witnesses. Go ahead."

Above the clamour rose Foma's loud voice:

"Instead of improving the world, you've turned it into a dung heap. You may be men of action, but all you've done is collect filth and raise a stench. Have you no conscience? Have you no God? Yes, gold is your god. And you've driven away your consciences. Where have you driven them to, you bloodsuckers? You live at other people's expense, you work with other people's hands. How many people have shed tears of blood because of your 'mighty works'! Hell is too good a place for swine like you. Not in clean flames, but in boiling dung ought you to be burned—tormented for centuries on end!"

256

In a sudden fit of laughter, Foma threw back his head, held his sides, and stood swaying on his feet. At that moment several of the men exchanged winks, then threw themselves at Foma, pressing down upon him with the weight of their bodies. A struggle ensued.

"Caught!" cried someone ecstatically.

"So . . . that's it!" gasped Foma.

The knot of black figures tussled briefly with Foma, stamping heavily with their feet and emitting smothered cries.

"Throw him down!"

"Hold his hand . . . his hand!"

"Oh, my beard!"

"Hands off! Hands off, I say!"

"Ready!"

"Good Lord, what muscles!"

They dragged Foma over the deck to the captain's cabin, then walked away straightening their clothes and wiping the sweat off their faces. Worn out by the struggle, stunned by the disgrace of defeat, Foma lay without a word. His clothes were torn and smeared with something unpleasant, his hands and feet were tightly bound with towels.

Now it was their turn to taunt him. Zubov began. He went over to him and kicked him in the ribs.

"So the thunderous voice of the prophet has been stilled?" he said mockingly, trembling all over with the joy of revenge. "How does it feel to be a prisoner of Babylon? Ha-ha-ha!"

"Just wait," said Foma without looking at him. "Just wait till I catch my breath. You haven't tied my tongue." But he knew there was nothing more he could say or do—not because he was bound, but because something had died inside him and his soul was dark and empty.

Reznikov came over and joined Zubov. Others drew near. Bobrov, Kononov and a few others followed Yakov Mayakin to the captain's bridge, where they stood discussing something in low tones.

The boat was making for the town at full speed. The throbbing of the engines caused the bottles on the tables to give out a high, thin complaint, and it was this sound that forced itself on Foma's ears above all others. Men were crowding about him and making vicious, insulting remarks.

But Foma saw their faces, as through a veil, and the words they spoke did not touch him. A great bitterness was welling up inside him. He felt it spread, and while the meaning of it was not clear to him, he was aware of his misery and his humiliation.

"Just see what you've brought yourself to, you fool," said Reznikov. "How are you to go on living after this? There's not a man of us who would take the pains even to spit on you now."

"Why, what have I done?" asked Foma. The merchants had formed a solid black ring round him.

"Everything's over with you now, Foma," said Yashchurov.

"We'll show you now," gloated Zubov softly.

"Untie me," said Foma.

"Oh, no; not on your life!"

"Call my godfather."

But Mayakin came up at this moment without being called. He stopped in front of Foma and gazed hard and steadily at him where he lay.

"Ah, Foma . . .!" he said with a deep sigh.

"Tell them to untie me," said Foma in an abject voice.

"So that you can run wild again? No, lie where you are awhile," said his godfather.

"I won't say another word . . . I swear to God. Untie me. It's shameful to lie here like this. I'm not drunk."

"Swear you won't make trouble?" asked Mayakin.

"Yes, of course. Oh, Lord!" moaned Foma.

They untied his feet, but not his hands.

When he got up, he looked at the faces round him and said softly, with a pathetic little smile:

"You've won."

"We always win," said his godfather with a harsh laugh.

Foma, his hands tied behind his back, slunk over to one of the tables without saying a word or raising his eyes. He seemed to have shrunk in height and grown thinner. His tousled hair fell over his forehead. His torn and crumpled shirt front was sticking out of his waistcoat and his collar covered his mouth. He twisted his neck to force it under his chin, but was unable to. Seeing this, the old man came up to him and set things right.

"It's got to be suffered," he said, smiling into Foma's eyes.

Now that Mayakin was on the scene, the people who had been taunting Foma grew silent and looked at the old man inquiringly, as if they expected him to do something. He still retained his composure, but his eyes had a gleam hardly in keeping with the occasion, so bright was it.

"Give me a drink," said Foma, sitting down at the table and leaning heavily against it with his chest. His crumpled figure looked pitiable and helpless. The people about him spoke in whispers and walked on tiptoe. And they kept stealing glances first at him, then at Mayakin, who had sat down opposite him. The old man was in no hurry to give Foma a drink. He studied him intently and took his time pouring him out a glass of vodka, which he held to his lips without a word. Foma drank.

"Another," he said.

"Enough," replied Mayakin.

There followed a moment of absolute, painful silence. People stole past the table, craning their necks to catch a glimpse of the culprit.

"Well, do you realize what you've done, Foma?" asked Mayakin. He spoke softly, but everyone heard what he said.

Foma nodded.

"Don't expect us to forgive you," said Mayakin firmly and in a louder voice. "We'll never forgive you, even though we are Christians, understand that."

Foma raised his head:

"I forgot to mention you, godfather," he said thoughtfully. "I didn't say a single word about you."

"Hear that?" cried Mayakin bitterly, pointing at his godson. There was a low murmur of indignation.

"But what of it?" said Foma with a sigh. "What of it? Why did I bother at all? Nothing came of it."

And he leant over the table again.

"What did you want to come of it?" asked his godfather sternly.

"What did I want?" Foma raised his head, glanced round at the merchants, and gave a sorry little laugh. "I wanted. . . ."

"You're a drunkard and a scoundrel!"

"I wasn't drunk," said Foma sullenly. "I had only had two glasses of wine. I was perfectly sober."

"That shows you're right, Yakov Tarasovich: he's insane," said Bobrov.

"I?" ejaculated Foma.

But they paid no attention to him. Reznikov, Zubov and Bobrov leaned down and began whispering to Mayakin.

". . . become his guardian. . . ." Foma heard them say.

"I'm in my right mind!" cried Foma, throwing himself back in his chair and glaring at them with troubled eyes. "I know what I wanted. I wanted to tell the truth. I wanted to expose you."

Once more his passions flared up and he wrenched at his bonds.

"Not so fast, not so fast!" said Bobrov, seizing him by the shoulders. "Hold him, gentlemen."

"Ah, well—hold me," said Foma in despair. "Hold me. . . ."

"Sit still!" cried his godfather harshly.

Foma said nothing. All he had done, he had done in vain. His words had not shaken these merchants in the least. Here they were, standing in a solid wall round him and he could see nothing but this wall. Calm and resolute, they looked upon him as a madman, and he knew they were plotting something against him. He was crushed by this dark wall of clever, self-confident men. He did not know himself at this moment—did not understand what he had done or why he had done it. He even resented what he had done and felt almost ashamed of himself. He was conscious of a burning sensation in his throat and his heart seemed to be buried under a layer of dust that made it beat slowly and irregularly.

"I wanted to proclaim the truth," he said thoughtfully, without looking at anybody.

"Fool!" said Mayakin contemptuously. "How can you proclaim the truth? As if you understood anything!"

"My heart was bursting. I felt the falseness of everything."

"It's clear from the way he talks that his mind is touched," said someone.

"It's not given to every man to tell the truth," said Mayakin instructively, raising one hand for emphasis. "It's not enough to feel things—even a cow can feel you twisting her tail. The thing is to *understand*. To understand everything. To understand your enemies—understand them so well you can guess what they dream about. Then you can go for them!"

Mayakin would have gone on expounding his philosophy with the usual zest if he had not been stopped by the realization that one does not teach strategy to the conquered. Foma looked at him dully.

"Leave me alone," he pleaded, giving an odd little shake of his head. "You've won. Isn't that enough for you?"

Everyone was on the alert the minute Foma opened his mouth and there was something evil and ominous in their unnatural attentiveness.

"What I saw going on round me made my blood boil," he said lifelessly. "And at last it boiled over. That's all. Now there's not a drop of strength left in me. It's all drained away."

He spoke in a colourless monotone, as if in delirium.

Mayakin laughed.

"Did you think you could lick a mountain away with your tongue? Threw yourself at a bear with the fury of a bedbug! Behold the prophet! Bah! If your poor father could see you now!"

"But you are to blame for it all!" said Foma in a loud resolute voice and with flashing eyes. "It's you who have spoiled everything. It's you who are squeezing people off the earth. It's you who are choking them to death. And weak though my truth may be against yours, still it is the truth. It's you, I say, curse you!"

He lashed about in the effort to free his hands.

"Untie my hands!" he roared, rolling his eyes in fury.

The merchants crowded more closely round him. Their faces wore a hard look now, and Reznikov said to him threateningly:

"Stop that noise! We'll soon be back in town. Don't disgrace yourself and us. Do you want us to take you straight from the pier to the asylum?"

"So that's it?" cried Foma. "So you want to put me in the asylum, do you?"

Nobody answered him. He looked into their faces a moment, then hung his head.

"If you behave yourself we'll untie your hands," somebody said.

"Don't bother," said Foma softly. "It doesn't matter."

And again be began speaking as if in delirium:

"I'm lost—I know it. Not because you're so strong, but because I'm so weak. You, too, are worms in the sight of God, and wait—you'll get your deserts. I'm lost because of my blindness. I saw so much it blinded me. Like the owl—the owl I chased in the gully when I was small. It kept darting up and bumping into things. The sun blinded it. It bumped itself so often that it was all bruised and bleeding, and then I lost it. I remember my father saying to me then: it's just like that with human beings—sometimes a man rushes here and there, bumping into one thing after another until he's so sick and sore he's ready to crawl into the

261

first hole he finds to get relief. . . . God! untie my hands, won't you?"

He turned white and closed his eyes and his shoulders shook. In his torn and crumpled clothes he began to rock back and forth on his chair, knocking his chest against the edge of the table and muttering to himself.

The merchants exchanged meaning glances. Some of them nudged their neighbours and nodded in Foma's direction without saying a word. Mayakin's face was as dark and rigid as if hewn out of granite.

"Perhaps we ought to untie his hands," whispered Bobrov.

"No, we oughtn't," said Mayakin under his breath. "We'll leave him here. Let someone go for the ambulance and we'll have him taken straight to the hospital."

He walked off in the direction of the captain's bridge, saying as he went: "Keep an eye on him; he may try to jump overboard."

"I feel sorry for the lad," said Bobrov as he watched Mayakin go.

"Nobody's to blame if he's a fool," said Reznikov tartly.

"But Mayakin—" whispered Zubov, nodding at the old man's retreating figure.

"What about him? He hasn't lost anything by it,"

"Quite right. He'll take over everything as the boy's guardian."

Their whispers and hushed laughter were drowned by the gasping of the engines. Foma could not have heard them. He sat taring dully into space, his lips twitching from time to time.

"His son has turned up," whispered Bobrov.

"I know him," said Yashchurov. "I met him in Perm."

"What's he like?"

"A clever chap. At the head of a big business in Usolye."

"In other words, Mayakin has no more need of this one. So that's how it is."

"Look, he's crying."

"What's that?"

Foma was leaning back in his chair with his head on one side. His eyes were closed and tears were welling out under his lashes. One by one they coursed down his cheeks and into his moustache. His lips twitched convulsively, and the tears dropped off his moustache on to his breast. The irregular heaving of his breast was the only movement he made. For a moment the merchants

watched his pale face, drawn with suffering, wet with tears—
then they quietly withdrew.

Foma was left alone with his hands tied behind his back,
sitting at the table covered with dirty dishes and the remnants
of the feast. From time to time he lifted his swollen eyelids and
gazed through his tears at the ruin and desolation on the table.

Three years went by.

Two years after the dedication of Kononov's steamer,
Yakov Mayakin died. His mind remained clear to the end, and a
few hours before he died he said to his son, his daughter and his
son-in-law, in true Mayakin manner:

"Live and prosper, my children. I've had my fill of the fruits
of life, so it's time for me to leave the orchard. See? I can even
die without complaining. God will count that to my credit. I
may have caused the Almighty some annoyance with my tricks,
but never with my moans and groans. Dear Lord, I'm happy
to say that, by Thy grace, I knew how to get on in this world.
Farewell, my children. Live in friendship, and don't ponder
things too much. Remember that he who hides from sin and
seeks a peaceful couch will never be a saint. Cowardice will not
save you from sin, as the parable of the talents tells us. If you are
bent on getting something out of life, you must not be afraid of
sinning. The Lord will forgive your errors. The Lord has appointed man to improve life, and yet He has not blessed him
with too much wisdom. And so He cannot expect too much of
him. Great is His mercy, and righteous His ways . . ."

Mayakin's death pangs were brief, but agonizing.

Soon after the events that took place on Kononov's steamer,
Yezhov was banished from the town.

A new company was formed with the trading name of "Taras
Mayakin and Afrikan Smolin".

For three years nothing at all was heard of Foma. It is said
that as soon as he came out of hospital Mayakin sent him to his
mother's relatives in the Urals.

But at the end of three years he was seen in the town again.
Ragged, unkempt and nearly always drunk, he did indeed give
the impression of being insane. Sometimes he would go about
with knitted brows and hanging head, looking very forbidding,
but at others he would wear the sad and touching smile of a
pious imbecile. There were occasions when he became violent,

but they were rare. Lyuba Smolina let him live in a little outhouse.

Townsmen and merchants who remembered him were inclined to make fun of him. On seeing him come down the street, they would cry:

"Hey, you prophet! Come here!"

He rarely came—he avoided people and could not bear to talk to them. But if he did, they would say to him:

"Tell us something about the Judgment Day, will you? Ha-ha! A prophet indeed!"